JEREMIAH: A STUDY IN ANCIENT

HEBREW RHETORIC

JEREMIAH: A STUDY IN ANCIENT

HEBREW RHETORIC

by

Jack R. Lundbom

Published by

SOCIETY OF BIBLICAL LITERATURE

and

SCHOLARS   PRESS

DISSERTATION SERIES, NUMBER 18

1975

Distributed by

SCHOLARS PRESS
University of Montana
Missoula, Montana   59801

JEREMIAH: A STUDY IN ANCIENT HEBREW RHETORIC

by

Jack R. Lundbom
Andover Newton Theological School
Newton Centre, Massachusetts

Ph.D., 1973   Advisors:
Graduate Theological   David Noel Freedman
Union, Berkeley   Wilhelm Wuellner

Library of Congress Cataloging in Publication Data:

Lundbom, Jack R
   Jeremiah : a study in ancient Hebrew rhetoric.

   (Dissertation series ; no. 18)
   Thesis--Graduate Theological Union, Berkeley,
1973.
   Bibliography: p.
   Includes indexes.
   1. Bible. O. T. Jeremiah--Language, Style.
2. Bible. O. T. Jeremiah--Criticism, interpretation, etc.   I.   Series: Society of Biblical Literature. Dissertation series ; no. 18.
BS1525.2.L85   224'.2'044   75-15732
ISBN 0-89130-011-2

Printed in the United States of America
Printing Department
University of Montana
Missoula, Montana   59801

To

James Muilenburg

Scholar, Teacher, Friend

PREFACE

The present study was presented as a dissertation to the San Francisco Theological Seminary and the Graduate Theological Union in the spring of 1973, and is here made available to a wider reading audience in essentially the form in which it was presented. The research upon which the study is built has a longer history, however, more like ten years from start to finish. During this time many have contributed to the final product and I now happily give them the credit which it is rightly theirs to receive.

My interest in structure predates any work in Jeremiah. While doing my B.D. work at North Park Theological Seminary I became introduced to a book by Nils W. Lund entitled *Chiasmus in the New Testament*. Lund taught at North Park from 1922-1953 and was its dean from 1925-1949. He was also a family friend, but unfortunately one I was never able to know as scholar and teacher. I nevertheless developed a quick kinship with him during my seminary days and his particular interest in "chiasmus" became mine as well.

The book of Jeremiah was opened up to me by William L. Holladay, another scholar for whom I have the highest regard. It was my privilege to study with Professor Holladay during 1964-1965 at the Near East School of Theology in Beirut. Already by then a scholar of Jeremiah, his interest in structure and style--not to mention his expertise in the biblical languages--was sufficient to push me further along a course I had already chosen. Together we set to work on Jeremiah and our labors, especially in the poetry, were more than amply rewarded. The reader will have no difficulty in seeing the extent to which he has put me in his debt. Professor Holladay, although not a member of my doctoral committee, has been supportive of my work all along the way. He encouraged the dissertation's publication and has rendered help in proofreading a portion of the final manuscript.

My doctoral work was done primarily under the direction of James Muilenburg. Professor Muilenburg had already distinguished himself as a scholar and teacher at Union Theological Seminary in New York, but in his later years at San Anselmo was still vigorous and much beloved by students, all of whom drank freely from his deep well of knowledge and were able to profit immeasurably from a mind that had now come to maturity. I am grateful to have been one of those students. Seminars in Deuteronomy and Jeremiah contributed to my research, not least of all in helping me to clarify my methodology. Dr. Muilenburg was chairman of my doctoral committee until his retirement in 1971. Because of failing health he was able to read only part of the dissertation in first draft. Nevertheless I continued to write as if he were still listening. Now it is to him I dedicate what is finally done. I owe him far more. Wilhelm Wuellner chaired my committee following Dr. Muilenburg's departure and handled the final stages of dissertation preparation and the oral defense exceedingly well.

The other scholar with whom I worked closely in my doctoral studies was David Noel Freedman. Professor Freedman is another outstanding Old Testament scholar who contributed much to the present work. His probing questions brought about a necessary refinement of my thinking, and his insistence that biblical scholarship employ a rigorous historical and scientific methodology helped bring a measure of objectivity to my work when I may otherwise have relied too much on strict intuition. I also received from him a better understanding of Hebrew poetry. Dr. Freedman supported the dissertation from the beginning and became its primary support in the final stages. He carefully read two drafts and made comments that improved the work greatly over what it might otherwise have been.

Others joined my committee at various points along the way and I owe each of them a word of thanks. Professor Edwin M. Good of Stanford and Professor Norman K. Gottwald were members of the dissertation committee in addition to being readers of the dissertation. Each in his own way contributed to the final product. I also wish to thank Professors Thomas Conley and William J. Brandt of the Rhetoric Department at the University of California, Berkeley, for their interest in my work. I profited from their insistence that a rhetorical study of Jeremiah be related to studies in rhetorical criticism currently being done outside biblical studies. The result is thus a work which is essentially inter-disciplinary. Professor Brandt kindly supplied me with a portion of the manuscript for his forthcoming book *The Rhetoric of Poetry*. This was much appreciated. I must convey thanks also to Professor Leonard Nathan of the

Rhetoric Department at UCB for allowing me the use of his article on Vedic poetry prior to publication.

I was privileged to have Professor Norbert Lohfink, who in 1973 was visiting the GTU from Germany, as reader and guest at my oral defense. He proved to be a stimulating critic, and he is one with whom I hope an ongoing dialogue can be maintained.

The San Francisco Theological Seminary graciously afforded me the place to do my study and I thank them for this. Their library was a great asset, and so also was the personal assistance rendered by Head Librarian David Green and Louise Beck. Both aided me in locating materials which might otherwise have remained inaccessible.

To George MacRae of Harvard Divinity School and the Society of Biblical Literature, my thanks for their decision to include this in the new Dissertation Series. Dr. MacRae has provided every possible assistance in the preparation of the dissertation for publication. I have also been fortunate indeed to have a most capable typist, Miss Dorothy Riehm, who with remarkable ease has prepared the camera-ready copy for Scholars' Press.

To Dean George Peck and the Andover Newton Theological School, my thanks for a generous grant of money with which to pay the cost incurred in preparing the dissertation for publication. This too was greatly appreciated.

Finally, my work on Jeremiah has taken me away from my good wife and children, and they are to be thanked for patience and understanding beyond measure. For a long time now they have wondered when the end would finally come. A good family--no less than a good teacher or a good friend--is indeed a gift from God, and it is to him ultimately that thanks must be given, even as it is to him in the end that all glory must be given for whatever good might come of a human effort such as this.

Newton Centre, Massachusetts   Jack R. Lundbom
Easter, March 30, 1975

TABLE OF CONTENTS

AB	The Anchor Bible, eds., W.F. Albright and D.N. Freedman
AJP	American Journal of Philology
AJSLL	American Journal of Semitic Languages and Literature (Continued by Journal of Near Eastern Studies)
ANE	Ancient Near East
AThR	Anglican Theological Review
AV	Authorized King James Version (1611)
BA	The Biblical Archaeologist
BDB	F. Brown, S.R. Driver and C.A. Briggs eds., A Hebrew and English Lexicon of the Old Testament (Oxford: Clarendon Press, 1962)
BH^3	Biblica Hebraica, 3rd edition, ed., R. Kittel
BHS	Biblica Hebraica Stuttgartensia: Liber Jeremiae, eds., K. Elliger and W. Rudolph, prepared by W. Rudolph (Stuttgart, 1970)
BJRL	Bulletin of the John Rylands Library
BWAT	Beiträge zur Wissenschaft vom Alten Testament
BZAW	Beihefte zur Zeitschrift für die alttestamentliche Wissenschaft
CB	The New Century Bible, ed., W.F. Adeney
CBQ	The Catholic Biblical Quarterly
CJ	Classical Journal
CP	Classical Philology
CTM	Concordia Theological Monthly
EJ	Encyclopaedia Judaica, eds., C. Roth and G. Wigoder (Jerusalem: Keter Publishing House, 1971)
ET	Expository Times
GRBS	Greek, Roman and Byzantine Studies
HDB	James Hastings ed., A Dictionary of the Bible, IV (New York: Scribner's, 1902)
HKAT	Handkommentar zum Alten Testament, ed., W. Nowack
HSCP	Harvard Studies in Classical Philology
HThR	Harvard Theological Review
HUCA	Hebrew Union College Annual
IB	The Interpreter's Bible, ed., G. Buttrick
ICC	The International Critical Commentary, eds., S.R. Driver, A. Plummer and C.A. Briggs
IDB	The Interpreter's Dictionary of the Bible (New York: Abingdon Press, 1962)
Int	Interpretation
JAOS	Journal of the American Oriental Society
JB	The Jerusalem Bible (Garden City, 1966)

JBL	Journal of Biblical Literature
JHS	Journal of Hellenic Studies
JJS	Journal of Jewish Studies
JMEOS	Journal of the Manchester Egyptian and Oriental Society
JNABI	Journal of the National Association of Biblical Instructors (Continued by Journal of Bible and Religion and currently Journal of the American Academy of Religion)
JNES	Journal of Near Eastern Studies
JPOS	Journal of the Palestine Oriental Society
JQR	Jewish Quarterly Review
JR	Journal of Religion
JSS	Journal of Semitic Studies
JThS	Journal of Theological Studies
KAT	Kommentar zum Alten Testament, ed., E. Sellin
KBH	W.L. Holladay, A Concise Hebrew and Aramaic Lexicon of the Old Testament, based upon Lexicon in Veteris Testamenti Libros of Ludwig Köhler and Walter Baumgartner (Grand Rapids: Wm. B. Eerdmans, 1971)
LB	Linguistica Biblica
LXX	Septuagint, according to Septuaginta, II, 8th edition, ed., Alfred Rahlfs (Stuttgart, 1965)
Ms(s)	Manuscript(s)
MT	Massoretic Text, according to BH^3 or BHS
NEB	New English Bible (Oxford, 1970)
OS	Oudtestamentische Studiën
OT	The Old Testament
PBA	Proceedings of the British Academy
QJS	Quarterly Journal of Speech
RGG^2	Die Religion in Geschichte und Gegenwart, 2nd edition
RQ	Revue de Qumrân
RSV	Revised Standard Version (New York, 1953)
SEÅ	Svensk Exegetisk Årsbok
SJT	Southwestern Journal of Theology
ST	The Speech Teacher
TAPA	Transactions and Proceedings of the American Philological Association
TS	Theological Studies
UUÅ	Uppsala Universitets Årsskrift
VT	Vetus Testamentum
VT Supp	Supplements to Vetus Testamentum
ZAW	Zeitschrift für die alttestamentliche Wissenschaft
ZDA	Zeitschrift für deutsches Altertum
ZNW	Zeitschrift für die neutestamentliche Wissenschaft

I INTRODUCTION

Call to Rhetorical Criticism

A renewed interest in rhetoric can be seen today in biblical as well as in non-biblical studies.[1] In the field of Old Testament, a keynote was sounded by James Muilenburg in his lecture "Form Criticism and Beyond," delivered to the Society of Biblical Literature at the University of California, Berkeley, in December 1968.[2] Muilenburg pleaded on that occasion for increased sensitivity to rhetorical features in the biblical text. The call was timely, even though it presented no major advance beyond the particular brand of literary criticism that has engaged him for the past 50 years.[3]

Yet Muilenburg's concept of rhetoric is unmistakably modern. Written compositions are as much the object of study as oral speeches. And poetry also comes within its province.[4] But more important, rhetoric is not defined merely in terms of *style*, which was its chief meaning in the Renaissance,[5] and one that continued through the end of the 19th century.[6] Rhetoric is also made to include *structure*.[7] Muilenburg says,

> What I am interested in, above all, is in understanding the nature of Hebrew literary composition, in exhibiting the structural patterns that are employed for the fashioning of a literary unit, whether in poetry or in prose, and in discerning the many and various devices by which the predications are formulated and ordered into a unified whole. Such an enterprise I should describe as rhetoric and the methodology as rhetorical criticism.[8]

Muilenburg is interested in "structural patterns" which make up a literary unit. One of these structural patterns is the "inclusio," which balances the end of a unit with its beginning.[9] Another means by which Muilenburg ferrets out structure is by observing *clusters* of bi-cola or tri-cola, which he defines loosely as "strophes."[10] These are a bit harder to determine, but we know they exist because of acrostics and refrains.[11] Many of the other features which

1

Muilenburg points to could be termed stylistic, e.g., author's
use of particles, figures of speech, repetition, etc., yet because these appear in "strategic collocations," or in "crucial
or climactic contexts"[12] they serve a structural function.
Actually, Muilenburg makes no attempt to distinguish structure
from style (classical *dispositio* and *elocutio*), but then neither
do other scholars working in the field such as Luis Alonso-
Schökel[13] and William L. Holladay.[14] This should perhaps be
done. But most important just now is that one realize how the
modern definition of rhetoric has been expanded. It is in fact
much more broadly defined, but discussion of this can wait until
later.

According to Muilenburg the priorities in rhetorical
criticism are 1) to define the limits of the literary unit,[15]
and 2) to determine the structure of the composition, or in
Muilenburg's words, "discern the configuration of its component
parts."[16] These are important methodological insights, and they
have been echoed in a follow-up article by David Greenwood.[17]

Modern literary criticism of the Bible has brought us
to this juncture. Despite all work previously done, we are
still uncertain about delimiting literary units. This is basic,
and explains in part why our knowledge of internal structures is
less than complete. Advances have been made, especially since
the 18th century, yet the precise understanding we seek is still
for the most part based on subjective judgments.[18]

Nowhere is this more true than in the prophetic books.
And yet it is to that corpus that we now turn to select the book
providing for us the best point of departure: Jeremiah. Jeremiah is the largest prophetic book[19] and contains substantial
amounts of poetry and prose. But more important, Jeremiah
stands close in time to Deuteronomy,[20] the rhetorical book *par
excellence* in the Old Testament. The stylistic affinities between these two books are well-known,[21] and we might expect
there to be structural affinities as well. But before we outline the course of our work, it is necessary to give a brief
survey of earlier attempts at literary criticism in the Old Testament. This we will do, paying particular attention to what
has been done in Jeremiah.

Survey of Earlier Literary Criticism

In one way or another, all modern study of the prophetic
books builds on the work of Robert Lowth. His *Lectures on the*

Sacred Poetry of the Hebrews (1753)[22] argued two basic points: 1) that Hebrew poetry was dominated by a feature which he called "parallelism,"[23] and 2) that the prophetic books consisted primarily of poetry, not prose as was previously thought.[24] These theses were expanded and given specific application in Lowth's *Isaiah*, which appeared in 1778.[25] In Jeremiah, Lowth correctly recognized that the beginning and end of the book contained large poetical sections. He judged about half of the book to be poetry, and half prose.[26] Following Lowth's lead, Benjamin Blayney published a new translation with commentary of Jeremiah (1784)[27] which was modeled on Lowth's *Isaiah*. This work has been virtually forgotten, and unfortunately so since it is surprisingly discriminate in separating poetry from prose.[28]

During the same period, a new movement in source criticism was underway in Germany. By the 19th century it would be dominating not only biblical studies, but Homeric studies as well.[29] In Jeremiah, source criticism was from the first done in close conjunction with text criticism. It could hardly have been otherwise, since the Hebrew and Greek texts of Jeremiah are the most widely divergent in the Old Testament. The Greek (*LXX*) is one-eighth shorter than the Hebrew (*MT*), but more important, the Greek orders its material differently after 25:13.[30] These factors alone explain why even in recent times attention continues to be paid to the Jeremianic text.[31]

Eichhorn proposed in his *Einleitung* (1783) that the divergencies originated with Jeremiah himself (which parallels his views on Moses and Genesis). He believed that Jeremiah prepared successive editions. The first, with some augmentation, was sent to the exiles in Babylon. The second was prepared from a copy of the first in Egypt, after which it was sent to Palestine where it became the prototype of the *MT*.[32] Later in the early 19th century F. C. Movers proposed six separate books of Jeremiah which he argued were brought together into one compilation after the exile by the author of Kings. This is supported by the fact that Jer 52 = II Kings 24:18-25:30, each being the concluding passage of the respective books. This view was the one adopted by De Wette.[33]

By the mid-19th century, when source criticism was well advanced, the same issues at stake in the Pentateuch were also at stake in the Prophets: authorship, composition and the dating of the sources. By 1850 the thesis for a "Second Isaiah" (Isa 40-66) had gained wide acceptance.[34] No "Second Jeremiah"

emerged, but it was readily agreed that not everything in the
book of Jeremiah was to be attributed to the 7th-6th century
prophet. Jer 10:1-16 was assigned to "pseudo-Isaiah,"[35] and
sections from the Oracles to Foreign Nations (chs. 46-51) were
denied Jeremianic authorship.[36]

Graf's commentary (1862) also reflected the view that
Jeremiah was a composite document.[37] Graf called attention to
the fact that in the early chapters, Jeremiah speaks in the
first person while he is referred to in chapters 20ff in the
third person. In the former we find the formulas ויהי דבר יהוה
אלי לאמר or ויאמר יהוה אלי, while in the latter the correspond-
ing formula is ויהי דבר יהוה אל-ירמיהו לאמר. Also in these later chapters, both in the superscriptions as well as in the narrative portions, the designation ירמיהו הנביא is used, which
Graf says, "in dem Munde des Jeremia selbst sonderbar wäre."[38]

By the end of the 19th century we see three sources
emerging: 1) the Jeremiah source, consisting primarily of the
early chapters; 2) a Baruch source, consisting of narrative
which refers to Jeremiah in the third person, and 3) a Later-
Compiler (*Bearbeiter*) source which supplements both Jeremiah
and Baruch. This breakdown is seen most clearly in Giesebrecht's commentary.[39]

Yet the most important scholar of this period was Bernhard Duhm. A contemporary of Julius Wellhausen, who championed
the cause of source criticism in the Pentateuch, Duhm wrote
major commentaries on Isaiah (1892) and Jeremiah (1901).[40]
Wellhausen limited himself to the Minor Prophets.[41] In Jeremiah
Duhm refined the three-source theory by shifting the discussion
to a new axis, viz., prose vs. poetry. The study of Hebrew
poetry had been given new impetus in Germany as a result of the
metrical theories of Julius Ley and Eduard Sievers.[42] Duhm was
influenced by Ley,[43] and as is well-known, applied Ley's theories to Jeremiah with astounding rigidity.[44] Nevertheless Duhm
can be credited with isolating the core of the Jeremianic message in the poetry.

This in part reaffirmed the distinctions made by Lowth
and Blayney more than a century ago, yet with the difference
that neither Lowth nor Blayney were concerned as Duhm was with
isolating Jeremiah's *ipsissima verba*. We must not overlook
Kittel's 1906 edition of the *MT*, which for the first time
printed poetry as poetry. Kittel himself did Jeremiah, and is
largely responsible for the way the poetry is still read.

The last stage of source criticism in Jeremiah came with the early works of Sigmund Mowinckel and T. H. Robinson. Both later joined the new school of form criticism, but in Jeremiah their work proceeds along the old lines. Mowinckel's monograph *Zur Komposition des Buches Jeremia* (1914) is the most advanced discussion on the subject. In it Mowinckel refines the three-source theory further. Source A consists of poetry and is the *ipsissima verba* of Jeremiah. Source B consists of biographical prose written chiefly in the third person by an admirer. Source C is sermonic prose similar to what we find in Deuteronomy, and written in the first person.[45] Mowinckel was skeptical about Baruch being the biographer (responsible for Source B), but he later gave that up.[46] Working independently of Mowinckel, Robinson came to similar conclusions.[47]

Source criticism has thus for the most part come and gone,[48] but not without leaving some lasting impressions. We are in the first place firmly committed to the idea that the book contains poetry and prose. Recent attempts by Holladay to identify presumed poetry within what has heretofore been taken as prose may alter the picture somewhat, but it does not bring into question the fact that both types of material are mani-fest.[49] This point must be made clear, for whether we realize it or not, our views of structure will be deeply influenced by what we take to be poetry and what we take to be prose. Where poetry and prose are interspersed, our judgments determine in many cases where we begin or end the literary unit. It is also clear that the core of the Jeremianic message is the poetry, and we will build on that assumption, even if we are not quite so concerned to recover the prophet's *ipsissima verba*.

Secondly, we are committed to the idea that Jeremiah is not the sole author of the book which bears his name. The view of total Jeremianic authorship is expressed in the Talmud.[50] A biographer was largely responsible for the book's composition (although Jeremiah cannot be excluded as collaborator), and Baruch is the likely candidate. Not only is it Baruch who pre-pares the first scroll dictated by Jeremiah (Jer 36), but Mowinckel seems to be quite correct in proposing that Jeremiah's personal word to him (Jer 45) was meant as an autobiographical postscript.[51] In the *LXX*, now generally regarded as the more original text,[52] this postscript concludes the book (less chapter 52 of course). This in no way precludes there being other biographers or editors who add and rearrange material later on.

But it does mean that the book in broad outline was close to being in its present form by the beginning of the exile.

More could be said about source criticism. It has made substantial gains[53] even though some of its assumptions have had to be modified.[54] Yet it has not been rendered unusable because of newer methods which have come to replace it.[55] We need say no more. Specific source-critical points can be discussed as they arise along the way.

We turn now to form criticism (*Gattungskritik*),[56] which has dominated biblical criticism since the turn of the century. Its prime exponent was Hermann Gunkel, who did major studies in both Genesis and the Psalms.[57] Gunkel was interested in the pre-literary stage of Hebrew literature, which made form criticism particularly an inquiry into folk literature. Although some would restrict its province to folk literature exclusively,[58] Gunkel explicitly rejected the suggestion when it was made to him.[59] In his characteristic eclectic fashion, he believed that the method could be applied *mutatis mutandis* to the Prophets, and subsequent form-critics agreed.[60]

The primary concern of the form-critic was the identification of *Gattungen*, or to use the more common term, *genres*. Gunkel's article "Die Grundprobleme der israelitischen Literaturgeschichte"[61] was programmatic. Gunkel was also concerned to find the genre's *Sitz im Leben* (setting in life). Hymns he said were sung in the temple, lawsuits originated in the city gate, and prophetic oracles were uttered in the outer court of the temple.[62]

Gunkel said very little about Jeremiah. Actually from a form-critical standpoint, he developed his thoughts very little on any of the prophets.[63] Yet the methodology which became so fruitful for the study of folklore,[64] together with Gunkel's few comments about the prophets, have set in motion a movement in prophetical criticism that is at best a mixed blessing. But much work has been done, so it is necessary to examine the most basic form-critical assumptions as they apply to the Prophets.

Since Gunkel was interested in the earliest forms of prophetic literature, it was natural to begin in the poetry. Gunkel accepted the axiom that poetry was older than prose,[65] and, following the source critics, he believed that this is where the core of the prophetic preaching would be found. Yet a problem arose in the investigation of the prophetic speeches which emerged in the investigation neither of Genesis nor of the Psalms, viz., how one delimits the literary unit. Gunkel used two criteria for delimitation: 1) stereotyped opening phrases, and 2) content. Genres begin in a certain way, e.g., the lament begins with "Woe," while the hymn begins with "Sing unto Yahweh."[66] Gunkel built here on the assumption of Norden that ancient man was more tied to convention than is modern man.[67] He nevertheless used *modern* examples to illustrate his point. The fairy tale begins with "Once upon a time," the letter with "Dear Sir," and the sermon with "Beloved in the Lord."[68] And scholars following Gunkel have made the modern evidence even more impressive.[69]

Content analysis provided other clues for genre classification. Gunkel's *Einleitung in die Psalmen*[70] classifies hymns in a way similar to what we find in our modern hymnbooks. Here content is quite clearly the main criterion for all Gunkel's genres and sub-genres. One cannot quarrel about basic categories (songs of praise, songs of thanksgiving, individual and communal laments), but neither can one confirm (or refute) the existence of all the sub-genres, if in fact they are sub-genres. In Genesis Gunkel was on better ground when he argued for legendary genres, for he had the extensive research of the Grimm brothers and Axel Olrik to build on.[71] Furthermore, legends and fairy tales provide all kinds of clues from their content about beginning and end. It is thus easy to understand how Gunkel could say of a Genesis legend, "Everyone can see that the story ends here."[72] But everyone cannot see where the prophetic speech ends, and form-critics realize this. This is why more recent form-critics find their outlines in the prose and work back to the poetry,[73] instead of allowing the poetry to articulate itself.

Additional evidence showing the inability of form-critics to delimit the prophetic speeches comes from their arguments about length. Two arguments were used by Gunkel in the main, and both are erroneous.

The first was a psychological argument. Men of antiquity were unable to remember long units, therefore the units must be brief.[74] Gunkel used the analogy of a child (ancient man was "child-like") who only gradually develops to the point where he can absorb more.[75] Herder, a like-minded romantic from another era, interestingly enough argued just the reverse, viz., that ancients were fond of prolonged discourse.[76] This appears to be the more valid psychological argument if one wishes to stay with

Gunkel's analogy, for children are able to remember much longer units than adults, everything else being equal. Dependence upon the written word impairs memory, and anyone who has read stories to a child who cannot read will attest to the fact that the child can reproduce the story from memory much better than the adult who reads it to him night after night.

The second argument was an evolutionary one. Gunkel assumed that since the earliest prophets were ecstatics, their speeches must be brief. The earliest prophetic utterances were single words such as "Jezreel," "Not my People," etc., the names which prophets gave to their children.[77] "Dann haben es die P[rophet]en gelernt, längere Reden zu schaffen, die etwa ein Kapitel umfassen."[78] In Amos we get poems of four cola or more; Jer 2:14-19 is cited as one longer yet.[79] Ezekiel's speeches are the longest. Gunkel attributes this change to a development in culture. As writing became more and more common, the prophets turned into authors.[80] This latter point cannot be dismissed out of hand, for the prophets beginning with Amos and Hosea are clearly a different breed from those who preceded them. And they may also have written their speeches in a way that earlier prophets did not. But this will not support the thesis that speeches increase in length from Amos to Ezekiel. Gunkel was highly selective in the examples which he chose, and left far more unexplained than he explained. There is no observable distinction, for example, between the length of poems in Amos and Jeremiah. If anything, Amos 1-2 is probably one of the longest speeches in any of the prophetic books.[81]

We must conclude then that form-critics are on very subjective grounds when they argue for brief speeches. Furthermore, we are still left with the obvious question of "How long is long?" or "How short is short?". In Jeremiah, Gunkel's delineations of 2:14-19[82] and 17:5-8[83] are perceptive enough, and I would say basically correct, but both of these poems are easily identifiable because of obvious poetic balance.

Another form-critical observation has been a mixed blessing. Gunkel realized that oral literature is characterized by loose connections. Legends are often brought together by a thematic principle, e.g., the central figure may provide the means of unification.[84] But by and large the various collections of legends, songs and proverbs are brought together without any discernible connection.[85] Form-critics believed the same to be true of prophetic speeches, and from time to time we hear these being compared to "pearls on a string,"[86] a phrase apparently stemming from Herder.[87] This claim has been substantiated by the traditio-historical school and others who show how "catchwords" link poems together into chains of tradition. We will say more about this in a moment. But later form-critics, on the other hand, all too often use this point to argue that the present text has no discernible order.[88] John Bright has adopted this line in Jeremiah.[89] This has brought discredit upon form criticism since one of the original strengths of Gunkel's work was that it was holistic and treated the text with much greater respect than earlier works done by the source-critics.[90]

Recent form-critical work in the Prophets and in Jeremiah is plagued by these difficulties. The most ambitious study of prophetic speech forms is by Claus Westermann.[91] Westermann sets forth what he believes to be the fundamental prophetic genre, viz., the "judgment speech." The judgment speech is directed at two main audiences: 1) the individual (JI), and 2) the nation (JN). Jeremiah contains both. Following Gunkel and Gressmann, Westermann accepted the idea that prophets were from oldest times foretellers of the future. Thus we could expect the true prophetic genre to be one which forecasts the future.[92] What resulted was two self-evident types: 1) predictions of salvation,[93] and 2) predictions of judgment. Westermann also used the Mari Letters as a basis of comparison.[94]

Thus far Westermann is on safe ground. There is no reason to object to the idea that prophets were foretellers of the future.[95] Neither is there any reason to quarrel over prophets making predictions of salvation and judgment. We can conclude both almost *a priori*. We need not even object to calling them separate genres. Perhaps they were.

But Westermann's work falls apart when he tries to set up structures for the prophetic speech. Two difficulties are apparent at once. In the first place, he is either unable or does not bother to defend the limits of his literary units. In his lone example of the JI from the Prophets (Amos 7:16-17), part of the known speech is excluded. That speech began in v. 14. In the poetry, which we agree is difficult to separate, Westermann could at least have availed himself of some outside help. But a comparison of his units with those in BH^3 and the modern versions, not to mention the commentaries, will show that the former seldom correspond with any of the latter.

A second major difficulty concerns the outline categories themselves. To say that a judgment speech has two main
parts, the accusation and announcement of judgment, is to accent
the obvious. Could it be otherwise? These and his other categories are so general that they become non-descript. Among the
JN's, Jer 5:10-14 is made to fit by using the words of judgment,
which should by his calculation come at the end, serve as "Introduction."[96] In Jer 7:16-18,20 a command to Jeremiah not to
intercede for the people is "Introduction." And other examples
outside Jeremiah make it even more clear that the texts have
been placed in a mould which just does not fit.[97]

When we look at the list of Jeremianic passages that
supposedly fit the JI, of which Westermann finds ten,[98] only one
of them, 36:29-30, corresponds tolerably to the outline given.
Some lack "Accusations,"[99] while on two occasions the judgment
is prophesied to *both* the nation and the individual.[100] In the
case of 29:24-32, the order does not conform to the outline.
Also there are many instances where one of the elements of the
speech is not present.[101]

Taken together, these weaknesses greatly diminish the
value of Westermann's work. Certainly his structural analysis
cannot stand for the Jeremianic speech, if indeed it can stand
for any of the prophetic speeches. So for our purposes, it provides virtually no help at all.

Other genres which the prophets supposedly borrowed[102]
have also been studied since Gunkel. Westermann gives scant
attention to them in his book,[103] while other scholars have
written up independent studies of them in the journals. In Jeremiah, most attention has been paid to a supposed "lawsuit"
genre, which also goes by the name of *rib* (ריב), the characteristic term of the genre meaning "contention."[104] Gunkel called
it the *Gerichtsrede*, an example of which he found in Psalm
82.[105] Gunkel also laid out the outline of the genre,[106] and
has since been followed by Herbert Huffmon.[107] Huffmon advanced
the study by tying the ריב in with George Mendenhall's classic
study of Law and Covenant.[108] Mendenhall had compared the covenant of the Old Testament with Hittite treaties and shown
striking similarities. Huffmon then interpreted the lawsuit in
the context of the covenant calling the ריב a "covenant lawsuit." The prophets were seen as bringing a lawsuit by Yahweh
against the people for breach of covenant. Huffmon also took
over the main passages which Gunkel used to illustrate his

Gerichtsrede, among them Jer 2:4ff. In addition he added Deut
32, which is important for us since it is now clear that this
poem had a decisive influence upon Jeremiah.[109]

Following Huffmon, Julien Harvey contributed to the
discussion by modifying the Gunkel-Huffmon outline and comparing
prominent biblical texts with a lawsuit from the Epic of Tukul-
ti-Ninurta I, found among the Assyrian documents at Nineveh.[110]
Both Jer 2 and Deut 32 are central to his "Rîb à condamnation."
Harvey also takes this form to have originated in international
law where it was used by a suzerain against his unfaithful
vassal.

Finally Joseph Blenkinsopp has written an article on
the "prophetic reproach"[111] which he takes to be similar to the
lawsuit, and includes among his examples Jer 2:4-13. The significance of his work is that he refrains from making an outline,
and recognizes further that in at least one case (though not in
Jeremiah), it is the repetition in the poem that provides the
poem with its structure.[112]

Again we do not quarrel with this general approach.
The idea that Jeremiah would use a lawsuit form in one of his
speeches is reasonable. We can readily imagine him denouncing
the people for breach of contract. The only possible objection
to the overall comparison might be that, of all the extra-bibli-
cal texts cited thus far, none refers to a divorce proceeding.
This is important, for Jeremiah often views the covenant in
marital terms. Jer 2:2-3, which is introductory, describes
the early relationship of Yahweh and Israel as a time of honey-
moon.[113]

The main criticism is again with structure. There is
no agreement among these scholars on what constitutes the literary unit.[114] Also explanations of the internal structure of
the Jeremianic lawsuit tend to leave one confused. Elements in
the Jeremianic text are again "out of order." Gunkel noted long
ago that the opening summons, instead of coming at the beginning
of the suit where it belonged, came instead at v. 12.[115] Huffmon admits also that the suit begins with a summons to the ac-
cused, which he says should come later.[116] Then there is the
same problem which we found with Westermann's work, viz., that
the categories in neither the Gunkel-Huffmon outline nor the
Harvey outline do an adequate job of explaining the Jeremianic
text.[117]

It is clear that the advocates of these "lawsuit" genres

have over-extended themselves in drawing their parallels. And
the most serious result is that they have thereby failed to il-
luminate the way in which the text articulates itself. Exegeti-
cally this method is almost of no value. Anyone who reads the
text carefully is constantly at pains to see how such outlines
are made to fit the evidence. That Jeremiah is using legal language we will not deny. Neither will we object to the thesis
that his speech contains allusions to legal proceedings from the
court.[118] But it remains unproven that Jeremiah is using a borrowed genre in chapter 2, and we are certain that the structure
of Jer 2 is not controlled by any of the outlines set forth in
the lawsuit proposals. It is to Blenkinsopp's credit that he
refrains from making an outline, and the same may be said of
Holladay, who proposes a lawsuit initiated by Jeremiah against
Yahweh in Jer 12:1ff.[119]

   With other genre studies the same situation obtains.
Thomas Raitt has argued for a "summons to repentance" genre,[120]
and Norman Habel has isolated what he believes to be a genre of
the prophetic "call."[121] Both take into account texts from Jeremiah. Raitt has no agreed-upon units in mind when inserting
texts into his scheme, nor does he keep the texts in their present order. This latter problem does not disturb Raitt, any
more than it disturbs other form-critics, for it is assumed that
the present order is one of disarray.[122] In Habel's study, the
outline fails in part when applied to Jeremiah's call, and fails
significantly when put to the call of Isaiah.[123] This is damag-
ing to the whole argument, since the calls of Jeremiah and
Isaiah are two of the most important in the prophetic corpus.

   Actually the most form-critical help for delimiting
literary units came as a result of the thesis of Ludwig Köhler
who argued that prophetic speech was essentially "messenger
speech."[124] The prophet now becomes a messenger who receives
his message in the council of Yahweh and then delivers it to the
people. Yahweh is the sender; the people are the sendee. The
prophet remains an intermediary whose only function is to deliver the message as directed. This model then replaces the
ecstatic model, which was accepted earlier on the basis of
Hölscher's work.[125] The model of the messenger is seen elsewhere in the ancient Near East, notably at Mari, where a proph-
etic-type figure functions as a divine messenger of the god
Dagan.[126] A comparison, moreover, of the formula "Thus says
Yahweh..." (כה-אמר יהוה) with such formulas as "Thus says the

king..." (כה־אמר המלך) or "Thus says Ben Hadad..." (כה־אמר
בן־הדד), both of which are used in messenger contexts,[127] suggests that the prophetic formula was appropriated by the prophets for a new use. The "call" passages of Isaiah and Jeremiah
further suggest that the commission to be Yahweh's messenger
was part of the prophetic self-understanding. Köhler pointed
this out in Isaiah 6. In Jeremiah, the call from Yahweh is made
in order that Yahweh may *send* Jeremiah (אשלחך), after which he
puts words into Jeremiah's mouth (1:7,9).[128] Thus recent scholarship has adopted the messenger model,[129] although it is readily acknowledged that not all prophetic speeches are messenger
speeches.[130] Meek isolates Jer 2:2-3 on these grounds since the
speech is framed by כה אמר יהוה at the beginning, and נאם־יהוה
at the end, the latter being another formula similar to כה אמר
יהוה.[131]

These formulas are then a help in delimiting the literary unit. Yet they are not always reliable. It is conceded
that some have been inserted by editors for later adaptations of
the material,[132] in which case the original beginning or end of
the speech is obscured. In actual practice the form-critics
disregard these forumlas almost as much as they follow them,
which means we should probably regard them in about the same way
as we regard chapter headings. They are useful ancient markers,
but they need corroborating data before they can be judged to
signal authentic breaks, or be in fact original messenger formulas. Also, we can get help from these formulas only when they
are present, and a good bit of the Jeremianic text is without
them.

Summing up then the contribution of form criticism, we
can agree that it has asked some important questions even if it
has not always been able to provide the correct answers. The
question of genre is not unimportant. It was fundamental for
Gunkel in Genesis, and it is equally fundamental in Jeremiah--
especially when we come to the prose material. There what the
source-critics called "biography," some latter-day form-critics
want to call "legend," which is clearly an error.[133] Gunkel's
comments about this material indicate that he did not consider
it to be legend,[134] and Muilenburg has recently affirmed the
same.[135] The prose of Jeremiah ought not be compared with
either the Genesis legends or the legends of Elijah and Elisha;
it is far more like the Court History in II Sam 7-20 I Kings
1-2.[136]

As for the prophetic speeches, we are still lacking models for a proper genre analysis.[137] The most promising model to be used of late, viz., the letter,[138] is only of help when comparing opening and closing formulas. We get no insight into the *body* of the speech. Here we must judge form criticism to have failed, for it has been unable to throw light on the structure of the prophetic speech.[139]

The form-critical emphasis on the prophet as *speaker* is important. It is also worthwhile to recover when possible the *Sitz im Leben* of the prophetic speech, or to use a more appropriate term now in use, the *audience*. The speech needs to be understood in the context of the audience for which it was originally intended. And we must also find out more about how the speech--together with other comment--was used to address audiences removed in time from the original delivery.

It remains only to comment briefly on the contribution of the traditio-historical school of Old Testament studies. This was another school of biblical criticism which flourished for a time at Uppsala, and like the school of form criticism, developed its own particular theories about oral tradition.[140] H. S. Nyberg began it all with some revolutionary comments at the beginning of a commentary on Hosea.[141] He argued in short that much of the Old Testament was transmitted in oral form until the exile, which was the crisis that forced it into writing. This amounted to a sweeping attack on source criticism, and with regard to the Prophets, it challenged the entire search for the prophet's *ipsissima verba*. All we have in the text are "tradition-complexes" which became fixed at the time when they were written down.

The upshot of this thesis was a lively debate which continued for a time on oral vs. written tradition. Today, however, it is generally agreed not only that writing was practiced quite early in Israel,[142] but also that *both* oral and written tradition existed side by side prior to the exile.[143]

With respect to the Prophets, the traditio-historical critics believed that a circle of disciples preserved the master's words for a time in oral form, after which they were eventually written down. Hosea has continued to have particular appeal for this methodology,[144] but Jeremiah is not neglected either despite the explicit statement in Jer 36 that Baruch wrote Jeremiah's speeches down. This is a crucial chapter, and Birkeland, Mowinckel and Engnell begin there too.[145] They point

out the fact that Jeremiah retained oracles for a long period
(23 years according to 25:3) before committing them to writing
(36:2-4). This alone says something about the preservation of
literature in non-written form. The other point used to support
their thesis is not so persuasive. Birkeland says that the
final words of chapter 36, "and many similar words were added to
them" cannot be ascribed to Baruch,[146] therefore someone else
must be the biographer. But this however does not follow. And
as we pointed out earlier, Mowinckel later gave up a similar
skepticism which he once had on the same point.[147] But in the
traditio-historical view, Baruch is just one member of a circle
of disciples who preserved the Jeremianic traditions into the
exile, at which time they were finally written down.

Thus in Jeremiah these scholars begin not with the Jeremianic speeches, but with what they believe to be large blocks
of tradition still observable in the final composition. Metho-
dologically they work just the reverse of the form-critics:
they begin with the latest stage of development and work back.
Four "tradition-complexes" are posited in Jeremiah:[148] 1) 1-24;
2) 25, 46-51; 3) 26-35/36; 4) 36/37-45. The complexes are isolated for rather obvious reasons. The break at 25:13 between
the *MT* and the *LXX* is considered significant, and thus aids in
marking off two blocks of tradition. Since 25:1-13 originally
introduced the Oracles to Foreign Nations (as it still does in
the *LXX*), it is grouped together with those oracles, which in
the *MT* are found in 46-51. This forms the second group. By
elimination, 1-24 becomes group one. The other two groups are
arrived at by taking what is left and dividing at chapter 36,
which is pivotal. Only agreement does not exist on whether 36
ends the earlier complex, or begins the complex that follows.
Engnell takes the first view, and Claus Rietzschel, a German
scholar working along similar lines, takes the latter.[149]
Kessler and Hobbs side with Engnell.[150]

The way these scholars continue their research into earlier stages of composition is worthy of comment. Like the form-
critics, scholars of this school emphasize that earlier complexes were formed by rather loose connections. This is due to
oral tradition, only the traditio-historical scholars are quick
to point out that such arrangements are not haphazard of illog-
ical.[151] Early units are grouped into chains by "catchwords,"
(Rietzschel: "thematischen Gesichtspunkten oder Stichwort-
verknüpfungen").[152] This is basically a sound observation,

except that it is unfortunate that the major attempts to find
such links in Jeremiah have been made in the prose. We reject
the assumption that the prose is legend, and we are not prepared
to grant the material any substantial period of oral transmission. Thus the prose does not contain catchwords.[153] The poetry
is the proper place to look for catchwords. But since the units
there are not firmly established, this would be a precarious
venture. One can hardly show what is linked together without
first knowing the limits of units being linked. Thus we can
only conclude that such a study has promise, but cannot be done
unless other controls are available.

This concludes our survey. It should be clear by now
that a structural analysis of Jeremiah is much needed. We need
to know the very things which Muilenburg listed as deserving top
priority: the limits of the literary units, and the structure
of those units, whether in the prophetic speech or in the larger
book of Jeremiah.

Outline of the Present Study

In order to speak to this problem, we are prepared to
argue that two known rhetorical figures, the inclusio and the
chiasmus, are important controlling structures in Jeremiah.
They control not only the prophetic speeches, but also larger
complexes which make up the *book* of Jeremiah.

We mentioned earlier that Muilenburg delimited units by
the inclusio. Leon Liebreich also found the inclusio in both
First and Second Isaiah.[154] In Deuteronomy a use of the inclusio has been recognized by Norbert Lohfink, although he has yet
to realize the full extent to which this figure is employed in
the composition of that book.[155] More recently Dahood has found
it in the Psalms,[156] and David Noel Freedman has shown it to be
present in the poetry of Job and Hosea.[157] In Jeremiah some
valuable insights can be gained from Condamin's commentary,[158]
although Condamin's strophic notions detract from the overall
value of this particular work. Not all inclusios are the same.
Most consist of repeated vocabulary or phraseology at the beginning and end of a unit. But in the case of Hosea 8:9-13, Freedman correctly points out that the final line is not mere repetition of the line which opens the poem;[159] the two lines are com-
plementary, being broken parts of a standard bi-colon which the
poet uses for purposes of inclusio. The inclusio must therefore

not be defined too narrowly. It is necessary only that the end
show continuity with the beginning, and that this continuity be
taken as a deliberate attempt by the author to effect closure.

Chapter II of our study will show how the inclusio is
used in Jeremiah. Examples will be grouped at three levels.
One level will be the larger book of Jeremiah. Here we will
show structures imposed on earlier material in the collection
process, whether originating from a period of oral tradition or
deriving from the hand of a writing scribe. The other two levels deal with the Jeremianic speech, both as a whole and in
part. The inclusio is the surest way to delimit the speech,
since, by definition, it ties the end together with the beginning. We will also show the inclusio functioning in units smaller than the speech. It will thus be seen to control certain
parts even when it does not control the whole. This suggests to
us that such units are stanzas within the poem.

The other rhetorical figure assuming a prominent role in
Jeremiah is the *chiasmus*, or as is sometimes called, the
chiasm.[160] In rhetorical handbooks, the chiasmus is an inverted
syntactic structure which occurs in parallel or linked phrases.[161] It is well-known from both classical and biblical sources.[162] In Hebrew poetry it was first cited as an inverted form
of Lowth's parallelism, and was soon found to control much
larger units also, both in poetry and in prose.[163] It is thus
an ABB'A' structure, or in more developed form, ABCB'A',
ABCC'B'A', etc. In larger units, it is also the name given to
ABA' structures. The classic study of chiasmus in large panels
was done by Nils W. Lund, who demonstrated that this was clearly
a structure to be reckoned with in the biblical text.[164] Although Lund did most of his work in the New Testament, he argued
that chiasmus was originally a Semitic form, and called it on
more than one occasion "the gift of the East to the West."[165]
Lund also maintained that the structure served a liturgical
function in the Jewish community.[166]

Since the time of Lund numerous studies of chiastic
structures have been done. The figure in one form or another
has been found throughout the Old Testament,[167] including the
Prophets.[168] Some impressive chiasmi have been shown by Lohfink
to exist in Deuteronomy.[169] Thus while form-critics have either
ignored or spoken disparagingly about such studies,[170] it is
still recognized by scholars sensitive to literary structure
that the quest for chiastic structures is far from being

completed.[171] In Jeremiah some impressive chiasmi have been
discovered by Holladay,[172] and he has recently called for a
full-scale study to be done in that book.[173] This thesis is an
answer to that call.

Chapter III will be on chiasmus, and like the chapter
on inclusio, examples will be grouped at three levels. The
first level in this case will be the sub-poem level. Since chiasmus is first known as a syntactic structure, we will show how
it is used in that manner. Then we will show how it functions
in larger units within the poem. These we also think to be
stanzas. Since our examples are few, additional research can
perhaps test this to see if such a conclusion is valid. The
second level will be the poem (or speech) level. There is no
a priori reason why the chiasmus should delimit the speech like
the inclusio, but for reasons which will be given along the way,
we believe that to be the case in the Jeremianic speeches. The
speech chiasmi will also give us valuable insight into stanza
formation, providing us with clues to the "clusters" that make
up the overall structure. The third level will be the larger
book of Jeremiah. Here our examples will be varied. In all but
one case, viz., the Letter to the Exiles (ch. 29), the chiasmus
will be a structure imposed on material in the collection process. And even with the Letter to the Exiles, a superstructure
has been imposed on the original letter to give it an expanded
form.

This thesis then will take its lead from scholars who
pursued similar lines of inquiry in the past. These scholars
have met with varying degrees of success, but the evidence which
has motivated them--be it little or much--is nevertheless incon-
trovertible. Jeremiah has been largely neglected, yet we aim to
show that it is indeed a rich mine for such study. Our work
will be based upon a close examination of the text, without
which no rhetorical theory can stand. We will cover the entire
book, presenting a systematic array of data from all levels.

In two respects we hope to go beyond previous work.
First of all, our desire is to be eclectic insofar as other
methodologies can contribute to overall understanding. Earlier
studies of structure have gone along too much on their own.
Even Lund, who hoped in his New Testament research to open dialogue with the form-critics,[174] stopped short of penetrating
debate with them about the text. Corroborating data provides a
control for one's research. Yet by being eclectic we do not

mean to imply that all methodologies can be melted together and used synthetically. Rhetorical criticism is a distinct method, and makes possible a distinct way of looking at the text. As we aim to show, it can provide fresh insight into the text. But, the time is ripe for dialogue among the various disciplines, and this piece of research is devoted to that end.

The other point at which this thesis will go beyond previous work is by looking for the *function* of the rhetorical figures. We must do more than be descriptive, which has been the tendency from Lowth on. Analyses of balancing patterns could go on *ad infinitum* without our knowing anything of their rhetorical value.

To begin to see what we mean by "function," let us compare the different ways of viewing parallelism. Lowth described a relationship which existed between parallel lines. They were synonymous, antithetical, or synthetic, the latter being a balance of rhythm only. Following Lowth, refinements of the "parallelism doctrine" have amounted to more precise statements on word balance, whether or not the parallelism is complete or incomplete, has compensation or lacks compensation, etc.,[175] but these still remain essentially descriptive.

Another way of looking at the same phenomenon is seen in the work of Christian Schoettgen, who discussed this very thing in a section of his two-volume work *Horae Hebraica et Talmudica*.[176] What Lowth described as parallelism, Schoettgen took to be an example of the rhetorical figure "exergasia," which is described in the rhetorical handbooks as a figure that "polishes" or "refines" by repetition.[177] Schoettgen equated it with the Latin "expolitio," which is similarly defined in the *Ad Herennium* (4.42). Schoettgen then set forth ten canons of "exergasia sacra" to show the different ways this is accomplished. In these canons he becomes analytical as Lowth was to be, but going further in anticipating those who issued correctives to Lowth later on. A translation of these canons together with biographical information and comment appears in the Appendix.

We shall then be more than descriptive with the inclusio and the chiasmus. We want to know how the figures *function* in rhetorical discourse, whether it be in the original speeches of Jeremiah, or in the later re-presentation of those speeches along with other material to a worshipping congregation. In the Jeremianic speeches we will be interested in another dimension of the New Rhetoric: argumentation.[178] Do these figures function for Jeremiah in his argument, and if so, how? In structures that tie together large and originally separate units, we want to do more than point out the sense of order and artistry which the structures display. Lund suggested that the chiasmus had a liturgical function, and we will build on this idea with both the inclusio and the chiasmus in Jeremiah. In any case, the material must be viewed against its audience, and we will try whenever possible to distinguish between an original audience and a later audience removed from the former in time. The concluding chapter will bring together all the research in order that some statement can be made about 1) the rhetoric of Jeremiah, and 2) the rhetoric of the book of Jeremiah.

In our discussion of poetic material, we will use the terminology set forth by Albright and Holladay.[179] The basic unit in Hebrew is the *word*, which includes its prefixes and suffixes, and in some cases such particles which are attached by a maqqeph, e.g., כל-, את-, etc. The basic thought unit is the *colon*, which consists in almost all cases of two or more words, but rarely more than five. Beyond the colon is the *line*, made up of two or three cola. A line of two cola may also be called a *bi-colon*, and a line of three cola a *tri-colon*. Beyond this is the *stanza*, which is a group of two or more lines. In Jeremiah the stanzas are usually four lines, rarely more. We will not retain the use of the term "strophe," even though for many it means essentially what our "stanza" means.[180] Too often it implies an antistrophe common to Greek usage, and it further suggests units which are always equal in length. Here is an element of Condamin's work in Jeremiah with which we do not want to be associated.[181] The stanzas in Jeremiah are sometimes of equal length, but frequently they are not.

With regard to Hebrew meter, we will assume as little as possible since its canons are still as obscure as they were in the time of Lowth.[182] Where it is advantageous to measure cola quantitatively, we will count the number of syllables in a manner currently being done by Freedman and others.[183]

We now proceed to our study, which is to exhibit and discuss two rhetorical structures in Jeremiah: the inclusio and the chiasmus. Stated in terms of a thesis, we will argue the following: *that rhetorical structures are controlling structures of the prophetic speeches in Jeremiah, and that any other structures, gained as they may be from various genres known to the poet Jeremiah, are clearly secondary in influence--if they have influence at all--and in no case do they supply the basic model for the speech.* A corollary to this will also be argued: *that rhetorical structures are controlling structures for collections of speeches and collections of other material about Jeremiah which go together to make up the composite work now known to us as the book of Jeremiah.*

II INCLUSIO

The largest number of inclusios to be found thus far in datable passages of the Old Testament occurs in Isaiah. Muilenburg noted the inclusio in the poems of II Isaiah, and Liebreich has argued for many more in Isaiah, both I and II. One of Liebreich's more impressive examples ties the whole book together: chapter 66 is made to balance chapter 1.[1] Adding then to these the inclusios already mentioned from Deuteronomy,[2] we see that the figure is well-established in Deuteronomic literature. This is most important for any study of the rhetoric of Jeremiah since Jeremiah too is part of that same Deuteronomic tradition.

At the present time we are able to do little more than show where the inclusio is concentrated in the Old Testament. While we might prefer a sketch of its development, any attempt at such would surely be premature. Albright sketched the evolution of stylistic features in Hebrew poetry,[3] but even there, despite the fact that much is already known, we are still less than certain about the results. Perhaps at some future date we can write a history of Hebrew rhetoric. But for now we will be content to plant our feet firmly in what is generally agreed to be *the* rhetorical literature of the Old Testament, and then to work out from there.

Deuteronomy is by far the most important comparative document for Jeremiah, thus a few words are in order about Deuteronomy's provenance, authorship and composition. Deuteronomy has long been recognized to consist primarily of rhetorical prose. Von Rad has said that Deuteronomy is not mere law, but parenesis on the law.[4] And because it is "preached law" it must be seen *vis à vis* a gathered congregation. Von Rad also believed that Deuteronomy was written by the Levites, i.e., the Levitical priests,[5] and had as its *Sitz im Leben* the covenant renewal festival at Shechem.[6] But recently these views, especially the latter, have been called into question. Many scholars now believe that Deuteronomy was written not by Levitical priests but by scribes.[7] Lohfink reflects this shift of opinion, nevertheless his position is more moderate. He sees

much truth in von Rad's theory and is perfectly willing to re-
late the text of Deuteronomy to earlier liturgy.[8] But he does
not believe that von Rad's theory explains the *final stage* of
the book's composition. In this final stage, Deuteronomy is a
scribal document modeled on an archive. Lohfink says,

> In archives are collected various written documents,
> placed one beside the other, each with its title
> to indicate the contents. This is very prosaic and
> common, but it seems to be the type of writing which
> the book of Deuteronomy follows. In its final form
> Dt presents itself as an archive, a collection of
> what Moses uttered during the last days of his life.[9]

Lohfink does not advance this as an original theory but rather
as one expounded long ago by P. Kleinert (1872). Lohfink supports this theory by arguing that four major headings in 1:1,
4:44, 28:69 and 33:1 isolate four separate collections making
up the archive. But in our view 4:44 and 28:69 are not headings
at all but conclusions. Each in its own distinct way forms an
inclusio with 1:1-5.[10] This appears to be the crucial point of
disagreement with Lohfink since he is not otherwise predisposed
to discount rhetorical structures in Deuteronomy. He readily
concedes that such structures exist and in fact has done more
than most to call attention to where they exist. Moreover, he
correctly perceives that such structures are auditory signals
for people who must listen to documents read to them aloud.
The ancients did not read Deuteronomy silently as we do today.[11]
Nevertheless Lohfink considers *the final stage of composition*
to be a scribal work, and given his interpretation of 4:44 and
28:69, we assume this means a *non-rhetorical* work.

In our view 1-28[12] is a rhetorical unit. The inclusio
functions here to signal to a gathered audience that the end
has come. The function of the other subscription in 4:44-49 is
to frame the Introduction of 1-4. It restores focus before the
main presentation of legal material in chs 5ff. Thus we believe that Deut 1-28 in its entirety was read to a gathered
group of people, possibly at Shechem, but more probably at the
temple in Jerusalem. If 1-28 dates from the time of Hezekiah,
which is most probable,[13] then the material was tailored for
temple use at that time. The compilers used the inclusio because it was used earlier to tie together sermons within the
collection. Also the people could be expected to respond again
to a rhetorical structure that was now well-known. This will
all be very important when we come to explaining the function

of the Jeremianic structures. Jeremiah uses structures already
in existence and so also does his scribe Baruch. Deuteronomy
was a model for both of them--for Jeremiah the sermons became
models for his speeches, and for Baruch the composition of this
book became a model for the book that he was to compile: the
book of Jeremiah.

Finally, concerning the Levite/scribe debate, we suggest
that the question is not properly put. According to II Chr 34:
13 some Levites were scribes (ומהלוים סופרים) which means that we
may in fact be talking about one and the same group of persons.

Inclusio in the Larger Book of Jeremiah

We begin with the larger entity: the *book* of Jeremiah.
All the inclusio structures in this section we judge to be editorial, whether they are to be attributed to Jeremiah, Baruch
or some other unknown. They are structures beyond the prophetic
speech *per se*.

1-51

Our first inclusio is found at the limits of the present
book--or at least almost at the limits. Jeremiah has a chapter
52 but this duplicates II Kings 24:18-25:30 and served as a historical epilogue in the exilic or post-exilic period (Jer 52:31
gives us a *terminus a quo* of ca. 561 B.C.). The book of Jeremiah proper ends at 51:64. There we find what is generally regarded as a scribal summary statement.[14] It is indeed that and
more. Taken together with the opening words of the book, the
two form an inclusio:

1:1   *The words of Jeremiah*, the   דברי ירמיהו בן-חלקיהו
        son of Hilkiah,....

51:64   Thus far *the words of Jeremiah*   עד-הנה דברי ירמיהו

Like Deut 1:1-5 and 28:69 this ties an entire composition together. Everything within these limits is taken to be דברי
ירמיהו, which includes Jeremiah's own words as well as words
about Jeremiah. We note too a chiasmus: דברי ירמיהו begins
1:1 and concludes 51:64.

This could be the work of any Deuteronomic scribe, and
we would leave it at that were it not possible in this case
to attach to the inclusio the name of an individual.

Immediately preceding the subscription is a personal note from
Jeremiah to Seriah (51:59-64a). This man is the brother of
Baruch,[15] Jeremiah's close friend and scribe. Seriah is desig-
nated "quartermaster" (שר מנוחה) in v. 59, but he is also no
doubt a Deuteronomic scribe the same as Baruch (scribes came in
families later on in the time of the Massoretes). Jeremiah then
is said to have given Seriah custody of a scroll that went to
Babylon. This personal word--which we believe Seriah adds--
functions the same way as the personal word given by Jeremiah
to Baruch (which in the *MT* comes in 45 but in the *LXX* comes *in
exactly this position*!). Both are autobiographical postscripts.
We are thus led to wonder if it is not Seriah who also adds the
subscription in 51:64b.

The matter can be pursued further by comparing the Hebrew and Greek texts more closely. We recall that the Greek
places the Oracles to Foreign Nations after 25:13. In the Hebrew they come in 46-51. Now if we take Baruch to be the custodian of the text which was the *Vorlage* to the *LXX*, and Seriah
to be the custodian of the text which became the *MT*, we can
then isolate the two text traditions originating in Babylon and
Egypt. Baruch went to Egypt while Seriah went to Babylon.[16]
We assume that the *LXX* has an Egyptian provenance, and a Babylonian provenance for the *MT* is also likely. Frank Cross has
recently argued that the *MT* is Babylonian,[17] and we believe he
is right.

The different positions of the Oracles to Foreign Nations can be explained as follows. Seriah took the oracles
from 25:13ff, which is where Baruch placed them originally, and
put them at the end of the book. He then took Jeremiah's personal word to him and placed it at the new end as an autobiographical postscript (in the *LXX* its position is of no special
importance).[18] Then he added the subscription עד-הנה דברי
ירמיהו at the very end to make an inclusio with 1:1. And here
is the most important point of all: *this subscription is lacking in the LXX*, which is precisely what we would expect if
Seriah's text is the expanded *MT*.[19] We should observe also
that although Seriah relocates the Oracles to Foreign Nations,
the rest of Baruch's book is left intact: Baruch's own postscript still comes at what was formerly the end of the book
(chapter 45).

What can we say about the function of this inclusio?
It clearly delimits the final book of Jeremiah, but are we to

assume that an entire 51 chapters were read to a sitting congregation as with Deut 1-28? This would be a long reading, but perhaps it is not altogether out of the question given the situation in exile. If this be the case, then Seriah too prepared his book for worship. For him the inclusio would function just as it had in Deuteronomy 28:69: to signal that the end had finally come.

49:34-39

This is our one specimen from the Oracles to Foreign Nations. The inclusio comes only in the Greek, where the superscription of the *MT* is divided in two and placed half at the beginning and half at the end. The oracle is against Elam, and the *MT* introduces it with the following:

49:34	The word of Yahweh that came to Jeremiah the prophet concerning Elam, in the beginning of the reign of Zedekiah king of Judah:	אשר היה דבר־יהוה אל־ירמיהו הנביא אל־עילם בראשית מלכות צדקיה מלך־יהודה לאמר

The oracle in the *LXX* is found in 25:14-20 and appears there as follows:

25:14	What Jeremiah said concerning the nation of Elam:	Ἃ ἐπροφήτευσεν Ιερεμιας ἐπὶ τὰ ἔθνη τὰ Αιλαμ
25:20	In the beginning of the reign of Zedekiah the king, this word came concerning Elam	ἐν ἀρχῇ βασιλεύοντος Σεδεκιου τοῦ βασιλέως ἐγένετο ὁ λόγος οὗτος περὶ Αιλαμ

It appears that the *LXX* reflects a text tradition in which some scribe took the usual superscription and divided it up between beginning and end. It is possible that the process could have worked in the reverse except for the fact that all poems in this collection are introduced with superscriptions, and none with the exception of the Moab poems have subscriptions. Also, the subscription to the Moab poems (48:47) is of the same type as 51:64 and does not read like the subscription we have here.

The Elam oracle occupies a strategic location in the *LXX*, being there the first of the Oracles to Foreign Nations.

But we can do little more than speculate as to why it has the inclusio. Perhaps it circulated independently for a time.

<u>1-20</u>.

Here we find an inclusio of major importance.[20] It is formed by linking the first fragment of poetry in chapter 1 with the last lines of the poem in chapter 20. And according to established custom the key words are inverted in the closing section.

1:5	Before I formed you in the belly I knew you and before *you came forth from the womb*, I consecrated you	בטרם אצורך בבטן ידעתיך ובטרם <u>תצא מרחם</u> הקדשתיך
20:18	Why *from the womb did I come forth* to see trouble and sorrow and have my days end in shame?	למה זה <u>מרחם יצאתי</u> לראות עמל ויגון ויכלו בבשת ימי .

The opening line is from Jeremiah's call. He says that his call took place before emerging from his mother's womb. The latter poem reflects a moment of great despair. Jeremiah asks why his birth was ever allowed to take place. With the exception of a brief reference in 15:10, these are the only instances in which Jeremiah refers to the event of his birth.

The poem of 20:14-18 is well-known, especially for its tone of despair. The last colon of 20:18 reads ויכלו בבשת ימי, where the verb כלה should be translated "end" rather than "spend" (so *RSV*). The *AV* translates "consume," which is literal enough. The point is that Jeremiah fears his days will be ended, i.e., he will die. At such a time it is natural to recall one's birth, for that was when life began. It was natural at least for Jeremiah, because as we shall see before this study is concluded, he more than most was particularly conscious of beginnings and ends.

Another point has also been made about his poem: it ends without any hope. This is unusual since in all the other confessions (e.g., 15:15-21; 20:7-13; etc.) where Jeremiah boldly confronts Yahweh we have an answer from Yahweh. It is true that Jeremiah does not here address Yahweh--he curses "the day" and "the man who brought his father the news"--nevertheless the passage is still generally agreed to be a confession in which

Jeremiah pours out his heart to Yahweh. Von Rad says, "the God whom the prophet addresses no longer answers him."[21] Our inclusio, however, makes possible another interpretation, viz., that the conclusion of the poem was perhaps meant to be read together with the opening words of the call. Jeremiah says, "Why did I come forth from the womb?" Answer: "Because Yahweh called me before I came forth from the womb." Whatever despair the original poem of 20:14-18 may have had, in the larger composition *it contains an answer* which is one of hope and affirmation. 1:5 also serves to give the larger composition its authority. In disguised form, Jeremiah is affirming his call to be a prophet. He is saying that he was born because Yahweh called him forth to be born. And the listener with an ear for this kind of rhetoric would be able to make the connection. It is quite likely too that such a unit was deliberately prepared for temple worship, in which case the call could be reread as a final conclusion. We know that later custom dictated the rereading of the penultimate verse in Isaiah in order to provide a "happy ending."[22] A similar return, only this time to the beginning, could have been employed here so as not to conclude the composition on a dismal note.

We have suggested that 1-20 is an early major composition. Corroborating evidence can also be brought forth to show that a major break comes after 20. We note that chapter 21 contains the first *dated* biographical prose in the book. None of the prose in 1-20 is dated, while in 21ff, almost all the prose is pegged either in the reign of Jehoiakim or in the reign of Zedekiah. (Actually, neither of these kings is even mentioned before 21, except in the superscription of 1:3). We will also demonstrate shortly how 21 serves as the beginning of the first of two appendices that follow 1-20.

A firm delimitation of this major unit invites a reopening of the question of the *Urrolle*. Scholars are generally agreed that the *Urrolle* is contained within 1-25,[23] but so far no objective data has been made available which would enable us to determine more precisely its limits. Now we can put forth 1-20 as the *Urrolle* since 1-20 is a clearly defined composition within 1-25. Also, what we have proposed in the way of structure fits well with the situation described in chapter 36. Baruch brings a scroll to the temple and reads it to the people who are assembled there. Jeremiah is not allowed to go but the structure of the scroll material makes clear his authorship as

well as his authority to the careful listener. Some may perhaps
think that 1-20 is too large to have been read three times within a short period. Maybe so, but it is not at least out of the
question. Also it is always possible that material was inserted
into 1-20 at a later time making the present composition larger.
Our only argument is that what is now 1-20 manifests the marks
of a distinct composition made in the Deuteronomic manner. It
is therefore a more likely unit than, say 1-6, for the *Urrolle*.[24]

8:13-9:21 [Eng. 9:22]

This has not been put forth as a unit before, but our
inclusio is supported by the fact that 8:12 ends a previous
unit[25] and 9:22-25 [Eng. 23-26] is prose expansion. The inclusio is made up of the verb אסף, "to gather", used together with
אין.

8:13 *Gathering* I will end them[26] says Yahweh   אסף אסיפם נאם־יהוה
      no grapes there are on the vine   אין ענבים בגפן
      and *no* figs there are on the fig tree   ואין תאנים בתאנה
      even the leaves are withered   והעלה נבל

9:21 The dead bodies of men shall fall   ונפלה נבלת האדם
      like dung on the open field   כדמן על־פני השדה
      like sheaves after the reaper   וכעמיר מאחרי הקצר
      and *no one* shall *gather* them   ואין מאסף

We can see how 8:13 calls attention to both key words which will
occur later in the words of closure. The verb is given attention by the word-play אסף אסיפם, and אין is equally prominent
appearing twice at the beginning of successive cola (anaphora).
Condamin has noticed the repetition of אסף,[27] but he goes astray
in forcing the text into a different order.

Since there is no real semantic link between the two
verses, it appears that the inclusio functions only to tie together poems originally separate into a larger collection. Perhaps it is also here a mnemonic device used by Jeremiah. We can
imagine that he needed some such devices to hold speeches together in his head for those 23 years before they were put into
writing (Jer 36). If the unit was not part of the dictated material which went into the *Urrolle*, then it could have been material added later. Poems within this unit are also nicely
structured as we shall see later on when we come to the chapter
on chiasmus.

21:1-23:8

      This collection forms one of two appendices which follow
1-20. It contains words which Jeremiah delivered specifically
to Judah's kings. The other collection is made up of words specifically directed to the prophets (23:9-40). As Westermann has
pointed out, the criterion for collection in both of these cases
is "audience".[28] In the latter collection the introductory
לנבאים identifies the audience. The "king collection" has no
such introduction, although Adam Welch suggested some years ago
that a title לבית מלך יהודה may originally have existed at 21:11.
This he took to be the beginning of the collection,[29] which he
thought was comprised primarily of the poetry. Welch likewise
ended the collection at 22:30 which is where the poetry ends.

      There is definitely a poetic core in the king collection
and we will discuss its structure in the next chapter. Here we
are only concerned with the outer frame, i.e., 21:1-10 and 23:
1-8. The problematic unit is 21:1-10, which appears to be
nothing more than an ordinary prose account about one of Jeremiah's encounters with Zedekiah. It need not be part of the
king collection at all since it is essentially no different from
chapters 34 or 37. Perhaps this is why Bright groups it with
those chapters.[30] Yet we will now argue that 21:1-10 is definitely meant to be a part of the king collection. A final editor
meant to balance this account with the messianic prophecy in 23:
1-8. Thus another inclusio.

      We notice first of all that prior to the messianic ver-
ses Judah's kings are listed in chronological order. Josiah is
referred to by implication in 22:10 (he is the one who is dead);
then comes Shallum (Jehoahaz) (vv. 11-12); Jehoiakim (22:18-19);
and finally Jeconiah (22:24-30). We now expect a word about
Zedekiah, but there is none. Instead comes the messianic prophecy. Yet it is in this messianic prophecy that we find the key
to our outer structure. It comes in the name of the future
king, which is to be יהוה צדקנו, "Yahweh is our righteousness"
(23:6). As commentators have already noted, this is an obvious
play on "Zedekiah", צדקיהו, which can be translated "Yahweh is
righteous", righteous of Yahweh", or something similar.[31] Comparing the two names we note a small difference, but it is important. The component parts are switched around. In the name
Zedekiah the Yahwistic appellative יהו comes in normal fashion
at the end. But in the name of the new Davidic king יהוה comes
first. The reversal must be deliberate.[32] Jeremiah wants to

point out the *discontinuity* between the present king and the
future king. The future king will be what Zedekiah ought to be
but is not, viz., a sign of Yahweh's righteousness. Or the new
king will be a complete "turn-around" from the present king.

Let us now return to the structure of the section.
Having seen what Jeremiah did with Zedekiah's name in the first
place, it should amuse us even more to see how *the very same
point is silently made* by the creator of our structure. The
word to Zedekiah about his fate, instead of being placed at the
end (after 22:30) where we anticipated it, is placed at the beginning. And at the end comes the messianic prophecy providing
the compiler with the contrast he wanted to make. The compiler
then in his final composition makes the same contrast which
Jeremiah made earlier in 23:6. The inclusio becomes a vehicle
for theology. It affirms something not too dissimilar from
what was affirmed by the Deuteronomic Historian when he set up
David as the model of the good king and Jeroboam as the model
of the bad king (cf. II Kings 14:3,24; 15:9,18,24,28; 17:21-23;
18:3 etc.). Zedekiah is now the antitype of the messiah, and
we can imagine that such a contrast could forcefully be made to
a worshipping congregation over and over and over again.

30-31

Chapters 30-33 form a separate collection containing
primarily words of hope, thus the name "Book of Comfort" or
"Book of Consolation". A superscription tells us that Jeremiah
was commanded by Yahweh to write these words in a book (30:2).
The limits of this book--in its various stages of growth--can
now be seen because a compiler (or compilers) made use of the
inclusio.

Within the collection is a poetic core extending from
30:5 to 31:22. This core to begin with is held together by an
inclusio: the end of the last poem balances the beginning of
the first.

30:5-6 We have heard a cry of panic	קול הרדה שמענו
of terror and no peace	פחד ואין שלום
Ask now and see	שאלו-נא וראו
can a *male* bear a child?	אם-ילד זכר
Why then do I see every *soldier*	מדוע ראיתי כל-גבר
with his hands on his loins	ידיו על-חלציר כיולדה
like a woman in labor?	

31:22b   For Yahweh has created a new
               thing on the earth:
       the *female* protects the *soldier*

כי־ברא יהוה חדשה
בארץ
נקבה תסובב גבר

This final bi-colon was considered an appendage by Duhm, but
Holladay has recently argued that it belongs with the poem which
it concludes.[33] The bi-colon is also a *crux interpretum*. Many
solutions have been proposed but none is completely satisfac-
tory.[34] I take the line as an ironic statement expressing shock
and surprise at the weakness of Israel's soldiers in defeat.
Jeremiah is saying, "My, a new thing on earth! the woman must
protect the soldier". It should of course be the other way
around, but Jeremiah can only articulate another of the incon-
gruous sights before his eyes. Full play is given to the sexual
distinction. The common term for "woman", אשה, is not used;
instead Jeremiah employs the generic נקבה, "female".

       In the counterpart passage the same is true. There
Jeremiah mocks the soldiers asking, "Can a male (זכר) bear a
child?" Taken together these verses form an inclusio for the
core. They say the same thing only in different ways. In 30:6
the soldiers are said to be behaving like weak women in labor;
in 31:22b they are depicted as being so weak that they need
women for protection.

       The inclusio also sets the controlling mood for the
core, which is not hope but despair. This has not been properly
recognized. The tendency is usually to read the core in light
of the rest of the material which is all hope. But the core is
a "mixed bag". Some of the poems are judgment pure and simple.
The opening poem in 30:5-7 is a clear example. Holladay shows
how the final colon of that poem, "Yet he shall be saved out of
it" was not originally meant this way at all. It was an ironic
question to which the answer was a firm "No!".[35] Other judgment poems are 30:12-15; 30:23-24 and 31:15. We must therefore
recognize that the core contains *both* poems of judgment and
poems of hope.[36]

       It has also been pointed out that at least some of the
hope poems in this collection derive from the *earliest* part of
Jeremiah's ministry when he awaited the return of the exiles
from Assyria.[37] Maybe all are early, i.e., pre-exilic, in
which case we would have an earlier collection than is usually
assumed.[38] My reading of 31:22b would support such an interpretation since I think this line cannot be a sober statement

about the "new age" even if it does belong with a poem which looks ahead to the return from exile. It is a word of desperation reflecting the present state of affairs. And in forming an inclusio with 30:5-6 it creates an entire mood of the same. To be sure the core certainly falls short of the confidence expressed in 31:23ff.

We spoke earlier of the desire to end a collection on a happy note, for that appears to have been the function of the inclusio which tied together 1-20. Now we are suggesting just the reverse, viz., that the inclusio which ties together the poetic core within the Book of Comfort creates an overall tone of despair. Is this possible? Our answer must be in the affirmative not only because we know that the canons of Hebrew composition made this allowable (Ecclesiastes, the Book of the Twelve and Isaiah all end on a note of judgment), but also because there is *a priori* no reason why an inclusio must function the same way every time it is used. If the core was put together when the outlook was not good it could be made to reflect such a time, and the compiler is then one who "tells it like it is". We may then have a basis for dating the core. The final years of Jehoiakim would fit perfectly culminating in the attack on Jerusalem in 597 B.C. and the exile of Jehoiachin with many of the leading citizens (cf. II Kings 24:10-17). These were the years when Jeremiah and Baruch were in hiding (Jer 36:19) and any circulation of this core at such a time would certainly serve to weaken the people's resistance. It would not give them hope. Only later when the people are broken and Jeremiah gives additional words of hope does this core get expanded into the Book of Comfort it becomes. Yet the marks of the earlier composition remain.

We will now look at the structure of a portion of that expansion. The remaining verses of chapter 31 are nicely framed and held together by an inclusio. Since there appears to be two stages of development we will discuss one at a time.

In the first stage material in vv. 23 to 34 was added. The stereotyped phrases making the frames and the inclusio will show the structure in outline:

23	Thus says Yahweh of Hosts God of Israel: *Again they* *shall speak* these words...	כה־אמר יהוה צבאות אלהי ישראל <u>עוד</u> <u>יאמרו</u> את־הדבר הזה
27	*Behold, the days are coming,* says Yahweh, when I will sow...	<u>הנה ימים באים</u> נאם־יהוה וזרעתי
29	In those days, *they shall not* *again speak:*...	בימים ההם <u>לא־יאמרו</u> <u>עוד</u>
31	*Behold, the days are coming,* says Yahweh, when I will make ...a new covenant...	<u>הנה ימים באים</u> נאם־יהוה וכרתי ...ברית חדשה
34a	And *they shall not again teach* each man his neighbor,...	<u>ולא ילמדו עוד</u> איש את־רעהו
34b	And their sin *I will not* *remember again*	ולחטאתם לא <u>אזכר־עוד</u>

The two sections in the center are framed by opening and closing
formulas. At the extremes (vv. 23, 34b) we have single closing
formulas which make the inclusio. One of the key words in the
closing formulas is עוד which I have translated in all cases
as "again" to accentuate the intended repetition. עוד occurs
with three different verbs, which, in all but the first instance
(v. 23) are coupled with the negative לא. The key words emphasize the theme of the unit, which is the discontinuity between
the future and the present. The future will be a new time when
old proverbs are abandoned and even a new covenant is made.

In the second stage of development the poetic fragment in
vv. 35-37 is added along with another framed prophecy much like
those added in stage one:

38	*Behold the days are coming,*[39] says Yahweh, when the city shall be rebuilt...	[39]<u>הנה ימים (באים)</u> נאם־יהוה ונבנתה העיר
39	And *it shall go out again* the measuring line...	<u>ויצא עוד</u> קוה המדה

Verse 40 concludes the material added in stage two and contains
a single stereotyped phrase like those found in vv. 23,29,34a
and 34b. It makes an inclusio with yet one more closing formula found in 30:3:

36

30:3	For *behold, the days are coming* says Yahweh, when I will restore the fortunes of my people...	כי הנה ימים באים נאם־יהוה ושבתי את־שבות עמי
31:40	And *it shall not be overthrown again* forever	ולא־יהרס עוד לעולם

Since there is the mention of a "book" immediately prior to the beginning formula in 30:3 (v. 2), we conclude that this book is delimited by the above inclusio. Thus while we have earlier compositions preceding it, the first Book of Comfort contains only the material in chapters 30-31. What appears in chapters 32-33 is added from yet a later time.

A concordance check on עוד in chapters 30-33 only adds to what we have already come to realize about its importance. In 31:4-5, which is poetry, it is used as an anaphora for three successive cola making it a key word in the poem. In chapters 32-33 it occurs five times: 32:15; 33:10,12,13,24, and in one of these, viz., 33:13, it may signal another conclusion. We note that in the *LXX* this verse concludes the chapter (*MT* 33: 14-26 is omitted). Chapter 33 is admittedly a difficult chapter to unravel so we can not say more than this at the present time.

In summary the core is an early compilation of poetry found in 30:5-31:22. It contains judgment and hope but the in-clusio gives the whole a tone of irony and despair. Neverthe-less the hope which it contained gave rise to two subsequent additions, which, when completed became the Book of Comfort re-ferred to in 30:2. This book consisted of chapters 30-31, but was later expanded to include chapters 32-33. And if 33:14-26 is taken to be yet another addition we have five stages of com-position instead of four.

Inclusio in the Poems of Jeremiah

We come now to the poetic speeches of Jeremiah. The main problem as we have said before is their delimitation. It will now be argued that 12 poems in Jeremiah employ the inclu-sio device. In a variety of ways, Jeremiah forces his audience to return at the end to the beginning. In so doing he uses a rhetorical technique already well-established, and one to which his audience can respond if they are so inclined.

We will now look at each poem separately. The struc-ture of the whole will be laid out including a breakdown into stanzas. In the chiastic poems to be looked at later our criteria for establishing the rhetorical structure will also aid us in stanza division. But here the stanza division is based not upon the controlling inclusio but upon other criteria, some rhetorical, e.g., balancing terms, repetition, both in some cases making smaller inclusios or chiasmi, and some non-rhetorical, e.g., a messenger formula, change of speaker, content, etc. These will be discussed but only in a cursory way since our main concern is with the controlling inclusio.

3:1-5

The limits of this poem are easily established. The chapter divisions mark the upper limit and most commentators take this as the beginning.[40] The lower limit is marked by the introduction of prose comment beginning in v. 6, although debate still goes on whether this is the end or whether the poetry in vv. 12-14 or vv. 19ff continues the poem.[41] This latter poetry does have affinities with 1-5 which means, I think, that we may have a larger editorial unit. But for now we will argue only that 1-5 was originally a separate poem, and indeed it was a poem of uncompromising judgment.

הן ישלח איש את־אשתו והלכה מאתו   1
והיתה לאיש־אחר הישוב אליה עוד
הלוא חנוף תחנף הארץ ההיא
ואת זנית רעים רבים ושוב אלי נאם־יהוה

שאי־עיניך על־שפים וראי איפה לא שגלת   2
על־דרכים ישבת להם כערבי במדבר
ותחניפי ארץ בזנותיך וברעתך
וימנעו רבבים ומלקוש לוא היה   3

ומצח אשה זונה היה לך מאנת הכלם
הלוא מעתה קראתי לי אבי אלוף נערי אתה   4
הינטר לעולם אם־ישמר לנצח   5
הנה דברתי ותעשי הרעות ותוכל

1   *Behold*, a man divorces his wife
    and she goes from him
And becomes the wife of another
    Will he return to her?
Would it not be greatly polluted
    that land?
But you have played the harlot with many lovers
    and would you return to me? Oracle of Yahweh

2   Lift up your eyes to the bare hills and see
    where have you not been ravished?
Along the roads you sat for them
    like an Arab in the wilderness
You have polluted the land with your harlotry
    and with your evil deeds
3   Therefore the showers have been withheld
    and the spring rain has not come

Yet you have a harlot's brow
    you refuse to be ashamed
4 Have you not just now called to me "My father,
    you are the friend of my youth,
5 Will he be angry forever,
    will he be indignant to the end?"
Behold, you have spoken but done
    all the evil that you could.

      The poem contains many nice balances. Stanza 1 balances
lines 2 and 4 with forms of the verb שׁוב, and stanza 3 has assonantal balance with וּמָצָה and לָנֶצַח. There is also a play on
sound in the last lines of stanzas 1 and 2: רַבִּים and רְבָבִים.
Finally, both stanzas 1 and 3 have double rhetorical questions
in the center. The inclusio is formed by "behold" which begins
the poem and is then repeated again at the end. Different
forms of the interjection are used, but it is nevertheless the
same word. Modern translators overlook the repetition completely translating הֵן in v. 1 with "If" (so *RSV*, *JB*, *NEB*).[42]
And Bright follows Volz in emending הִנֵּה in v. 5 to הָנֵּה which
does away with the final "behold".[43] Both should be left intact.
Neither reading is problematic, and rhetorically the repetition
is significant.

      Jeremiah is here making a case for judgment and he be-
gins by citing the only law in the Old Testament dealing with
divorce: Deut 24:1-4. This law states that a man cannot re-
unite with a divorced wife if she has contracted another marriage.[44] Jeremiah then uses this law to make an analogy--
actually he does more than that since the argument contains in
addition an inference *a minori ad maius*, or to use talmudic
terminology, a *kal vechomer* (cf. 12:5).[45] The man cannot return to his former wife because she has known (or been known)
by *one* other man; in Jeremiah's argument Israel has had *many*
lovers (רעים רבים).[46] Thus Jeremiah's audience would have to
answer "No" to the question ending verse 1. Israel certainly
cannot return now to Yahweh after being so polluted by foreign
affairs.[47] What follows in stanza 2 is more indictment.
Stanza 3 ends the poem by pointing up an incongruity between
what the people say and what their actions betray, and the
final "behold" brings the hearer back to the beginning. It
reminds him of the "No" answer he just gave. The inclusio
thus forces the application which Jeremiah intends, viz., that
Israel--on the basis of old friendship--cannot now plead for-
giveness after violating so completely her vow to be faithful

to Yahweh in marriage. That the line "and would you return to
me?" was later read as a call for restoration is easy enough to
understand,[48] but we do not believe it to be consonant with Jeremiah's original intent.

This analysis has given us additional insight into Jeremiah's rhetoric. We said earlier that this was a poem of uncompromising judgment, yet it is to be noted that the judgment
is never explicitly given. The rhetorical question ending v. 1
may evoke a judgment, and the conclusion may also "beg" judgment as it returns the hearer to v. 1; but in each case the
hearer must furnish the answer of judgment himself. Jeremiah
does not give it. He gives the hearer plenty of indictment,
but no judgment. Thus while we recovered a much harsher tone
in the poem, at the same time we showed Jeremiah to be more
subtle, less judgmental and rhetorically more astute. He engages his audience at a point of common agreement--citing a law
which all know well--and then makes a quick application by
analogy. A final rhetorical question together with a repetition making an inclusio forces the hearer to *himself* bring the
matter to completion. The real twist of course does not come
until the end. After hearing many examples of wayward behavior
which embellish the indictment, the hearer is forced to see
the impossibility of expecting acquittal for wrongdoing. This
kind of rhetoric will not be grasped by everyone. Only those
who are perceptive will pick up the judgment Jeremiah intends.
Others must wait for someone to explain it to them.

5:10-13

The versions and the commentaries do not give much help
in delimiting this unit. Rudolph, Volz, Condamin and Bright
all extend through v. 14. And Rudolph and Volz begin back at
5:1. Condamin takes 10-14 as a strophe of a much larger unit.
The *RSV* breaks before v. 10 and after v. 13, but also after v.
11. Bright too says that 10-14 is composed of separate fragments.[49] Our only support for isolating 10-13 comes from the
Massoretes who marked the ends of verses 9 and 13 as closed
(ס) sections.[50] We take these verses then to comprise a poem
of 2 stanzas, each having 3 lines. The main division points
up a change of speaker. Yahweh speaks in the first stanza
(v. 11 ends with נאם-יהוה), and Jeremiah in the second. There
also appears to be cresendo in the stanzas for each has a long
final line.[51]

עֲלוּ בְשָׁרוֹתֶיהָ וְשַׁחֵתוּ וְכָלָה אַל־<u>תַּעֲשׂוּ</u> 10
הָסִירוּ נְטִישׁוֹתֶיהָ כִּי לוֹא לַיהֹוָה הֵמָּה
כִּי בָגוֹד בָּגְדוּ בִי בֵּית יִשְׂרָאֵל וּבֵית יְהוּדָה נְאֻם־יְהֹוָה 11

כִּחֲשׁוּ בַּיהֹוָה וַיֹּאמְרוּ לֹא־הוּא 12
וְלֹא־תָבוֹא עָלֵינוּ רָעָה וְחֶרֶב וְרָעָב לוֹא נִרְאֶה
וְהַנְּבִיאִים יִהְיוּ לְרוּחַ וְהַדִּבֵּר אֵין בָּהֶם כֹּה <u>יֵעָשֶׂה</u> לָהֶם 13

10 Go up through her vinerows and destroy
    and *make* a full end[52]
    Strip away her branches
    for they are not Yahweh's
11 For they've been utterly faithless to me
    the house of Israel and the house of Judah
       oracle of Yahweh

12 They've spoken falsely of Yahweh
    and said "Surely not he;
    Evil will not come upon us
    and sword and famine we will not see"
13 The prophets will become wind
    the word is not in them
       thus *he will make* them[53]

The inclusio is formed by the verb עשה, meaning "make".
There is no reason to follow the Alexandrinus and Arabic which
omit the last colon (so Rudolph and Bright). It does not "fit
poorly";[54] rather it gives a poem the closure which Jeremiah
intended.

Like 3:1-5, this poem has also had the judgment
softened. Whether the אַל in v. 10 is to be read as an ancient
asseverative, or is a negative added later to harmonize the
poem with 30:11 (cf. 4:27; 5:18)--in either case the colon did
not originally read "but make not a full end."[55] The whole
poem is strong judgment and can hardly admit such immediate
qualification.

How then does the structure give insight into the in-
teraction between Jeremiah and his audience? Jeremiah averts
any immediate wrath by beginning with generalities. The object
of Yahweh's attack is stated metaphorically, and the audience
is not yet offended because the "branches" are not identified.
But at the end Jeremiah becomes specific. The culprits turn
out to be the prophets (v. 13), and we are even given their
words before they themselves are specified. The inclusio helps
make the desired connection: יעשה in the final colon echoes
תעשו at the beginning. And what might otherwise be an ambigu-
ous conclusion is now very clear. The antecedent of כה, "thus"
is כלה, "full end". Yahweh will make a full end of the

prophets. Now we know that *they* are the dead branches in Yahweh's vineyard.

This type of argument has subtlety. Jeremiah does not come right out and damn the prophets; he uses his structure in such a way that the audience can end up doing it. And Jeremiah is also able to keep his audience with him because the total message does not come across until the end, or perhaps we should say, after the end.

5:26-31

Chapter 5 ends with v. 31 and most commentators (except Volz) break there. The beginning has been less clear. Only Volz breaks before v. 26, but neither he nor anyone else makes the divisions we propose. Verse 29 is the same stereotyped refrain found in 5:9 and 9:8. Condamin places it after v. 31. We take it as an insertion, and therefore omit it. What remains then is a nicely balanced 3:3:3 poem with inclusio.

כי־נמצאו בעמי רשעים ישור כשך 26
יקושים הציבר משחית אנשים ילכדו
ככלוב מלא עוף כן בתיהם מלאים מרמה 27

על־כן גדלו ויעשירו *שמנו עשתו 28*
גם עברו דברי־רע דין לא־דנו
דין יתום ויצליחו ומשפט אביונים לא שפטו

שמה ושערורה נהיתה בארץ 30
הנביאים נבאו־בשקר והכהנים ירדו על־ידיהם 31
ועמי אהבו כן ומה־תעשו לאחריתה

26 For scoundrels are found among *my people*
    they lurk like fowlers[56]
  Bait-layers setting their traps
    it is men they catch
27 Like a basket full of birds
    so their houses are filled with deceit

  Therefore they've become great and rich
28   they are fat and sleek
  Yes, they overlook bad deeds
    not judging with justice
  The cause of the orphan to win it;
    they defend not the rights of the needy

30 An appalling and horrible thing
    has happened in the land
31 The prophets prophesy falsely
    and the priests rule at their direction[57]
  But *my people* love it *so*
    therefore what will you do when the end comes?

Despite some textual difficulties, we generally know what the poem is about. The prophets and priests are being flayed for acting in self-interest. They disregard the admonition of Deuteronomy to help the orphan and the needy (cf. Deut 10:18; 14:29; 16:11,14; etc.). Jeremiah again is slow to identify them specifically. The poem begins by referring to רשעים (scoundrels). But we soon know from the description in stanza 2 who these are. Now one might think that the poem is exclusively about prophets and priests, but it is not. The inclusio gives a peculiar twist in that it shifts the focus *off* the *prophets and priests* and *on* to the *people*. These people—who had been prey to the scoundrels—*they* "love" it this way. The verse is also ironic. Jeremiah says that the people do not really mind injustice prevailing. So understood, the part about prophets and priests is merely *foil*; the *preferred subject* is the people themselves, making the last two cola the *cap* of the poem.[58] If the "people" happen to be the audience, we can see how they might cheer Jeremiah along most of the way. But the cap makes them accomplices with the prophets and priests, meaning that they too must share the blame. What we have is an "unholy alliance" between clergy and people against society's helpless. Thus the concluding question "And what will you do when the end comes?" addresses *both* clergy and people.

9:9b-10 [Eng. 9:10b-11]

This is a brief 4-line poem. Verse 11 begins prose comment establishing the lower limit. The upper limit is not so clear. Condamin and Bright begin with 9a (verse 8 is again the stereotyped refrain seen earlier in 5:29, and in this context signals the conclusion of the poem preceding). Volz completely rearranges the text and therefore is of no help. Our inclusio argues for 9a being outside the poem and thus an introductory line. In the next chapter we will explain why it is there.

9b כי נצתו מבלי-איש עבר ולא שמעו קול מקנה
מעוף השמים ועד-בהמה נדדו הלכו

10 ונתתי את-ירושלם לגלים מעון תנים
ואת-ערי יהודה אתן שממה מבלי יושב

9b   For they are laid waste *without man* passing through
     and the lowing of cattle is not heard
    Both birds of the air and beasts
     have fled and are gone

10   I will make Jerusalem a ruin-heap
     a lair for jackals
    And the cities of Judah I will make a total waste
     without inhabitant

     The poem is also divided in half by speaker. Jeremiah
speaks in the first stanza, and Yahweh in the second. The one
in fact echoes the other. Jeremiah says he sees a land "without inhabitant," and Yahweh says that is what he sees too.
The function of this inclusio appears to be simple reinforce-
ment. Yahweh echoes Jeremiah's thought like in 1:12 ("You
have seen well"). The inclusio builds here on similar--not
identical--expressions, yet we prefer *MT* מבלי in v. 10 to
מאין, the latter occuring in 24 Mss.

10:6-7

     As we mentioned earlier, 10:1-16 is not usually attri-
buted to Jeremiah. Nevertheless we have in vv. 6-7 an unusually intricate poem that deserves to be seen. These verses
can be isolated form-critically. They comprise one of two
doxologies that follow separate poems mocking false gods.
These poems come in vv. 2-5 and vv. 8-9. The other doxology
praising Yahweh is in v. 10. The entire unit of 10:2-10 al-
ternates, then, between a mocking poem to false gods (2-5);
a doxology praising Yahweh (6-7); a mocking poem to false
gods (8-9); and a doxology praising Yahweh (10). In its present form it appears to be a liturgy recited antiphonally.
We now look to the doxology of 6-7. It is 3 lines with each
line a tri-colon.

מאין כמוך יהוה גדול אתה וגדול שמך בגבורה   6
מי לא יראך מלך הגוים כי לך יאתה   7
כי בכל־חכמי הגוים ובכל־מלכותם מאין כמוך

6   *There is none like you*
    Yahweh you are great
     and great is your name in power
7   Who would not fear you
    King of the Nations
     for that is your due
  For among all the wise men of the nations
    and among all their kingdoms
     there is none like you

The subject of the doxology is in the exact center:
King of the Nations. And the inclusio repeats words which are
the poem's theme, i.e., the incomparability of Yahweh.[59]   If
then 10:2-10 is a liturgy, our doxology with its inclusio gives
the whole even greater suitability for use in temple worship.

14:7-9

This next poem can also be isolated form-critically.
It is a liturgy of penitence to be recited by the people in the
temple.[60]   It follows a judgment oracle (2-6) and was probably
used together with it. Condamin has again noticed the key words
making up the inclusio.

7   אם־עוניני ענו בנו יהוה עשה למען שמך
כי־רבו משובתינו לך חטאנו

8   מקוה ישראל מושיעו בעת צרה
למה תהיה כגר בארץ וכארח נטה ללון

9   למה תהיה כאיש נדהם כגבור לא־יוכל להושיע
ואתה בקרבנו יהוה ושמך עלינו נקרא אל־תנחנו

7   Though our iniquities testify against us
     act *Yahweh* for *your name's* sake
   For our backslidings are many
     against you we have sinned

8   O Hope of Israel
     its savior in time of trouble
   Why are you like a stranger in the land
     like a traveler who stops only for a night?
9   Why are you like a man surprised
     like a soldier who cannot save?
   Yet you *Yahweh* are in the midst of us
     we are called by *your name*
       do not leave us.

Taken by itself the second colon of stanza 1 sounds a
bit altruistic: "act Yahweh for your name's sake." The inclusio however focuses on the poet's main intent, i.e., to per-
suade Yahweh that only *by saving Israel* he will save his own
name. Yahweh's name is inextricably tied up with the fate of
his people, and their defeat will harm his as well.

20:4,6

This is a poem which Holladay recently uncovered in
the prose of 20:1-6.[61]   He calls attention to its inclusio,
even as Condamin did much earlier. I take the poem as 6 bi-
colic lines, the last being very short because of the poem's
diminution.

הנני נתנך למגור לך ולכל־אהביך   4
ונפלו בחרב איביהם ועיניך ראות
ואתה פשחור וכל ישבי ביתך   6
תלכו בשבי ובבל תבוא
ושם תמות ושם תקבר
אתה וכל־אהביך

4 Behold, I make you a terror[62]
    yourself and all your 'dear ones'
  And they shall fall by the sword of their enemies
    while your eyes are looking on
6 And you Pashur
    and all the inhabitants of your house
  You shall go into captivity
    to Babylon you shall enter
  And there you shall die
    and there you shall be buried
  You
    and all your 'dear ones'

Holladay eliminated vv. 4b-5 and the final phrase of v. 6 as
expansion. Perhaps this expansion merely attempts to explain
the term אהביך, which is ironic.[63] There seems to be two groups
of "dear ones." The first are those mentioned in v. 4 who will
die violently before Pashhur's eyes. The second group in v. 6
go into exile and will die there. They are members of Pashhur's
house. At any rate, Pashhur and his colleagues will all suffer
an ignominious fate, and the inclusio functions to reinforce the
comprehensive quality of Yahweh's judgment.

20:7-10

      Condamin correctly sees the limits of this poem and
also its inclusio. But we do not agree with him that it is an
antistrophe to vv. 4-6.[64] It goes instead with vv. 11-13 following, which some commentators include with 7-10 to make one
poem.[65] In our view, 11-13 is a companion poem to 7-10, and
the two were probably meant to be read together at some later
stage. Let us now look at the inclusio in 7-10.

פתיתני יהוה ואפת חזקתני ותוכל   7
הייתי לשחוק כל־היום כלה לעג לי
כי־מדי אדבר אזעק חמס ושד אקרא   8
כי־היה דבר־יהוה לי להרפה ולקלס כל־היום

ואמרתי לא־אזכרנו ולא־אדבר עוד בשמו   9
והיה בלבי כאש בערת עצר בעצמתי
ונלאיתי כלכל ולא אוכל

כי שמעתי דבת רבים מגור מסביב   10
הגידו ונגידנו כל אנוש שלומי שמרי צלעי
אולי יפתה ונוכלה לו ונקחה נקמתנו ממנו

7   *You deceived me*, Yahweh, and *I was deceived*
        you seized and *overcame* me
     I have become a joke all the day
        everyone mocks me
8   For whenever I speak, I cry out
        'Violence and destruction' I shout
     For the word of Yahweh has become for me
        a reproach and derision all the day

9   If I say 'I'll not remember him
        and not speak anymore in his name'
     In my heart there is like a burning fire
        shut up in my bones
     And I weary of holding it in
        and I cannot

10   For I hear many whispering
        'Terror On Every Side,[66]
     Denounce him, let us denounce him'
        say all my friends of shalom who wait for my fall
     'Perhaps *he will be deceived* and *we can overcome* him
        and take our revenge on him'

        This is one of the Jeremianic confessions. It is a
brutally frank word to Yahweh accusing him of deception and
also of being overpowering. The inclusio gives added theological insight. Yahweh is here charged with the very thing that
comes to Jeremiah from his opponents. Jeremiah calls these
opponents אנוש שלומי, "my friends of shalom" (v. 10), suggesting some concern on his part about their genuineness. Only if
he suspects that they perhaps be right and he perhaps be wrong
can Jeremiah turn to accuse Yahweh. Were he sure of his right-
ness, he would instead write them off and be confident. His
confidence does come in vv. 11-13, but this we take to be later
since Yahweh has by then delivered him from the grip of these
men (v. 13). Taken by itself, however, the poem of 7-10 preserves the ambiguity so often existing in real life situations.
Certainty must come sometime later.

20:14-18

        This final poem in the 1-20 collection is the most
moving in Jeremiah, and perhaps one of the most moving in all
of ancient literature. Its unity is contested by no one since
the poem is easily delimited by content. In this poem Jeremiah
curses his birth. We saw earlier how this poem was made to

balance the call in chapter 1. Now we can see its own structure, which also has an inclusio made up of "day" and "days." These key terms are noted by Condamin. For reasons which will be given later, we believe that the poem divides up into stanzas of 2 lines each.[67] With also the position of אשר beginning each second colon, we propose that the poem in its original form was 5 stanzas (2:2:2:2:2) which means that two of the cola have fallen out.[68] This would further explain the abrupt beginning of v. 17.[69]

אָרוּר הַיּוֹם אֲשֶׁר יֻלַּדְתִּי בּוֹ
יוֹם אֲשֶׁר־יְלָדַתְנִי אִמִּי אַל־יְהִי בָּרוּךְ

14

אָרוּר הָאִישׁ אֲשֶׁר בִּשַּׂר אֶת־אָבִי לֵאמֹר
יֻלַּד־לְךָ בֵּן זָכָר שַׂמֵּחַ שִׂמְּחָהוּ

15

וְהָיָה הָאִישׁ הַהוּא כֶּעָרִים אֲשֶׁר־הָפַךְ יְהוָה וְלֹא נִחָם
וְשָׁמַע זְעָקָה בַּבֹּקֶר וּתְרוּעָה בְּעֵת צָהֳרָיִם

16

[..........] אֲשֶׁר לֹא־מוֹתְתַנִי מֵרָחֶם
וַתְּהִי־לִי אִמִּי קִבְרִי וְרַחְמָה הֲרַת עוֹלָם

17

לָמָּה זֶּה מֵרֶחֶם יָצָאתִי [אֲשֶׁר..........]
לִרְאוֹת עָמָל וְיָגוֹן וַיִּכְלוּ בְּבֹשֶׁת יָמָי

18

14 Cursed be *the day*
        on which I was born
    The day when my mother bore me
        let it not be blessed

15 Cursed be the man
        who brought the news to my father
    'A son is born to you'
        making him very glad

16 Let that man be like the cities
        which Yahweh overthrew without pity
    Let him hear a cry in the morning
        and an alarm at noon

17 ....
        who did not kill me in the womb
    So my mother would have been my grave
        and her womb forever great

18 Why did I come forth from the womb
        ....
    To see toil and sorrow
        and end in shame *my days*?

Jeremiah begins the poem by recalling the *day* of his birth. He ends it with a reference to the most recent of *days*, which apparently were very trying. The poem is probably to be

dated from the time around 605-604 B.C. when Jehoiakim was
threatening his life, and if so, we can well understand Jeremiah's fear and despair. The inclusio puts in tension his beginning and what Jeremiah feared would be his end. And at such
a time his thoughts return to the beginning: "Why did I come
forth from the womb.." (v. 18). Verse 15 suggests that for Jeremiah's father at least, his birth was a joyous event. Indica-
tions elsewhere in the poetry suggest that for Jeremiah too the
early years of his life were filled with happiness.[70] But now
in light of present despair, what originally was a happy event
becomes tragic, and Jeremiah curses the event strongly. History
has a way of changing one's perspective, and that appears to
have been the case here with Jeremiah.

We discussed earlier how the inclusio tying this poem
together with the call *did just the opposite*. It made over
time what was originally a desperate cry into a larger statement of hope. The compiled form then gives us the "long view"
of Jeremiah, which is the more balanced view. He is not just
the prophet of doom; he both breaks down and builds up (cf.
1:10).

<u>22:6-7</u>

This is a short poem of 4 lines framed by prose comment
on either side (so Volz, Condamin and Bright). It is one of
three main poems in the "King Collection" (21:1-23:8), all of
which play upon the luxury of Jerusalem's royal complex. The
other two are 22:13-17 and 22:20-23. So plush were these build-
ings with their cedar interiors that Jeremiah addresses them
metaphorically as "Lebanon."[71] This poem forms its inclusio
by using words of common association: "Lebanon" and "cedars."
They may even be a fixed pair (cf. 22:23), although their use
in the Old Testament is usually in the construct chain ארזי
הלבנון (Psalm 29:5; 104:16; etc.).

6	גלעד אתה לי ראש <u>הלבנון</u>
	אם־לא אשיתך מדבר ערים לא נושבה
7	וקדשתי עליך משחתים איש וכליו
	וכרתו מבחר <u>ארזיך</u> והפילו על־האש

6   You are as Gilead to me
      as the summit of *Lebanon*
    Yet I will surely make you a desert
      uninhabited quarters[72]
7   I will sanctify destroyers against you
      each with his weapons
    And they shall cut down your choicest *cedars*
      and cast them into the fire

Jeremiah could have placed the line about the "cedars" immediately following the line about "Lebanon," but instead he delays it until the end. And if the key terms are a fixed pair, he is also playing with the hearer's expectations: the second of the pair is bound to be anticipated soon after the first is given.

22:20-23

This is the third poem on "Lebanon," and its limits are agreed upon by all commentators.[73] It contains other metaphorical terms, e.g., "shepherds," which is a favorite Jeremianic term for kings (cf. 2:8; 23:1-4; etc.). The inclusio here is formed by the repetition of "Lebanon" with an added "cedars" at the end.[74] And each stanza has its own inclusio as we will see in the next section.

```
20   עלי הלבנון וצעקי ובבשן תני קולך
         וצעקי מעברים כי נשברו כל־מאהביך
21   דברתי אליך בשלותיך אמרת לא אשמע
         זה דרכך מנעוריך כי לא־שמעת בקולי

22   כל־רעיך תרעה־רוח ומאהביך בשבי ילכו
         כי אז תבשי ונכלמת מכל רעתך
23   ישבתי בלבנון מקננתי בארזים
         מה־נחנת בבא־לך הבלים חיל כילדה
```

20   Go up to *Lebanon* and cry out
         and in Bashan lift up your voice
     Cry out from Abarim
         for all your lovers are destroyed
21   I spoke to you in your prosperity
         but you said, 'I will not listen'
     This has been your way from your youth
         that you have not obeyed my voice

22   The wind shall shepherd all your shepherds
         and your lovers shall go into captivity
     Then you will be ashamed and confounded
         because of all your wickedness
23   O inhabitants of *Lebanon*
         nested among the *cedars*
     How you will groan when your pangs come upon you
         pain as of a woman in travail

The poem begins with Jeremiah ironically telling the king to go ahead with his pagan worship on "Holy Hill." This is the classical figure called *epitrope*. Now if the hearer does not detect the irony with which Jeremiah begins, he might catch the word-play in כל־רעיך תרעה־רוח beginning stanza 2. There is more irony in the next colon where Jeremiah uses "lovers" as he did in v. 20.[75] In the final lines of the poem

Jeremiah is still using metaphors to indicate how royalty will
suffer in the coming day of judgment. These figures--especially
the metaphors--all create *distance* between Jeremiah and his
audience. Perhaps such a stance was the only safe one to take.
It is dangerous to come right out and tell the king and his
court that they will be defeated, although Jeremiah was evidently able to speak this candidly with Zedekiah (see chs. 21,34 &
37).

51:11-14

In spite of some prosaic-sounding lines (11bcd), we
nevertheless take this to be a 3-stanza poem of four lines each.
The lower limit is established by the doxology in vv. 15-19
(=10:12-16) and commentators generally take v. 11 as the beginning.[76] Condamin has again caught the key word מלא, which
means "to fill" or "to supply."

הברו החצים מלאו השלטים	11
העיר יהוה את־רוח מלכי מדי	
כי־על־בבל מזמתו להשחיתה	
כי־נקמת יהוה היא נקמת היכלו	
אל־חומת בבל שאו־נס החזיקו המשמר	12
הקימו שמרים הכינו הארבים	
כי גם־זמם יהוה גם־עשה	
את אשר־דבר אל־ישבי בבל	
שכנתי על־מים רבים רבת אוצרת	13
בא קצך אמת בצעך	
נשבע יהוה צבאות בנפשו	14
כי אם־מלאתיך אדם כילק וענו עליך הידד	

11 Sharpen the arrows
        supply the shields
    Yahweh has stirred up
        the spirit of the kings of the Medes
    For his purpose against Babylon
        is to destroy it
    For that is the vengeance of Yahweh
        the vengeance for his temple

12 Signal attack against Babylon's walls
        make the watch strong
    Set up watchmen
        prepare the ambushes
    For even Yahweh has planned
        even he has done
    That which he said
        concerning the inhabitants of Babylon

```
13    You who dwell by many waters
         rich in treasures
      Your end has come
         the thread of your life is cut
14    Yahweh of Hosts has sworn
         by his own very self
      Surely I will supply you with men like locusts
         and they will raise the victory shout over you
```

Any translation of the two uses of מלא will be inade-
quate because of the shift in meaning. The verb normally means
"to fill," which fits well into v. 14, but not into v. 11. Our
use of "supply" follows Condamin who translates with "remplir."
This tension only serves to point up again how Jeremiah plays
with word meanings, and since the less common usage occurs at
the beginning, the audience will be alerted to notice the term
when it appears again at the end. The inclusio helps to focus
on a battlefield filled with armor and men and thereby functions to emphasize what is meant to be the main point, viz.,
that Babylon will soon be faced with an enemy whose strength
is nothing less than overpowering.

This concludes our section on the use of the inclusio
in the Jeremianic speeches. Yet we have not exhausted the
number of speeches that end by a return to the beginning.
Chiastic speeches to be shown in the next chapter do this and
more. But we have made a beginning. And we have also for the
first time discovered strategies of argumentation used by Jeremiah against his audience.

Since the inclusio was employed in the earlier rhetoric
of Deuteronomy and is now found quite frequently in the rhetoric of Jeremiah, we may perhaps be permitted some speculation
about Jeremiah's dependence on Deuteronomy. It would appear
that Jeremiah appropriated the structures of Deuteronomy for
his own use. Why? A slightly revised answer of Herman Gunkel's would be suitable enough. When asked why the prophets
borrowed certain genres, Gunkel answered that they did so in
order to win over the hearts of a people who were already receptive to those genres.[77] We think rather that Jeremiah used
the rhetorical structures of Deuteronomy because *they* were
already familiar to the people, and were no doubt structures
to which the people could conceivably respond.

Inclusio Within the Jeremianic Poems

We have seen that the inclusio delimits whole poems.
Now, as we look within various poems, we see the inclusio again
where it appears to delimit certain parts. These we offer as
stanzas within poems. As we mentioned earlier, stanzas are already conceded in Hebrew poetry, and we think that the inclusio
can now be listed as another criterion for their delimitation.
It is of course possible that some of the units to be discussed
here are in reality whole poems; we cannot be sure, but our
present judgment is that they are not. Most important is that
Jeremiah structured smaller segments of his poems in the same
way that he structured whole poems. That is the point we wish
to make clear.

4:22

This unit is usually taken to be a part of 4:19-22
(so Condamin and Bright). Volz, however, separates it out as
being independent. We take it as a 3-line stanza of 4:19-22
with לא ידעו at the end of lines 1 and 3 making the inclusio.

22 כי אויל עמי אותי לא ידעו
בנים סכלים המה ולא נבונים המה
הכמים המה להרע ולהיטיב לא ידעו

22 For my people are foolish
  me *they do not know*
Stupid children are they
  no understanding have they
Wise are they to do evil
  but to do good, *they do not know*

To lack a knowledge of Yahweh is to lack a knowledge of
how to do good. The people lack both. This entire unit is
finely constructed: the center cola balance one another by both
ending in המה. The final bi-colon is a chiasmus, and the positive "Wise are they.." sets up the negative "they do not know,"
which enables the tie-up with the beginning.

4:29

This is a 3-line stanza in the poem of 4:29-31.[78] The
rest of the poem divides up into two additional stanzas of 3
lines each making the whole a 3:3:3 structure.[79] The inclusio
here is made by the repetition of כל-העיר. It appears at the
end of the first line and at the beginning of the third. We

see no reason to emend (with Rudolph) the first of these to
כל־הארץ (Greek: πᾶσα χώρα). Bright says כל־העיר in line 1 is
an intrusion from line 3, but we disagree.[80] We also find it
unnecessary to expand the center of the unit as the Greek does.
The Hebrew has here a nice syntactic chiasmus giving the stanza
added structure.

29　מקול פרש ורמה קשת ברחת כל־העיר
באו בעבים ובכפים עלו
כל־העיר עזובה ואין־יושב בהן איש

29　At the noise of horseman and archer
　　　every city takes to flight
　　They enter into the thickets
　　　and into rocks they climb
　　Every city is deserted
　　　and no man dwells in them

When Jeremiah first speaks of "every city," he is using "city"
as a metonymy for "people of the city." But in the second instance "every city" means every *place* where people so live together. Thus after *every city* evacuates, *every city* is deserted.

5:21

　　　　5:21, though a brief 2 lines, contains a nice inclusio
using שמע (hear):

21　שמעו־נא זאת עם סכל ואין לב
עינים להם ולא יראו אזנים להם ולא ישמעו

21　*Hear* this please
　　foolish people without sense
　　Who have eyes but do not see
　　who have ears but do not *hear*

It is ironic. Jeremiah asks a people to hear who cannot hear.
Perhaps by placing the key term at the extremes he will make
an impression on the *ear*, in which case their deafness can be
penetrated. A comparison of this verse with Isaiah 6:9-10 and
Psalm 135:16-17 shows that the thought was not original to Jeremiah, but the structure which he gave it was.

8:4-5

　　　　This is the first of four stanzas in the poem of 8:4-
9, and three make use of the inclusio in one way or another.
The key term in this stanza is שוב (to return). Not only does

this verb make the inclusio, but together with its cognate nouns
it occurs in the stanza no fewer than five times. In Holladay's
major study of שוב[81] this text is crucial for determining the
root's basic meaning.[82]

4   היפלו ולא יקומו אם־ישוב ולא <u>ישוב</u>
5   מדוע שובבה העם הזה ירושלם משבה נצחת
         החזיקו בתרמת מאנו <u>לשוב</u>

4   When men fall, do they not rise again?
      If one turns away, does he not *return*?
5   Why then has this people turned away
      Jerusalem, the 'turncoat pre-eminent'?
    They hold fast to deceit
      They refuse *to return*

My translation differs from most in that it follows the *MT* in
line 2 which includes "Jerusalem." One Ms. and the *LXX* omit,
and so also does the *RSV*. Commentators are similarly divided.[83]
This line, however, is a syntactic chiasmus: Why then/ turned
away/ this people// Jerusalem/ the 'turncoat/ pre-eminent'.
The second colon in the line is ironic: Jerusalem (=the people
of Jerusalem) is "exhibit A" of apostasy. She is outstanding
in her field.

      The inclusio in this brief stanza reveals a rhetorical
strategy seen earlier in the full poem of 3:1-5. Jeremiah begins with a rhetorical question, to which his audience can be
expected to give an obvious answer. He then goes on to use a
link term to point up an incongruity. The obvious answer to
the question in colon 2 is, "Of course such a person will return" (although in 3:1 it was just the opposite!). Then at the
end comes the twist: but this people *refuses* to return. Here
lies the incongruity Jeremiah wants his audience to see. We
have here from Jeremiah no "authority preaching." He appeals
only to the listener's sense of order, and after an analogy
pointing up the incongruity, the listener is left with the decision to accept or reject.

<u>8:7</u>

      This is the third stanza of the same poem and plays on
the verb ידע. That same verb formed the inclusio in 4:22.
Here Jeremiah uses it to contrast people with birds, and in a
way very typically Jeremianic, it is unfavorable to the
people.

גם חסידה בשמים ידעה מועדיה   7
ותר וסוס ועגור שמרו את-עת באנה
ועמי לא ידעו את משפט יהוה

7   Even the stork in the heavens
       knows her times
    And the turtledove, swallow and crane[84]
       keep the time of their coming
    But my people do not *know*
       the ordinance of Yahweh

Again Jeremiah uses an argument from the natural order. The
repetition of "know" helps underscore the contrast and also to
point up the incongruity which Jeremiah has come to see. How
different a view of man within the created order from what is
found in Gen 1:26ff and Psalm 8:6!

8:8-9

The final stanza of this poem is 4 lines, and the inclusio here is made up of balancing terms in *both* cola of the
opening and closing lines.

איכה תאמרו חכמים אנחנו ותורת יהוה אתנו   8
אכן הנה לשקר עשה עט שקר ספרים
הבישו חכמים חתו וילכדו   9
הנה בדבר-יהוה מאסו וחכמת-מה להם

8   How can you say, 'We are *wise*
       and the *law of Yahweh* is with us?'
    But, behold, the false pen of the scribes
       has made it into a lie
9   The wise men shall be shamed
       they shall be dismayed and taken
    Behold they have rejected the *word of Yahweh*
       so what *wisdom* is in them?

Here Jeremiah quotes his opponents in order to engage them, or
perhaps he may be putting words in their mouth. Then by showing that their claim is mere pretension, he uses synonymns and
cognate terms to turn and accuse them. But the question at
the end still leaves the answer with the audience.

10:20-21

This cluster of 4 lines is usually taken to be part of
a 6-line poem beginning at v. 19.[85] Yet they may be independent. We are faced at the outset with textual difficulty
primarily because of some metaphors. Verse 20 begins by mentioning a "destroyed tent," which is followed by "destroyed

children" no longer able to set up a tent (is it Yahweh's tent?).
Without discussing other alternatives the following solution is
proposed. First we must omit אהלי שדד, "my tent is destroyed"
as a gloss (so Rudolph).[86] What emerges then is an inclusio that
helps clear up the sense.

וכל־מיתרי נתקו בני יצאני ואינם   20
אין־נטה עוד אהלי ומקים יריעותי
כי נבערו הרעים ואת־יהוה לא דרשו   21
על־כן לא השכילו וכל־מרעיתם נפוצה

20   *All my cords* are broken
    my children have left me and are not
  There is no one to spread again my tent
    and to set up my curtains
21   For the shepherds are stupid
    and of Yahweh they do not inquire
  Therefore they have not prospered
    and *all their flock* is scattered

The problematic term is מיתר, which is an uncommon word meaning
"cord" or "string."[87] It usually refers to a "tent cord" (Ex
39:40; Isa 54:2; etc.) which no doubt explains the attempted
gloss: the tent cords are broken//the tent is destroyed. But
if one reads "All my cords are broken" with the colon *following*,
then "cords" ends up in parallelism with "children." This
would require a metaphorical use of "cords"--albeit a rare one
(but again who knows since the term is uncommon to begin with).
Yet if the inclusio is made up of equivalent terms, i.e., if
both metaphors refer to *people*, then this interpretation is
substantiated. The "cords" become the same as the "flock,"
which is also equivalent to the "children." Jeremiah is of
course responsible for the confusion, but he seems to want to
say something like "My cords are no longer able to set up my
tent. Why? Because they are broken, i.e., they are gone away."

Such a pattern of thought is true to form. Jeremiah
begins with an obscure term--in this case a metaphor--and one
that does not reveal his preferred subject. The "broken cords"
only enlist the audience's sympathy. The preferred subject is
"shepherds" (i.e., the kings). *They* have become alienated from
Yahweh, and as a result the flock/children/cords are scattered.
The end of the unit in this way brings us right back to the beginning.

22:20-21

We looked earlier at this stanza when we discussed the
whole poem.[88] Now we can see how an inclusio isolates vv. 20-
21 into a stanza of four lines, making the poem a 4:4 structure.
Stanza two also has an inclusio and will be our next example.
Here the structure is created by "your voice/my voice," which
comes at the end of lines 1 and 4.

עלי הלבנון וצעקי ובבשן תני קולך 20
וצעקי מעברים כי נשברו כל-מאהביך
דברתי אליך בשלוחיך אמרת לא אשמע 21
זה דרכך מנעוריך כי לא-שמעת בקולי

20 Go up to Lebanon and cry out
    and in Bashan lift up *your voice*
    Cry out from Abarim
    for all your lovers are destroyed
21 I spoke to you in your prosperity
    but you said, 'I will not listen'
    This has been your way from your youth
    that you have not obeyed *my voice*

The repetition making this inclusio brings out the lack of com-
munication between Yahweh and the personified daughter of Jerusalem. The whole is of course ironic. Jeremiah tells her to
go ahead and *continue* crying to her deity (so also Elijah on
Mt. Carmel; cf. I Kings 18:27), while at the same time reminding her of her *continual* refusal to listen to the voice of
Yahweh.

22:22-23

Inclusios which tie together stanzas of poems seem to
be appearing in clusters. We found three such stanzas in 8:4-
9, and now two are present in 22:20-23. These four lines contain an inclusio which is assonantal. We give the Hebrew only.

כל-רעיך תרעה-רוח ומאהביך בשבי יֵלֵכוּ 22
כי אז תבשי ונכלמת מכל רעתך
ישבתי בלבנון מקננתי בארזים 23
מה-נחנת בבא-לך חבלים חיל כַּיֹּלֵדָה

The play on sound is made by two words containing יל followed
by a sere vowel. In addition we have כ following the combination in the first term, whereas it precedes the combination in
the final term. Assonantal balance is common in Jeremiah as
Holladay has already shown us.[89] Thus far in this study we

have put the emphasis on *key words*, which in turn create semantic links. But the possibilities of *sound* for making associa-
tions should not be minimized. Here by sound alone Jeremiah
associates "travail" with "going into captivity," the former
very clearly describing what the latter will be like.

30:12-14

This is the larger of two stanzas which make up a poem
in 30:12-15. That poem, taken as a whole, is a companion piece
to 30:16-18.[90] The inclusio here is formed by the repetition
of מכה (wound), which is a central term of the poem. This word
in fact also links the poem to its companion piece (v. 17:
(וממכותיך ארפאך).

אנוש לשברך נחלה מכתך 12
אין־דן דינך למזור רפאות תעלה אין לך 13
כל־מאהביך שכחוך אותך לא ידרשו 14
כי מכת אויב הכיתיך מוסר אכזרי

12 Your hurt is incurable
 your wound is grievous
13 No salve for your sore[91]
 no healing for you
14 All your lovers have forgotten you
 they care nothing for you
 An enemy's wound I dealt you
 a cruel chastisement

The movement is again from the general to the specific. Only
in the final line does Jeremiah make it clear that the wound is
from Yahweh. And if the "wound" stated at the beginning is not
readily perceived to be at the same time a wound from the enemy,
then the hearer must wait until the end for this revelation
also.

31:35-36

This stanza is another cluster of 4 lines in a 4:2 poem.
31:35-37 was inserted into the Book of Comfort in what we determined earlier to be the third stage of its growth. Such shapes
of unequal but proportional stanzas are now commonly seen in
Jeremiah--the 4:2 and 2:4 structures being most prevalent in
the Book of Comfort.

נתן שמש לאור יומם חקת ירח וכוכבים לאור לילה 35
רגע הים ויהמו גליו יהוה צבאות שמו
אם־ימשו החקים האלה מלפני נאם־יהוה 36
גם זרע ישראל ישבתו מהיות גוי לפני כל־הימים

35 Who gives the sun for light by *day*
      and the ordered moon and stars to illumine the night?
   Who lashes the sea to make its waves roar?
      Yahweh of Hosts is his name
36 If this fixed order should vanish
      from before me--oracle of Yahweh
   Then Israel's descendants will cease
      from being a nation before me, *all the days*

The balance of "day/days" is exactly what we had in 20:14-18.[92]
There Jeremiah cursed the *day* of his birth at the beginning,
and concluded with a lament about ending his *days* in shame. It
would appear that Jeremiah not only uses the same structures
more than once, but even some of the same word-pairs over again.

        The "if/then" form at the end leaves the final answer
again with the audience. If the fixed order departs, then Israel's descendants will cease from being a nation. We can hear
the audience respond to this with a loud "No!". The people are
now broken and Jeremiah must raise them up, so he uses the same
strategy of former times when he gave them a message of judgment. Before the people needed to supply an answer that would
break them; now they need to articulate words that will sustain
them in the days ahead.

46:20-21

        Our final example is a cluster of 4 lines which comes
from a speech given by Jeremiah against Egypt. I take the
speech to include all of 46:18-23, and since this cluster com-
prises the middle 4 lines, the poem appears to be a 4:4:4
structure.[93] The verb בוא makes the inclusio.

                    עגלה יפה־פיה מצרים קרץ מצפון בא בא[94]   20
                    גם־שכריה בקרבה כעגלי מרבק   21
                    כי גם־המה הפנו נסו יחדיו לא עמדו
                    כי יום אידם בא עליהם עת פקדתם

20 A beautiful heifer is Egypt
      but a fly from the north has *come* upon her[94]
21 The mercenaries too in her midst
      are like fatted calves
   They too have turned and fled together
      they did not stand
   For the day of their disaster has *come* upon them
      the time of their punishment

Jeremish begins again with metaphors, only when speaking
against Egypt it is apparently safe to identify her from the
start. Yet we still move from the figurative to the literal:

a fly has come/ the day of disaster has come.

This concludes our section on inclusio within the Jeremianic poems and also the chapter. We have seen that parts of
poems are structured the same way as whole poems. Occasionally
same words are used. For Jeremiah the inclusio is not merely
a device enabling him to repeat himself. It is a tool of argumentation, and as such becomes something it was not in Deuteronomy. Deuteronomy's audience needed reminding, and occasionally some gentle admonition. Jeremiah's audience, however, was
of a different sort. It required for the most part penetrating
arguments gauged to break the will.

Editorial structures in Jeremiah have been seen to have
a close affinity with the structures of Deuteronomy. In some
cases, e.g., 1-20, the harshness of the original is toned down
making the final compilation more suitable for temple worship.
And we are not thinking of worship in the exilic and post-exilic
community. The process of adaptation began immediately. The
scroll which Baruch reads in the temple in 604 B.C. is already
modified in order that it may end with hope instead of despair.

Although a variety of larger chiastic structures have
been found in Deuteronomy and the Deuteronomic literature,[1]
there appears to be no concentration of the figure in this literary corpus. Lund showed numerous examples of the chiasmus in
Leviticus and he found it also in material as early as the Yahwistic account of the Fall (Gen 3).[2]

Arguments for a chiasmus usually build upon the distribution of key words or what is believed to be a "thought pattern." Lund argued that the chiasmus was a thought pattern[3]
though it is true that most of his structures had key words for
undergirding. When these were not present the chiasmus became
infinitely more difficult to objectify. While it may be conceded that an author can deliver a concept without using the
key word for that concept, e.g., a passage written about love
need not have the word "love" in it, nevertheless the possibility that the author had another basic concept in mind or perhaps more than one concept is always present. The danger then
is that an outline, if based *only* upon a "thought pattern," all
too easily becomes the creation of the modern scholar who im-
poses on the text something that was never intended to be there
in the first place. Numerous discoveries of chiasmi fail because of this and they must be judged no less severely than the
so-called genres about which we spoke earlier.

In our present study we will require that speeches have
at least some key words before a chiasmus of thought is proposed. In the larger editorial structures too, key words can
almost always be found which make the chiasmus more certain.
We would like to know more about ancient Hebrew thought patterns, but this much we do know, that verbal association was
widely used in all levels of discourse, and we are therefore
well-advised to stay close to the specific vocabulary of the
text in attempting to find out rhetorical structures.

Another kind of chiasmus not recognized by Lund has
been observed by Lohfink, and significantly for us it appears
in Deuteronomy. This is a chiasmus of *speaker*. In Deut

61

1:20-31, Moses narrates in the first person introducing the
direct address of each of the participants in a discussion--in-
cluding himself--in chiastic fashion:[4]

> A   Moses speaks   (20-21)
>   B   People speak   (22)
>   C   Explorers speak   (25)
>   B'   People speak   (27-28)
> A'   Moses speaks   (29-31)

Lohfink of course does not consider this order fortuitous.
Structures in Deuteronomy are intended by their authors to be
auditory signals for a people who must listen to material being
read to them aloud.[5] We will see this same type of chiasmus in
Jeremiah where it becomes almost as important as the key-word
type in structuring the Jeremianic speech.

Chiasmus Within the Jeremianic Poems

In Hebrew poetry chiasmus is a syntactic structure at
base which inverts normal word order. It works especially well
in a poetry which makes use of parallelism. Holladay says it
serves to "vary the steady drumbeat of the normal [i.e., paral-
lel] pattern."[6] Syntactic chiasmus is commonly found in all
Old Testament poetry so we need not make too much of its existence in Jeremiah. But since we are going to show how Jeremiah
expands the figure, it would be well to see how he uses the
figure in its most basic form.

We shall begin with the smallest unit of the poetry,
the bi-colon. The greatest number of syntactic chiasmi in Jeremiah are bi-cola which position verbs at the extremes:

2:9	Therefore I still contend	לכן עד אריב
	with you	אתכם
	and with your children's children	ואת-בני בניכם
	I will contend	אריב
2:19a	It will chasten you	תיסרך
	your wickedness	רעתך
	and your apostasy	ומשבותיך
	will reprove you	תוכחך
4:5a	Declare	הגידו
	in Judah	ביהודה
	and in Jerusalem	ובירושלם
	proclaim	השמיעו

4:7a	It has gone up	עלה
	a lion from his thicket	אריה מסבכו
	and a destroyer of nations	ומשחית גוים
	has gone forth	נסע

4:9c	And they shall be appalled	ונשמו
	the priests	הכהנים
	and the prophets	והנביאים
	shall be astounded	יתמהו

5:6a	Therefore it will slay them	על־כן הכם
	a lion from the forest	אריה מיער
	and a wolf from the desert	זאב ערבות
	will destroy them	ישדדם

5:12b	It will not come upon us	ולא־תבוא עלינו
	evil	רעה
	and sword and famine	וחרב ורעב
	we will not see	לוא נראה

6:21b	And they shall stumble against them	וכשלו בם
	fathers and sons together	אבות ובנים יחדו
	neighbor and friend	שכן ורעו
	shall perish	יאבדו

6:25a	Do not go forth	אל־תצאי
	into the field	השדה
	and by the way	ובדרך
	do not walk	אל־תלכי

14:2a	She mourns	אבלה
	Judah	יהודה
	her gates	ושעריה
	languish	אמללו

18:23b	Do not forgive	אל־תכפר
	their iniquity	על־עונם
	and their sin from your sight	וחטאתם מלפניך
	do not blot out	אל־תמחי

20:6	You shall go	תלכו
	into captivity	בשבי
	and Babylon	ובבל
	you shall enter	תבוא

30:17a	For I will restore	כי אעלה
	health unto you	ארכה לך
	and from your wounds	וממכותיך
	I will heal you	ארפאך

30:18b And it shall be built
    the city upon her mound
    and the palace where it used
                    to be
shall stand

ונבנתה
עיר על־תלה
וארמון על־משפטו
ישב

46:14b Proclaim
    in Memphis
    and in Tahpanhes
say[7]

והשמיעו
בנף
ובתחפנחס
אמרו[7]

48:11c Therefore it remains
    his taste in him
    and his scent
is not changed

על־כן עמד
טעמו בו
וריחו
לא נמר

48:41a They will be taken
    the cities
    and the strongholds
will be seized

נלכדה
הקריות
והמצדות
נתפשה

51:58c And they toil
    the peoples for nought
    and the nations only for fire
indeed they weary themselves

ויגעו
עמים בדי־ריק
ולאמים בדי־אש
ויעפו

Using Lowth's terminology these would all be examples
of synonymous parallelism. For Schoettgen they would illustrate
the rhetorical device "exergasia" (see Appendix). The repetition functions to embellish the idea and the chiasmus merely
adds variation.

In only a few instances does Jeremiah use the small
chiastic structure for contrast:

4:22c Wise are they
    for evil
    and for good
they do not know

הכמים המה
להרע
ולהיטיב
לא ידעו

12:13a They have sown
    wheat
    and thorns
they have reaped

זרעו
חטים
וקצים
קצרו

In 4:22c Jeremiah was perhaps forced into such a construction
because of his desire to create balance with an earlier colon
in the stanza.[8]

Lowth would have called these antithetical parallelisms
but again that definition is not exhaustive. The sequence of

expression in 4:22c is worthy of a closer look because it appears elsewhere in different kinds of parallelistic structures.
Jeremiah often in stating things twice first uses *positive* and
either *ironic* or *mildly humorous* terms, and second *negative* but
sober terms.[9] In this line to say that the people are "*wise* for
(doing) evil" is humorous, whereas the following remark "and for
good they do not know" is brutal frankness, perhaps even sarcasm.
But Jeremiah's mind typically works in this sequence and we must
be on the lookout for it in other places where it occurs.

In 12:13a we find an element of sequentiality present:
sowing and reaping. The combination of sequentiality and contrast sets up incongruity: thorns are reaped where wheat was
sown. This type of thinking too, as we have already seen, is
characteristically Jeremianic.

Only rarely do we find chiasmi with verbs at the center:

2:36b	So by Egypt	גם ממצרים
	you will be shamed	תבושי
	as you were shamed	כאשר־בשת
	by Assyria	מאשור

10:11[10]	The gods which the heavens and earth	אלהיא די־שמיא וארקא
	did not make	לא עבדו
	shall perish	יאבדו
	from the earth and under the heavens	מארעא ומן־תחות שמיא אלה

51:38	Together like lions	יחדו ככפרים
	they shall roar	ישאגו
	they shall growl	נערו
	like lion's whelps	כגורי אריות

Sometimes the use of a "double-duty" subject[11] in the
center makes an even more impressive pattern:

4:2b	And they shall bless themselves	והתברכו
	in him	בו
	nations	גוים
	and in him	ובו
	shall they glory	ותהללו

4:30c	They despise	מאסו־
	you	בך
	lovers	עגבים
	your soul	נפשך
	they seek	יבקשו

In one instance Jeremiah manages a word-play:[12]

8:5a   Why then has it turned away   מדוע שובבה
          this people   העם הזה
          Jerusalem   ירושלם
          the 'turncoat' pre-eminent!   משבה נצחת

     Particles are also structural indicators in Jeremiah.
In 4-cola units they frequently repeat at the beginning of the
center cola creating a partial chiasmus:

6:8   Be warned O Jerusalem   הוסרי ירושלם
          lest I be alienated from you   פן־תקע נפשי ממך
          lest I make you a desolation   פן־אשימך שממה
          an uninhabited land   ארץ לוא נושבה

8:13   Gathering I will end them   אסף אסיפם
          no grapes on the vine   אין ענבים בגפן
          no figs on the fig tree   ואין תאנים בתאנה
          even the leaves are withered   והעלה נבל

9:21   The dead bodies of men shall fall   ונפלה נבלת האדם
[9:22] *like* dung on the open field   כדמן על־פני השדה
          like sheaves after the reaper   וכעמיר מאחרי הקצר
          and none shall gather them   ואין מאסף

13:16a Give glory to Yahweh your God   תנו ליהוה אלהיכם כבוד
          before it grows dark   בטרם יחשך
          before your feet stumble   ובטרם יתנגפו רגליכם
          on the mountains at twilight   על־הרי נשף

17:1   The sin of Judah is written   חטאת יהודה כתובה
          with a pen of iron   בעט ברזל
          with a point of diamond   בצפרן שמיר
          it is engraved on the tablet   חרושה על־לוה לבם
               of their heart

     A construction of the same type is found in Deut 32:27, which
may perhaps have provided Jeremiah with a prototype.[13]

Deut 32:27   לולי כעס אויב אגור
                              פן־ינכרו צרימו
                         פן־יאמרו ידינו רמה
                      ולא יהוה פעל כל־זאת

       Had I not feared provocation by the enemy
         lest their adversaries should judge amiss
         lest they should say, 'Our hand is triumphant
       Yahweh has not wrought all this'

Key nouns can also come at the end of center cola in partial chiasmi.

4:19   My bowels, my bowels, I am sick   מעי מעי אחולה
        Oh, the walls of *my heart*   קירות לבי
        a commotion within *my heart*   המה־לי לבי
    I cannot keep silent   לא אחריש

12:10   Many shepherds have destroyed my רעים רבים שחתו כרמי
           vineyard   בססו את־חלקתי
        they have trampled down *my portion* נתנו את־חלקת
        they have made my pleasant *portion* חמדתי
    a desolate wilderness   למדבר שממה

These partial chiasmi function to retard movement. The repetition at the center gives the thought pause for embellishment before it is then carried on to completion in the final colon.

In 9:3 [Eng. 9:4] key nouns provide balance in all four cola. This chiasmus was noted long ago by John Forbes.[14]

9:3   איש מרעהו השמרו ועל־כל־אח אל־תבטחו
           כי כל־אח עקוב יעקב וכל־רע רכיל יהלך

      Let everyone beware of *his neighbor*
        and put no trust in *any brother*
        for *every brother* is a 'Jacob'
      and *every neighbor* goes about as a slanderer

Jeremiah has another characteristic way of using the chiasmus to balance contrasting terms while keeping the thought the same. Holladay first noted this in 14:2.[15]

14:2   Judah mourns   אבלה יהודה
        her gates languish   ושעריה אמללו
        they lament on the ground   קדרו לארץ
      and the cry of Jerusalem goes up   וצוחת ירושלם עלתה

As Holladay points out the recognition of a chiasmus here clears up finally the subject of the third colon. It is not "people," which the *RSV* supplies as a bonus, but "gates." Jeremiah is speaking figuratively of "gates lamenting on the ground."[16] The middle cola are then parallel. Holladay also calls attention to Jeremiah's play on the vertical. Cola 1-3 depict people and gates lying *down* while colon 4 speaks of the cry of the people going *up*. Nevertheless 1 and 4 convey the same idea making the whole a chiasmus.

68

A similar structure occurs in 20:14, which opens the
poem in which Jeremiah curses his birth:

20:14   Cursed be the day   ארור הירם
            on which I was born   אשר ילדתי בו
            the day when my mother bore me   יום אשר־ילדתנ׳ אמי
            let it not be blessed   אל־יהי ברוך

Like 14:2, the center cola balance and colon 4 repeats colon 1
only casting the thought in the negative. The contrast is seen
in the beginning and ending words "cursed/blessed," which, if
taken alone, make an inclusio. We therefore think that the unit
is self-contained making a stanza within the poem. The next cluster of four cola (20:15) is similar with the terms ארור (cursed)
and שמח שמחהו (making him very glad) appearing in the same collocations. This we take to be a second stanza in the poem. With
these two stanzas thus delimited we can therefore propose a 2:2:
2:2:2 structure, which is how we took the poem earlier.[17]

The preceding opens up yet another line of research for
the Jeremianic speeches. Because 14:2 and 20:14 are both
regarded as beginning their respective poems in addition to
their being similarly structured, we should not seem to be going
too far amiss if we suggest that perhaps the poems *en toto* were
written alike. It seems that such is the case. Like 20:14-18,
14:2-6 is easily delimited. Verse 2 is preceded by a superscription and chapter number in v. 1, and the lower limit is fixed at
v. 6 because of the liturgy isolated in vv. 7-9.[18] Now if 14:2
is also a stanza of two lines as it appears, we can break down
the remaining verses into stanzas of two lines each, which then
results in 14:2-6 being a 2:2:2:2:2 structure just like 20:14-
18.[19] The implications of this should be obvious. For the
first time we are now able to see Jeremiah the poet writing at
least two of his poems alike, i.e., with similar beginnings and
the same number of 2-line stanzas. We know that modern poets
and song-writers allow structures to repeat from one work to
another, and it should come as a surprise to no one that the
same obtained with the ancients. As we increase our understanding of Hebrew poetic structure we will probably find even more
structures which repeat from poem to poem.

We will now look at a few instances where Jeremiah
creates a chiasmus by assonance. Assonance is a major stylistic
feature in Jeremiah, but when it provides poetry with balance
it becomes a structural feature as well.

5:22　　　　　　　　האותי לא־תיראו　נאם־יהוה אם מפני לא תָחִילוּ
　　　　　　　　　　אשר־שמתי חול גבול לים חק־עולם ולא יעברנהו

6:1c-2a　　　　　　　כי רעה נשקפה מָצָפוֹן ושבר גדול
　　　　　　　　　　הנוה והמענגה דמיתי בַּת־צִיוֹן

20:11　　　　　　　　ויהוה אותי כגבור עריץ על־כן רדפי יִכָּשְׁלוּ ולא יֻכָלוּ
　　　　　　　　　　בשו מאד כי־לא הִשְׂכִּילוּ כלמת עולם לא תשכח

48:3-4　　　　　　　קול צְעָקָה מחרונים שד וָשֶׁבֶר גדול
　　　　　　　　　　נִשְׁפְרָה מואב השמיעו זְעָקָה צעוריה

　　　　Our two final examples of chiasmus within the Jeremianic
poem are slightly larger. Here we begin to see how balanced
terms throughout the unit create a pattern that is commonly
found in whole poems. Chiasmus is now more than syntactic re-
versals or inversion patterns within the 2-line stanza; it becomes a structure by which large panels are ordered.

2:27b-28a　　　　　　　　　　ובעת רעתם יאמרו
　　　　　　　　　　　　　　קומה והושיענו
　　　　　　　　　　　ואיה אלהיך אשר עשית לך
　　　　　　　　　　　　יקומו אם־יושיעוך
　　　　　　　　　　　　　בעת רעתך

　　　　But *in the time of their trouble* they say
　　　　'*arise* and *save us*'
　　　　　　but where are your gods which you made for yourselves?
　　　　let them *arise* if they can *save* you
　　　　in your time of trouble

Here Yahweh takes the people's own words to use against them.
But the climax is still in the center where the people are given
a "loaded question" which they cannot answer without first ad-
mitting their guilt.

　　　　The chiastic structure in 4:19c-21 also appears to delimit a stanza within a poem. Since 4:19-22 is generally taken
to be a unit (so Condamin and Bright) and we have earlier isolated both 19ab and 22,[20] our poem thus becomes a 2:4:3 structure, which again should warn us not to be overly predisposed
to finding stanzas of equal length.

4:19c-21

כי קול שופר שמעתי
נפשי תרועת מלחמה
שבר על־שבר נקרא
כי שדדה כל־הארץ
פתאם שדדו אהלי
רגע יריעתי
עד־מתי אראה־נס
אשמעה קול שופר

> For the *sound of the trumpet/* you have *heard*[21]
> O my soul, the *alarm* of battle
> disaster comes hard on disaster
> for the whole land is *laid waste*
> suddenly my tents are *laid waste*
> in a moment my curtains
> how long must I see the *standard*
> must I *hear/* the *sound of the trumpet?*

Here Jeremiah is in conversation with himself. Key terms at
the extremes and in the center make the chiasmus, with an added
feature being the inversion of terms in the final colon. We
may also have a fixed pair in תרועת (alarm) and נס (standard).

These examples should suffice to show how Jeremiah uses
the chiasmus in building smaller portions of the prophetic
speech. We will now go on to whole poems where the chiasmus
becomes the controlling structure.

Chiastic Poems in Jeremiah

Two criteria can be used to identify chiastic poems in
Jeremiah: 1) key words and 2) speaker. If either alternate
to form an ABA' or expanded type arrangement, we call this a
chiasmus. Some poems have only key word balance while others
only a balance of speaker. But many have both working simul-
taneously to create coterminous stanzas. The one then becomes
a control for the other giving added support for the divisions
made. We will look at 12 chiastic poems in all.

2:5-9

We begin with a poem which has been unsuccessfully modeled
by form-critics on the lawsuit genre. It might have been analyzed form-critically as a "letter" since it has *both* the opening and closing messenger formulas, but form-critics generally
ignore these. Actually there is no agreement on how the material in chapter 2 is to be delimited. Volz takes 1-19 as a unit,
Rudolph 2-13. Bright ends at 13 but considers 2-3 separate.

As we mentioned earlier, Meek isolated 2-3 because they are
also framed by opening and closing formulas.[22]   We will argue,
however, that 5-9 is an independent poem since its controlling
structure is a chiasmus, both of key words and of speaker.[23]

כה אמר יהוה   5

A   מה־מצאו אבותיכם בי עול   כי רחקו מעלי
ﬥﬥ וילכו אחרי ההבל   ויהבלו

B   ולא אמרו איה יהוה   המעלה אתנו מארץ מצרים[24]
באַרץ ערבה ושׁוחה בארץ ציה וצלמות[25]   6

C   ואביא אתכם אל־ארץ הכרמל   לאכל פריה וטובה
תבאו ותטמאו את־ארצי   ונחלתי שמתם לתועבה   7

B'   הכהנים לא אמרו איה יהוה   ותפשי התורה לא ידעוני
והרעים פשעו בי   והנביאים נבאו בבעל   8

A'   ואחרי לא־יועלו הלכו
לכן עד אריב אתכם נאם־יהוה   ואת־בני בניכם אריב   9

5   Thus says Yahweh

A   What wrong did *your fathers* find in me
        that they wandered far from me?
      They went/ after worthlessness
        and became worthless

6   *They did not say, 'Where is Yahweh*
B   who brought us up from the land of Egypt[24]
      Into a land of deserts and pits
        into a land of drought and death shadows'[25]

7   And *I brought you into* a garden *land*
C   to enjoy its fruits and its good things
      But when *you came in* you defiled *my land*
        and made my heritage an abomination

8   The priests *did not say, 'Where is Yahweh?'*
B'   those who handle the law did not know me
      The shepherds transgressed against me
        the prophets prophesied by Baal

      And *after what does not profit/ they went*
A'   [......................?]
9   Therefore I still contend with you--oracle of Yahweh
        and with *your children's children* I will contend

•

       The key words give the structure of the poem in outline.
Let us look at them. In A "your fathers" balances "your children's children" in A'.[26] Jeremiah uses the extremes here to
state the prevailing theology that the sins of the fathers are
meted out on their children (but see later 31:29-30 where the

Jeremianic theology changes). Also in AA' our stanzas are balanced by the verb הלך with אחרי and different expressions meaning "worthlessness": הבל and לא־יועלו. The inverted syntax is also nice. We saw this frequently in the inclusio and it works in the chiastic return as well. B' repeats "they did not say 'Where is Yahweh?'" from B. The center (C) has its own internal balance repeating בוא and ארץ.

The stanza division rests thus far upon the distribution of key words. Breaking down stanzas in this way would perhaps seem a bit unjustified were it not known that stanzas in Lam 1-2 also contain key words arranged chiastically.[27] But there an acrostic form provides us with a welcome control. In Jeremiah there are no acrostics--at least so far as we know-- yet we have a control of another kind. That control is a co- existing chiasmus of speaker. It can work one of two ways. If a single speaker is narrating throughout, the direct address of various speakers is introduced in balancing stanzas making the whole a chiasmus. This is what we have here in 2:5-9. Yahweh is the narrator. In B he introduces the direct speech of the fathers and in B' the direct speech of the priests. Thus Yahweh speaks in A; the fathers in B; Yahweh in C; the priests (=the fathers) in B'; and Yahweh concludes in A'. This chiasmus of speaker is very similar to the one in Deut 1:20-31 which Moses narrated. In these instances the chiasmus of speaker is not always coterminous with the stanza divisions delimited by key words. This is most noticeable in B' where Yahweh narrates the rest of the stanza (and in B Yahweh also begins with "They did not say"). But we can say that here as well as in other poems where the same occurs, the quotes of the various speakers never violate stanza divisions, and in most cases they balance each other within the poem rather nicely. The second way a chiasmus of speaker can work is in dialogue poems where two or three parties are in conversation--sometimes with each other, sometimes with an audience who does not parti- cipate--in which cases the chiasmus of speaker *is coterminous* with the key-word divisions. Here then we have an excellent control every bit as good as the acrostic for our division of poems into stanzas.

Now a word about the poem's original form. It will be noted that without the proposed deletions B would be more than three full lines. Since the remaining stanzas are all two lines it is reasonable to suppose that B has been expanded.

The deletions we propose appear to us to be scribal glosses
added either for purposes of clarification or because an expanded form of the confession was desired at a later time in worship. This is discussed more fully in the notes. The poem in
its original form was then 2:2:2:2:2 just like 14:2-6 and
20:14-18.[28]

Finally we must see how structure affects meaning. Jer-
emiah begins by asking a question about the "fathers." Who are
they? Are they fathers of those present in Jeremiah's audience?
Or are they fathers from the distant past, say the fathers of the
Exodus? We don't know. The second stanza narrows it down some
by saying that these fathers did not remember Yahweh who brought
Israel out of Egypt. The fathers must then be at least "post-
Exodus."

The third stanza (C) brings us up to the Conquest. This
is when things began to go bad and the center of the chiasmus
underscores the turning point. Yahweh brought the people into
a "garden land" but in due time they ravaged it. B' returns to
pick up the thought of B and expands upon it. It also identifies
the fathers. They are the nation's leaders, i.e., the priests,
scribes, kings (=shepherds) and prophets. *All* can be faulted in
one way or another for not asking "Where is Yahweh?". The identification is made more sure by the words of A': ואחרי לא־יועלו
הלכו. A' contains judgment which is both contemporary and fu-
turistic. Yahweh will judge those listening as well as their
children for the sins of Israel's "fathers."

If the audience was made up of ordinary citizens they
would realize, but only at the poem's end, that judgment was
aimed at *them*. The part about the fathers, the nation's leaders,
was foil. The last line is the cap. Jeremiah wants most of all
to say that judgment is to come to the common people. These
would no doubt support Jeremiah as he flayed the nation's leaders, because if the leaders can be blamed for the nation's ills
the rest of the people can rest secure in their innocence. But
Jeremiah counters this with "Therefore I still contend with *you*--
oracle of Yahweh--and with *your children's children* I will contend." We saw this same strategy employed in 5:26-31.[29] The
real "twist" is saved for the very end, and even then, only
those with ears to hear are likely to perceive it.

One final point before leaving this poem. A comparison
of key phrases with phrases in the poem that precedes and the
poem that follows shows how three poems have been linked into a

chain. The line ...כתך אחרי במדבר בארץ (2:2) is a link to
וילכו אחרי ההבל (2:5) making a chain of 2:2-3 and 2:5-9. The
second link is made by the phrases לא-יועלו (2:8) and בלוא יועיל
(2:11). These make a chain of 2:5-9 and 2:10-13.[30] Such links
can best be explained as mnemonic devices which Jeremiah used to
keep these early poems together (for 23 years; cf. 25:3; 36:2).
Otherwise we must suppose that someone else created a chain of
poems for an early period of oral transmission.

2:33-37

Commentators are likewise not in agreement on the literary unit here. The conclusion of the poem is fairly well established because v. 37 ends the chapter. Bright takes 29-37 as a
unit which follows the Massoretic division, but says that this
is composed of two parts each having a separate origin. One of
these is 33-37.[31] Condamin also takes 33-37 as a unit and even
notices some of its balancing terms, but he characteristically
misses the proper structure because of his strophic biases.[32]
Actually, upon close examination this poem can be shown to be
one of the most fully and intricately balanced in the book. It
breaks down into three unequal but proportioned stanzas with the
center stanza one half the length of the stanzas on either side.
The poem is then 4:2:4, an enlarged form of a rhythmic pattern
discovered by Dahood in the bi-colon.[33]

מה-תיטבי דרכך לבקש אהבה		33
לכן גם את-הרעות למדתי את-דרכיך	A	
גם בכנפיך נמצאו דם נפשות אביונים נקיים		34
לא-במחתרת מצאתים כי על-כל-אלה		
ותאמרי כי נקיתי אך שב אפו ממני	B	35
הנני נשפט אותך על-אמרך לא חטאתי		
מה-תזלי מאד לשנות את-דרכך		36
גם ממצרים תבושי כאשר-בשת מאשור	A'	
גם מאת זה תצאי וידיך על-ראשך		37
כי-מאס יהוה במבטחיך ולא תצליחי להם		

33   *How* well you direct *your way*
      to seek love
    So *even* to wicked women
      you have taught your ways
34 A *Even* on your skirts is found
      the blood of innocent men[34]
    Not breaking in you found them
      for yet in spite of all these things

<pre>
35   You say, 'For I am innocent
        B   surely his anger has turned from me'
             Behold I will sentence you
                for your saying 'I have not sinned'

36   How lightly you gad about
               .to change your way
             Even by Egypt you will be shamed
               as you were shamed by Assyria
37   A'   Even from this you will come away
               with your hands upon your head
             For Yahweh has rejected your 'trusted ones'
               not letting you prosper by them
</pre>

The poem literally teems with balanced terms. AA' both begin their first lines ...ל ....מה, and alternate the position of דרכך. Each second and third line begin with גם except line 2 of A which modifies to לכן גם. Then stanza 1 ends with ......כי .....לא, while stanza 3 inverts to .....ולא .....כי. The center (B) is framed nicely by the repetition of אמר in the first and last cola. Also in the center we have another *speaker* introduced: Yahweh quotes the people who twice protest innocence, first in positive then in negative terms.

This poem begins by ironically applauding Israel's efforts to find a 'love.' She was apparently successful although we are not told at the beginning who the lover or lovers might be. Bright thinks they are the fertility gods[35] which is likely enough since idolatry is the major theme of chapter 2. But the structure of the poem forces a connection between A and A' suggesting that Israel's love affair is with Egypt. All the echoes of A in A' help make the connection. The affair with Assyria is over and Egypt is the new lover. But Jeremiah says the new love will end just as the old one did--in shame. Yahweh's sentence of judgment comes in the center, but the audience is not lost because the lover is yet to be named. After the identification the poem ends much the way it began, ironically mentioning Israel's "trusted ones" (מבטחיך).

5:1-8

This poem is rather easily delimited. The chapter division marks the upper limit while the Massoretes close a section at the end of v. 9. Since v. 9 is that stereotyped verse found elsewhere in 5:29 and 9:8, we take it as a later addition. The structure of this poem is seen correctly if not in detail at least in broad outline by both Condamin and Bright. Condamin notes some of the key terms, and Bright recognizes also that the

phrase "Why should I forgive you" in v. 7 resumes a theme stated
in v. 1. Bright also recognizes that a dialogue is going on between Yahweh and Jeremiah.[36] Jeremiah is faced with the challenge of finding a righteous man in Jerusalem much in the same
way Abraham was challenged when Sodom's fate was in the balance
(Gen 18:22-33). Both precede Diogenes in Athens, yet Jeremiah
by a mere 250 years.

שוטטו בחוצות ירושלם   וראו־נא ודעו   1
ובקשו ברחובותיה אם־תמצאו איש
אם־יש עשה משפט מבקש אמונה ואסלח לה
ואם חי־יהוה יאמרו לכן לשקר ישבעו   2

יהוה עיניך הלוא לאמונה   3
הכיתה אתם ולא־חלו כליתם מאנו קחת מוסר
חזקו פניהם מסלע מאנו לשוב

ואני אמרתי אך־דלים הם נואלו   4
כי לא ידעו דרך יהוה משפט אלהיהם
אלכה־לי אל־הגדלים ואדברה אותם   5
כי המה ידעו דרך יהוה משפט אלהיהם

אך המה יחדו שברו על נתקו מוסרות   6
על־כן הכם אריה מיער זאב ערבות ישדדם
נמר שקד על־עריהם כל־היוצא מהנה יטרף
כי רבו פשעיהם עצמו משבותיהם

אי לזאת אסלוח־לך בניך עזבוני וישבעו בלא אלהים   7
ואשבע אותם וינאפו ובית זונה יתגדדו
סוסים מיזנים משכים היו איש אל־אשת רעהו יצהלו   8

A (lines 1-2), B (line 3), C (lines 4-5), B' (line 6), A' (lines 7-8)

1   Run back and forth in the streets of Jerusalem
      look please and take note
    Search in her squares (to see)
      if you can find a *man*
A If one exists who does justice
      searching for truth, that *I may pardon her*
2   For if they say, 'As Yahweh lives'
      surely in vain *they swear*

3   O Yahweh, your eyes
      do they not look for truth?
    You have smitten them, but they felt no anguish
B   you annihilated them, but they refused to take
                 correction
    They have made their faces harder than rock
      they refuse to repent

4   Then I thought, but these are the *poor*
      they have no sense
    For they know not Yahweh's way
      the law of their God
C I will go to the *great*
      and I will speak to them
5   *For they know Yahweh's way*
      the law of their God

But both alike had broken the yoke
   they had burst the bonds
6   Therefore *it will smite them*, a lion from the forest
  B'   and a wolf from the desert will devour them
    A leopard is watching over their cities
     anyone going out from them will be torn apart
    For their crimes are many
     their regressions great

7   How then can *I pardon you*?
     your sons have forsaken me
     and *have sworn* by 'no gods'
  A' When I fed them to the full they fornicated
     and to whore-houses they trooped
8   They were well-fed lusty stallions
     each *man* neighing for his neighbor's wife

This emerges as a nicely formed 5-stanza poem with a 4:3:4:4:3 structure. Here we see the key word and speaker chiasmi coinciding perfectly, the latter clearing up what has otherwise been a speaker problem in the poem.[37] Yahweh is the speaker in A and A' and Jeremiah the speaker in B, C and B'. The audience varies but for the most part can be quite easily identified. Yahweh speaks to Jeremiah in A, although the plural imperatives, שוטטו...וראו־נא ודעו etc. indicate that Jeremiah must be part of a larger search company. In B Jeremiah addresses Yahweh; in C he is in conversation with himself; and in B' he is either addressing Yahweh again or speaking in a non-direct way to the people. Yahweh concludes the poem by speaking to the people in A'. The use of the second person "you" in "How can I pardon you?" makes the final words very direct. We see again a type of rhetoric that begins at a distance but comes in close at the end.

The people presumably know the Yahweh-Abraham dialogue (Gen 18:22-33), and knowing also the outcome they may perhaps wonder if history will not be repeated. Yet the dialogue unfolds in its own unique way. The answer and added subtleties of interpretation come gradually. The repetition at the center marks the turning point even if it does not contain the actual judgment. The poor have been examined and now also the great, which means that *everyone* has been seen. The indictment and judgment follow swiftly in B'. The key word נכה (smite) in B' creates an added subtlety. Yahweh has *smitten* the people previously (B) but now Jeremiah uses metaphors (lion, wolf and leopard) to speak of the enemy poised for attack on Jerusalem. The enemy thus remains unnamed, but if we associate B' with B as Jeremiah intends, it then becomes clear that *Yahweh is the one coming again to smite*; he is the enemy even more than the bands of marauders or the Babylonian army.[38] Jeremiah thus understands full well the theology of the Sodom and Gomorrah incident (Gen 19:24).[39]

The key words in the final stanza force an association with stanza 1 making the judgment certain. Yet the final word from Yahweh is a question, "How then can I pardon you?" to which the people must supply an answer. If they concede that a righteous man has not been found they can only answer "No" to this question. But the audience is still left with a choice--even though it is not really much of a choice--and this is what distinguishes the Jeremianic speeches from those which are dogmatically judgmental. Dialogue is open to the very end--and even after the end.

This poem has a center very much like 2:5-9. In both the normal kind of alternating parallelism acts as a hinge upon which the whole poem can swing. This would seem to support Lund who made a definite point about the centers of chiastic structures being pivot points.[40]

6:1-7

This poem and the one following (6:8-12) have the same number of lines and both are 4:4:4. They also have same words and sounds in identical collocations, besides containing a chiasmus of speaker. We are justified then in calling them companion poems. Not only were they written alike, but it appears that because of their similarities they were also grouped together in the collection process. After we have analyzed each poem separately we will discuss the two together.

The beginning of this poem is marked correctly by the chapter division, but most commentators break after v. 8 because of the introductory formula כה אמר יהוה צבאות beginning v. 9. This suggests that 9ff is a new poem which it is not. After we have outlined 8-12 this will become clear. For now let us look at 1-7.

העזו בני בנימן מקרב ירושלם		1
ובתקוע תקעו שופר ועל־בית הכרם שאו משאת	A	
כי רעה נשקפה מצפון ושבר גדול		
הנוה והמענגה דמיתי בת־ציון		2
תקעו עליה אהלים סביב רעו איש את־ידו[41]		3
קדשו עליה מלחמה קומו ונעלה בצהרים	B	4
אוי לנו כי־פנה היום כי ינטו צללי־ערב		
קומו ונעלה בלילה ונשחיתה ארמנותיה		5

כרתו עצה ושפכו על-ירושלם סללה ⁴²
היא העיר הפקד כלה עשק בקרבה
A'
כהקיר בור מימיה כן הקרה רעתה
חמס ושד ישמע בה על-פני תמיד חלי ומכה

1		Flee for safety, O people of Benjamin
		from the midst of *Jerusalem*
		Blow the trumpet in Tekoa
	A	and on Beth-hak-kerem raise a signal
		For evil looms out of the north
		and great destruction
2		The comely and delicately bred I will destroy
		the daughter of Zion

3		⁴¹They shall pitch their tents around her
		they shall pasture, each in his place
4		'Sanctify war against her
	B	*up, and let us attack* at noon'
		'Woe to us, for the day declines
		for the shadows of evening lengthen'
5		'*Up, and let us attack* by night
		and destroy her palaces'

6		⁴²Cut down her trees and pour up
		against *Jerusalem* a siege mound
		This is the city to be punished
	A'	there is nothing but oppression *in her midst*
7		As a well keeps its water fresh
		so she keeps fresh her wickedness
		Violence and destruction are heard within her
		before me continually, sickness and wounds

Antiphony of speaker in vv. 4-5 has been noticed by
Robert Gordis who cited this as an example of how the speaker
can change without there being any obvious notations in the
text.⁴³ Lines 2 and 4 of B are the words of the enemy while
line 3 articulates the cry of the frightened people inside Jerusalem. Yahweh is otherwise the narrator throughout ("I will
destroy" in v. 2; "before me continually" in v. 7). Jeremiah
does not interject himself at all into the poem unless we take
him to be the voice of the people in the center ("Woe to us...").

Jeremiah's audience here appears to be the country folk
from Benjamin who are living in Jerusalem. These are some of
Jeremiah's own people (cf. 1:1) and Yahweh tells them to flee
because the wealthy elite (הנוה והמענגה cf. Deut 28:54-56) are
about to be destroyed. There is no argument here, no subtlety,
no wait until the end to see who is really being addressed. The
poem from beginning to end is very straightforward. The key
words in A' merely break up the construct chain of A for varia-
tion.⁴⁴ We are thus looking at a different use of chiasmus. It
functions not for argument but mainly for the sake of reinforce-
ment.

6:8-12

      In this poem we must argue for beginning and end. Verse
8 is not normally included because of the introductory formula
כה אמר יהוה צבאות placed before v. 9. And because v. 12 is similar in content to 8:10a, and also because both introduce a stereotyped unit immediately following (6:13-15 = 8:10b-12), commentators take these verses as variants of a common original. Rudolph, for example, proposes that we delete the last line in v.
12 since it is not present in 8:10. In BH[3] his reason was that
"propheta loquitur," but this is dropped in the new BHS. Our
structure however will argue for the inclusion of both vv. 8 and
12.

הוסרי ירושלם פן־תקע נפשי ממך	8
פן־אשימך שממה ארץ לוא נושבה	A
45עולל יעוללו כגפן שארית ישראל	9
השב ידך כבוצר על־סלסלות	
על־מי אדברה ואעידה וישמעו	10
הנה ערלה אזנם ולא יוכלו להקשיב	B
הנה דבר־יהוה היה להם לחרפה לא יחפצו־בו	
ואת חמת יהוה מלאתי נלאיתי הכיל	11
שפך על־עולל בחוץ ועל סוד בחורים יחדו	
כי־גם־איש עם־אשה ילכדו זקן עם־מלא ימים	A'
ונסבו בתיהם לאחרים שדות ונשים יחדו	12
כי־אטה את־ידי על־ישבי הארץ נאם־יהוה	

8   Be warned O Jerusalem
        lest I be alienated from you
    Lest I make you a desolation
        an *uninhabited land* 45
9 A Glean thoroughly as a vine
    the remnant of Israel
    Like a grape-gatherer pass *your hand* again
        over its branches

10   To whom shall I speak and give warning
        that they may hear?
    Behold, their ears are uncircumcised
        they cannot listen
  B *Behold*, the word of Yahweh is to them
        an object of scorn, they take no pleasure in it
11   Therefore I am full of the wrath of Yahweh
        I am weary of holding it in

    Pour it out upon the children in the street
        and upon the gatherings of young men also
    Both husband and wife shall be taken
        the old folk and the very aged
12 A' Their houses shall be turned over to others
    their fields and wives together
    For I will stretch out *my hand*
        against the *inhabitants of the land*--oracle of Yahweh

So arranged this poem is 4:4:4 with key word and speaker chiasmi coinciding. The phrase ארץ לוא נושבה in A balances ישבי הארץ in A'. The other key word is יד (hand). In A it is the hand of the enemy and in A' the hand of Yahweh. In the center הנה repeats as anaphora making this the pivot point of the poem.

Bright recognizes that a dialogue is going on, and so it turns out that the speakers break precisely where the stanzas break. Yahweh speaks in A and A', Jeremiah in B. Yahweh shifts his audience however in A: he addresses the people in v. 8 and the enemy (not Jeremiah) in v. 9. The נאם־יהוה formula belongs right where it is at the end of v. 12, this time confirming the poem's end.

We must now look at 1-7 and 8-12 together. Both are 12 lines and 4:4:4. Both have chiastic structures based on key words and both have a chiasmus of speaker. In each case Yahweh begins and ends the dialogue with Jeremiah speaking in the center. Certain key words--in some cases those making the chiasmus, in other cases different words entirely--appear in identical collocations. "Jerusalem" is mentioned in the first line of each poem (in 1-7 it helped form the chiasmus). Next we note that the third stanza of each poem begins with the verb שפך (pour out/up). Equally impressive are plays on the same sounds.[46] First the verbs תקע and יקע. In 1-7 the second line of the poem begins וּבִתְקוֹעַ תִּקְעוּ creating a word-play on תקע acknowledged by all. This same verb begins the next stanza (v.3) only the meaning there is different making then another word-play. In 8-12 the first stanza opens with פֶּן־תֵּקַע נַפְשִׁי מִמֵּךְ. Here we have the similar sounding verb יקע. Now if we can presuppose some sophistication on the part of Jeremiah's audience, it is possible that the audience would hear not only word-plays within a specific poem, but would also recognize when similar sounds are repeated from poem to poem. There are more parallels. Throughout both poems the על and עול sounds reverberate. The preposition על occurs no fewer than five times in each. A look at the final stanza of each poem will show also that it is this preposition which gives the stanza its own internal balance. Finally we have וְנָעֲלָה repeated twice in 6:4,5, and עוֹלֵל עוֹלֵל (or עוֹלֵל יְעוֹלְלוּ if one can make sense out of the *Kethib*) in 6:9 balancing עַל־עוֹלָל in 6:11b. It becomes quite obvious then that these poems had a much greater impact on the ancient ear than they have on the modern eye.

What do these similarities tell us? Were the poems

delivered together, i.e., did they have a common *Sitz im Leben*?
Possibly, but not necessarily so. Because of their juxtaposition
in the text it seems safe to conclude that they were *collected*
together. Their similarities in structure would make them a
pair for mnemonic reasons. But we must not pass over lightly
the fact that two poems *were written alike*. We have been saying
all along that Jeremiah wrote poems with fixed structures, e.g.,
4:4:4, 4:2:4; etc., but we now realize in addition that vocabulary and even certain sounds can remain constant from poem to
poem.

8:13-17

The limits of this poem are easily established. The
preceding unit (8:10-12) is found elsewhere in 6:13-15 which
argues for its independence. We also have both opening and
closing formulas.[47] Bright takes these verses as a unit but
says they are composite. Volz and Condamin reflect the same
opinion relocating all or parts of vv. 14-15. We see no reason
for relocating v. 14, but v. 15 could be independent since it
is found again in 14:19 where it functions as the transitional
verse of a liturgical unit. It fits here, as our analysis will
show, so we had best reserve judgment as to whether it is original to the poem or editorially inserted. The poem is 2:3:1:3:2
and nicely balanced by key words and change of speaker. All
point to a controlling chiasmus. One single theme is reiterated:
destruction is coming. And like 6:1-7 we hear it discussed from
both sides: Yahweh (the enemy) on one side, and the people of
Judah on the other.

13	A	אסף אסיפם נאם-יהוה אין ענבים בגפן ואין תאנים בתאנה והעלה נבל ואתן להם יעברום48
14	B	על-מה אנחנו ישבים האספו ונבוא אל-ערי המבצר ונדמה-שם כי יהוה אלהינו הדמנו וישקנו מי-ראש כי חטאנו ליהוה49
15	C	קוה לשלום ואין טוב לעת מרפה והנה בעתה
16	B'	מדן נשמע נחרת סוסיו מקול מצהלות אביריו רעשה כל-הארץ ויבואו ויאכלו ארץ ומלואה עיר וישבי בה
17	A'	כי הנני משלח בכם נחשים צפענים אשר אין-להם לחש ונשכו אתכם נאם-יהוה

13
A
Gathering I will end them
  oracle of Yahweh
    there is *nothing* on the grape vine (16)
And *nothing* on the fig tree
    even the leaves are withered
      and what I gave them has passed away from them[48] (23)

14
B
Why do we sit still?
  gather together (12)
And let us *enter* the fortified *cities*
  and be silent there (14)
For Yahweh our God has silenced us
  given us poisoned water to drink
    because we have sinned against Yahweh[49] (23)

15
C
We looked for peace, but *nothing* good came
  for a time of healing, but behold, terror (18)

16
B'
From Dan is heard
  the snorting of their horses (8)
At the sound of their neighing stallions
  the whole land quakes (15)
They enter to devour the land and all that fills it
  the *city* and those who dwell in it (19)

17
A'
For behold I am sending among you
  poisonous serpents (14)
Nothing you do can charm them
  and they shall bite you
    oracle of Yahweh (16)

Stanzas 1 and 2 of this poem have long final lines which
may indicate expansion. The final colon of stanza 1 is lacking
in the Greek, and the final colon in stanza 2 sounds prosaic
(cf. 3:25). Yet a syllable count shows that all the stanzas
have cresendo which means that at minimum the long final lines
fit the poem in its final form.

Key words and antiphony of speaker delimit the stanzas.
Yahweh is the speaker in A and A'. BB' and C are the people, or
more probably Jeremiah for the people. The particle of negation
אין is a key word in AA' and C, and I have exercised more than
the usual amount of freedom in translation in order to keep this
term constant. If the center stanza is original to the poem,
then Lund would be supported in his contention that key words of
chiastic structures frequently appear at the extremes *and at the
center*.[50] We also noted earlier[51] that אין together with אסף
formed an inclusio for the complex 8:13-9:21. In BB' we have
the verb בוא (to go, enter) and the noun עיר (city). And as we
have seen happen before, one stanza breaks up the terms of the
other. This is becoming a common feature now in the Jeremianic
poems.

This poem is really one of despair. Jeremiah is advising the people to return to the city, but with the knowledge that the security it ordinarily affords will not be enough to save them. His remark in v. 14 ונדמה־שם (let us be silent there) is thus paraphrastic (*RSV* translates "perish"). In case B does not make it clear that Jeremiah has given up hope, B' does. The repetition of עיר forces the conclusion that the *cities*--to which they are fleeing--will not be spared. The metaphors of A and A' do not coalesce, but the repetition of אין brings the argument together: since Yahweh found *nothing* when he went to harvest his crop, there is now *nothing* the people can do to escape the enemy come to destroy. Note too the shift from "them" in A to "you" in A' making Yahweh's word more direct.

8:18-21

The beginning of this poem is not seriously in doubt. It follows the poem just discussed and most commentators take v. 18 as the beginning. Only the first word is emended by some and placed with the final line of the previous poem (so Bright following the *LXX*). This however is unnecessary. Agreement does not exist on where the poem ends. Bright following the German commentators extends through v. 23 [Eng. 9:1].[52] The *RSV* breaks after v. 21 which we take to be correct. The poem is 5 lines, which is another fixed type used more than once by Jeremiah.

מבליגיתי עלי יגון עלי לבי דוי	A	18
הנה־קול[53]היהוה אין בציון אם־מלכה אין בה	B	19
מדוע הכעסוני בפסליהם בהבלי נכר	C	
עבר קציר כלה קיץ ואנחנו לוא נושענו	B'	20
על־שבר בת־עמי השברתי קדרתי שמה החזקתני	A'	21

18
  A
    My joy is gone
      grief is upon me
        my heart is sick   (14)

19
  B
    Hark a cry[53]
      'Is Yahweh not in Zion?
        Is her King not in her?'   (15)

  C
    Why then have they provoked me to anger with their images
      and with their foreign idols?   (16)

```
20          The harvest is past
      B'        the summer is ended
                and we are not saved  (18)
```

```
21        For the wound of the daughter of my people I am wounded
      A'      I mourn
                dismay has taken hold of me  (20/21)
```

The controlling structure here is a chiasmus of speaker: Jeremiah speaks in A; the people in B; Yahweh in C;[54] the people again in B'; and Jeremiah finally in A'.

Two text problems merit attention. First the phrase מבליגיתי עלי beginning the poem. Unsuccessful attempts to translate this go back at least to the *LXX*. The noun מבליגיתי is a *hapax legomenon* but comes from an attested verb בלג, which means "to smile" or "to look cheerful."[55] One can thus translate מבליגיתי "my cheerfulness," or as I have rendered it, "my joy." The problematic term is actually the following עלי. Rudolph says we should take this to be the verb עלה but emend to either עָלָה or יַעֲלֶה. A better suggestion comes from Professor Freedman who says that עלי could be the archaic form of the infinitive absolute (normally עָלֹה). This would obviate the need to emend and would also preserve what appears to be a word-play between this term and another עלי two words hence. That עלי is the preposition with its suffix, עָלַי, "upon me." The line is thus a tri-colon instead of a bi-colon. For that matter all the lines except the one in the center are tri-cola. Jeremiah is here playing with *space* in the first two cola as he did in 8:4 and 14:2. He says, "My joy has gone *up*,[56] grief is upon me," i.e., come *down* upon me.

The second problem of text comes in line 2. The phrase מארץ מרחקים (from a land far off) is frequently taken as a gloss because it makes what otherwise appears to be a poem uttered in Judah sound exilic.[57] When the people say "Is Yahweh not in Zion? Is her King not in her?" they are expressing the commonly held idea that Zion was Yahweh's eternal dwelling place. Ever since the deliverance of Jerusalem during the reign of Hezekiah it had become dogma that Yahweh's temple was inviolable.[58] Jeremiah of course refutes this dogma in his Temple Sermon (Jer 7, 26), and it is refuted here by Yahweh's interruption in C. I would propose only one change, and that is that we take all of שועת בת-עמי מארץ מרחקים as the gloss. The proper place to break is between קול and שועת since the two terms are redundant together. This has the added advantage of further reducing the

length of the line so a cresendo can be seen in the poem as a
whole. The syllable count will show this. To find cresendo
here in a 5-line poem is significant since Holladay observed
gradation in *another 5-line poem*, 4:23-26, only it was not
cresendo but diminution.[59]

This poem is a well-structured chiasmus without the help
of key words.[60] The center is clearly the climax. There Yahweh
interrupts to answer the people's questions with one of his own.
The break-up of the ...מדוע... אם... ה formula, which Holladay
has called a "signature" of Jeremiah,[61] makes this clear. The
people ask the first two rhetorical questions and Yahweh finishes
with the third. Judgment is not given, but if the audience answers Yahweh's question they will be forced into making judgment
themselves. Jeremiah meanwhile stands outside the argument and
grieves. We hear from him at the beginning and again at the end.
But in remaining outside he is not an onlooker, as A' makes perfectly clear: "For the wound of the daughter of my people I am
wounded."

9:2-5 [Eng. 9:3-6]

Since the text here is troubled with various problems,
the commentaries give us no help in delimiting this poem even
though both vv. 2 and 5 have concluding formulas.[62] In their
own way these adequately mark the limits of the poem. This has
not been sufficiently recognized but will become clear after
our analysis is completed. There is, however, some uncertainty
about stanza formation. If we take the text as it stands the
poem would divide 3:3:3. Yet we propose an original 3:2:2:3
because it seems as if a line has fallen out. Verse 3 was
found earlier to be chiastic,[63] so we are inclined to take it
as an independent stanza. This decision is not however crucial
since in either case we have a chiastic structure; in one case
it is ABA', in the other ABB'A'. The poem has no obvious chiasmus of speaker; balanced vocabulary alone shows the poem's
structure in outline.

וידרכו את־לשונם קשתם שקר		2
ולא לאמונה גברו בארץ	A	
כי מרעה אל־רעה יצאו ואתי לא־ידעו נאם־יהוה		
איש מרעהו השמרו ועל־כל־אח אל־תבטחו	B	3
כי כל־אח עקוב יעקב וכל־רע רכיל יהלך		

ואיש ברעהו יהתלו ואמת לא ידברו   B'   4
[............. ....]

למדו לשונם דבר־שקר
העוה נלאו שבתך בתוך   A'   5
מרמה במרמה מאנו דעת־אותי נאם־יהוה

2   They bend *their tongue*
            their bow is a *lie*[64]
    A And not for truth
            are they mighty in the land
         For *from evil to evil* they go
           me/they do not know--oracle of Yahweh

3   *Each man* beware of his *neighbor*
    B   and put no trust in any brother
         For every brother is a 'Jacob'
           and every neighbor goes about as a slanderer

4   *Each man* deceives his *neighbor*
    B'   and no one speaks the truth
        [........................
        ....]

         They have taught their *tongues*
            to speak *lies*
         Iniquity they commit
5   A'   (..................?)[65]
         More evil on more evil
           refusing to know/me--oracle of Yahweh

      Since the Hebrew text is difficult most modern ver-
sions seek help from the Greek. Yet for a number of reasons
we believe the Hebrew text to be more original even if it is
more corrupt. Let us begin at the beginning. The translation
of line 1 in A is Holladay's. He recognized that "bow" and
"tongue" were meant to be synonyms and that the line is to be
read as a partial chiasmus. Thus we do not need to follow the
Greek which presupposes כקשת (like a bow). Jeremiah has broken
up two very straightforward expressions: "they bend their bow"
and "their tongue is a lie." The result is that *bow* becomes
a metaphor for *tongue*. A' contains something of an echo:
"They have taught their tongues to speak lies." This movement
from the figurative to the literal is what we now expect from
Jeremiah. So the translators must not be unduly faulted for
their imprecise renderings. There were probably many in Jeremiah's original audience who also missed line 1. Actually the
LXX translator did realize that the bent tongue was like a bent
bow, and so he preserved the essential meaning. Unfortunately
we cannot say more about the connection between A and A'

because the text in A' is also in poor condition. There is a
reference to "your house" which is unclear. Is this Yahweh's
house? Perhaps the verse contained something too offensive for
later scribes to let stand. In 23:11 wickedness in Yahweh's
house is mentioned. In any event the poem is primarily concerned with the mistrust between persons who are normally very
close to each other: neighbor and brother. Some malicious talk
was evidently circulating among the clergy which Jeremiah interpreted as evidence of a real lack of the knowledge of Yahweh on
their part.

The poem is well-supplied with balancing terms, and we
should note too how the final colon in A' reverses the key words
from A. We said earlier that there was no obvious alternation
of speaker. The נאם-יהוה formulas ending A and A' indicate
that Yahweh speaks at beginning and end (against Rudolph and
Bright), and he is probably the speaker throughout. But if
Jeremiah be the speaker in BB', then we also have a chiasmus
of speaker. The content gives no clue either way, so we offer
this only as a suggestion.

17:13-16a

Here is another 5-line poem with chiasmus of speaker
only. It is similar to 8:18-21 just discussed. The commentaries give us no help in delimiting the poem. Bright says
the whole chapter could have come from Jeremiah's miscellaneous
file or else from some cupboard in the editor's home where odds
and ends were stored.[66] Verses 12-13 are taken to be one fragment and 14-18 is thought to be one of Jeremiah's *bona fide*
confessions. We think, however, that the basic confession is
13-16a which has then been expanded at a later time to include
16b-18. Verse 12 then becomes another fragment. Let us now
look at the confession in 13-16a.

מקוה ישראל יהוה כל-עזביך יבשו	A	13
יסורי בארץ יכתבו כי עזבו מקור מים-חיים[67]	B	
רפאני יהוה וארפא הושיעני ואושעה כי תהלתי אתה	C	14
הנה-המה אמרים אלי איה דבר-יהוה יבוא נא	B'	15
ואני לא-אצתי מרעה אחריך ויום אנוש לא התאויתי	A'	16

13   O Yahweh, the hope of Israel
  A   all who forsake you shall be put to shame

B Those who turn away from me shall be written in the
earth
for they have forsaken the fountain of living water[67]

14
C Heal me O Yahweh and I shall be healed
save me and I shall be saved
for you are my praise

15
B' Behold they say to me
'Where is the word of Yahweh, let it come'

16
A' I have not pressed you to send evil
and the day of disaster I have not desired

Commentators have long been troubled by the first person suffix on יסורי in line 2.[68] But if we take Yahweh to be the speaker of this line the problem disappears. Jeremiah narrates the whole speaking in A, C and A'. Then in B he speaks for Yahweh and in B' his opponents are quoted. This also enables us to take את־יהוה at the end of line 2 as a gloss.[69] It has in fact created the confusion in the first place by making Yahweh object as well as subject. Perhaps the gloss originally sought to explain the metaphor מקור מים־חיים (fountain of living water).

The poem procedes much in the way we would expect. Jeremiah tells Yahweh in A that the infidels will be shamed. We don't yet know who the infidels are; we only know that their future is none too bright. In B Yahweh echoes Jeremiah saying the same thing again only in different words. In C Jeremiah asks to be delivered. This is the climax and is Jeremiah's preferred subject. What follows now is like what followed after the climax of 8:18-21, viz., embellishment of what has already been said. The taunt of the opponents is quoted in B' and if we knew who said these words we would know the identity of the infidels. A' is merely supportive argument used by Jeremiah in his defense before Yahweh. The climax has passed and Yahweh's promise of 1:19 was no doubt foremost in his mind at the time.

23:18,21-22

The structure of this poem is marred by expansion and textual problems, yet we can see its original shape quite nicely after removing vv. 19-20. These verses occur elsewhere as a unit (30:23-24) and we take them here to be a later insertion.[70] There is no reason to rearrange the text as Volz does.

The poem is 2:2:2 with good balance throughout.

כי מי עמד בסוד יהוה וירא את־דברו[71]   A   18
מי־הקשיב דברי וישמע

לא־שלחתי את־הנבאים והם רצו   B   21
לא־דברתי אליהם והם נבאו

ואם־עמדו בסודי וישמעו דברי את־עמי   A'   22
וישבום מדרכם הרע ומרע מעלליהם

18   For who has *stood in the council* of Yahweh
         and seen *his word*?[71]
  A Who has hearkened to *his word*[72]
         and *listened*?

21   *I did not send the prophets*
         yet they ran
  B *I did not speak to them*
         yet they prophesied

22   Now if they had *stood in my council*
         and *listened* to my *word* to my people
  A' Then they would have turned them from their evil way
         and from the evil of their doings

There is no problem with the center. The text is fine and the parallelism makes this compare nicely with other centers we have seen, e.g., 2:7; 5:4-5; 6:3-5; 6:10-11. A and A' are also meant to balance each other. In the poem's original form Yahweh was probably the speaker throughout which means that the Kethib דברי in v. 18 is original.

Yahweh begins by asking whether any have stood in his council. In B he says that prophets were quick enough to run but they were not sent. Then in the return (A'), assuming that his original question remains unanswered, Yahweh goes on to tell what would have happened had the prophets been present in council. The wicked people would then have been turned around. Who might the audience have been? If Jeremiah was speaking directly to the prophets his attack is admittedly brutal. But since the prophets are referred to in the third person it is likely that Jeremiah is here addressing the ordinary people. If so, there is subtle judgment for *them* at the end making all but the last line foil and the last line cap. Ordinary people may not have minded an attack on the false prophets, but they would hardly be receptive to the suggestion that they constitute an unredeemed populace, whether because of the negligence of the prophets or for some other reason.

51:20-23

Here is a catalogue poem which gives Jeremiah the perfect opportunity to use a chiastic structure. And use it he
did. The poem is easily delimited from its context. The Massoretes mark the end of v. 19 as a closed section making the
upper limit secure. They also close a section at the end of
v. 24. Verse 24 is generally considered to be prose expansion
so we are left with 20-23. Even without this help we could most
likely conclude from content alone that 20-23 is independent.
Probably no other poem which we have looked at, with the possible exception of 2:33-37, is so carefully done.

מפץ־אתה לי כלי מלחמה		20
ונפצתי בך גוים והשחתי בך ממלכות		
ונפצתי בך סוס ורכבו	A	21
ונפצתי בך רכב ורכבו		
ונפצתי בך איש ואשה		22
ונפצתי בך זקן ונער	B	
ונפצתי בך בחור ובתולה		
ונפצתי בך רעה ועדרו		23
ונפצתי בך אכר וצמדו	A'	
ונפצתי בך פחות וסגנים		

20   You are my hammer and weapon of war:

     I shatter with you *nations*, and I destroy with you
                                                kingdoms
21 A I shatter with you *horse* and *its rider*
       I shatter with you *chariot* and *charioteer*

22   I shatter with you *man* and *woman*
     B I shatter with you *old* and *young*
        I shatter with you *young man* and *maiden*

23   I shatter with you *shepherd* and *his flock*
  A' I shatter with you *farmer* and *his team*
      I shatter with you *governors* and *commanders*

Repetition and variation here work together for the
poet. The repeated ונפצתי at the beginning of each successive
line creates the sound of the hammer, which, according to the
introduction (v. 20), Jeremiah is himself supposed to be. It
is then not only with words but also by his rhetoric that Jeremiah *shatters* the people. A variation in the pattern occurs
at the beginning where line 1 is expanded to include בך והשחתי.
It is hard to know whether this is original or due to expansion.

The verb שחת (to destroy) links this poem into a chain with
three others.[73] The verb could thus have been added for such a
purpose or else it could be original, in which case the chain
was created because it was already there. We will leave והשחתי
בך in because while Hebrew poetry is fond of repetition it is
also fond of variation,[74] and examples of the latter are not
wanting elsewhere in the poetry of Jeremiah.[75]

The real variation of the poem, however, comes in the
distribution of its key words. We begin at the center. The
Greek omits the center line but that can be attributed to haplography.[76] Its key words זקן (old) and נער (young) make it a
pivot point for B, distinguishing those persons in the previous
line from those in the line following. The איש is the old man
and the בחור is the young; the אשה is the old woman and the
בתולה the young.[77] The Greek also transposes lines 1 and 3,
but with such a structure there is no net loss. The same kind
of transposition occurs in the liturgies found in Deut 6:6-9
and 11:18-20[78] and it is attested elsewhere in Scripture.[79]
Perhaps the centers of chiastic structures enjoyed a measure of
fluidity before the written tradition became fixed.

The key terms of A and A' are not necessarily fixed
pairs, but we notice some deliberate inversions being made. In
A the human figures, i.e., the rider of the horse, and the rider of the chariot, come *second*. In A' they come *first* (shepherd and farmer). The reverse is of course true for the non-
human figures. The opening and closing lines of the poem break
up a standard bi-colon and make an inclusio: the *governors* and
commanders (A') are the leaders of the *nations* and *kingdoms*
(A). Here there is inversion also. Jeremiah chooses terms
which make their plurals in ים and וֹת, and switches them
around. All in all a perfectly balanced poem.

The chiasmus here seems to be mainly for the sake of
variation. And it also shows artistry. But there is no argument going on. The repetitions and variations all contribute
to an impression of total destruction which Jeremiah means to
convey. No person will be spared regardless of age, sex or
social status. Even the animals will be destroyed.[80]

51:34-45

No commentator has yet seen this as an independent
poem. Bright following Volz takes the verses as smaller
units,[81] and Condamin, who usually notices key words, misses

the structure completely. The poem is a long 20 lines which
divide up 4:4:4:4:4. Key words in each stanza form the chiasmus
while the center has its own peculiar balance. Of special interest is the נאם־יהוה formula in the center. We are used to
seeing messenger formulas at the beginning or end--and this particular formula at the end--but here for the first time it occurs
in the center. Since there is no reason for omitting it we can
take this to be its original position. Yahweh is speaker in all
stanzas but the first so as the poem now stands there is no chiasmus of speaker. Yet the very *direct* words at the end of A and
A' give the whole an antiphonal effect. In A the people articulate the curse to be hurled at Babylon and in A' an urgent call
is sent throughout Babylon telling Yahweh's people to flee.

אכלנו[82]הממנו נבוכדראצר מלך בבל הציגנו כלי ריק		34
בלענו כתנין מלא כרשו מעדני הדיחנו	A	
חמסי ושארי על־בבל תאמר ישבת ציון		35
ודמי אל־ישבי כשדים תאמר ירושלם		
הנני־רב את־ריבך[83] ונקמתי את־נקמתך		36
והחרבתי את־ימה והבשתי את־מקורה	B	
והיתה בבל לגלים מעון־תנים		37
שמה ושרקה מאין יושב		
יחדו ככפרים ישאגו נערו כגורי אריות		38
בחמם אשית את־משתיהם והשכרתים למען יעלזו	C	39
וישנו שנת־עולם ולא יקיצו נאם־יהוה		
אורידם ככרים לטבוח כאילים עם־עתודים		40
איך נלכדה ששך[84] ותתפש תהלת כל־הארץ		41
איך היתה לשמה בבל בגוים	B'	
עלה על־בבל הים בהמון גליו נכסתה		42
היו עריה לשמה ארץ ציה וערבה[85]		43
ופקדתי על־בל בבבל והצאתי את־בלעו מפיו		44
ולא־ינהרו אליו עוד גוים	A'	
גם־חומת בבל נפלה *צאו מתוכה עמי		45*
ומלטו איש את־נפשו מחרון אף־יהוה		

34	He has eaten me,[82] he has crushed me
	Nebuchadrezzar, king of Babylon
	he has made me an empty vessel
	He has swallowed me like a monster
A	he filled his belly
	from my luxuries he rinsed me out
35	'My broken flesh be upon Babylon'
	let the inhabitant of Zion say
	'And my blood on Chaldea's inhabitants'
	let Jerusalem say

36   [83]Behold, I will plead your cause
                and take vengeance for you
             I will drain her *sea*
         B   I will dry up her fountain
37   Babylon will become a *heap*
                a lair for jackals
         A   *horror* and a hissing
                without inhabitant

38   Together *like* lions they shall roar
                 they shall growl *like* lions' whelps
39   While they fret I'll prepare them a feast
         C   I'll make them drunk till they talk loudly
               They'll sleep a perpetual sleep
                 they will not waken--oracle of Yahweh
40   I will bring them down *like* lambs to the slaughter
                 like rams and he goats

41   How Babylon[84] is taken
                the praise of the whole earth is seized
             How she has become a *horror*
         B'   Babylon among the nations
42   The *sea* has come up upon Babylon
                with its noisy *heaps*, she is covered
43   Her cities have become a *horror*
                a land of drought and desert[85]

44   So I will punish *Bel* in *Babylon*
                and take out what *he swallowed* in his mouth
             They shall not flow to him
         A'   the nations any longer
             Even the wall of Babylon has fallen
45   'Go out from her midst, my people
             Let everyone save his life
                from the fierce anger of Yahweh'

The Greek omits "Bel" at the beginning of v. 44 and in
addition the remainder of this verse and the verse following.
"Bel" belongs in the text but Rudolph is probably correct in
thinking that "Nebuchadrezzar" in v. 34 is added. In the poem's
original form the subject of v. 34 was not revealed until v.
44. *Bel was the king in Babylon*. The poem is really telling
us about the future cosmic battle about to take place between
Yahweh and Bel, otherwise known as the Babylonian god Marduk
(cf. Isa 51:9-11).

The chiasmus is well-marked by key words. In A and A'
the balancing verb is בלע (to swallow). The king of Babylon,
who like a sea monster has swallowed Israel (A), will soon be
forced to disgorge what he has swallowed (A'). B and B' tell
of the future "horror" in store for Babylon. Babylon's own
"sea" will be drained (B) but another "sea" will come up and
inundate her (B'). The noun גל (heap) is also used in BB' with

different meanings. In B Jeremiah speaks of a heap of dry rubble while in B' the heap is a heap of water, i.e., waves. The center of the structure has its own internal contrast signaled by the 4-fold use of the preposition כ (like). The enemy will cry out like the fiercest of animals but Yahweh will bring her down as if she were the most docile. The chiastic structure then, carries well Jeremiah's message, i.e., that the future promises to be a complete *turn-around* of the past.

We have now completed our look at the chiastic speeches in Jeremiah. We have seen that like the inclusio, the chiasmus allows Jeremiah to withhold key information until the end and also on occasion to set up a foil for his preferred subject. But the chiasmus does more. Because movement is directed both towards and away from the center, the center becomes a kind of hinge on which the whole poem swings. Not infrequently it is the place of *climax*. But the chiasmus can be used in non-argumentative poems for the simple purpose of providing variation, e.g., 51:20-23, and together with other patterns of repetition, it helps to achieve the Hebrew desire for totality.

The key word chiasmi in Jeremianic poems are most like those found in Lam 1-2, while certain speaker chiasmi appear to have their affinity with the chiasmus in Deut 1:20-31. Thus we find that our best comparative material is to be dated about the same time as Jeremiah, which must mean that such structures were well-known in the 7th and 6th cc. B.C. and appreciated at that time by the people who heard them.

We concluded earlier that Jeremiah was a prophet of dialogue, and the chiastic structures have only confirmed this conclusion all the more. The many changes of speaker show that he was as much a dramatist as he was a speaker. Yahweh, Jeremiah and the people are continually talking to each other. On occasion the enemy is even heard from. Jeremiah is thus a true mediator between Yahweh and the people because he converses with Yahweh. Yahweh for Jeremiah is someone approachable and in conversations with him Jeremiah is alarmingly frank. He is frequently compared along with Job to the Greek Prometheus.[86] With the people he is no different. He is frank but he is also open. Jeremiah is not a prophet who simply calls out the divine word. He is a person willing to discuss--indeed to argue-- with the people. But his aim is not to overpower. There is always the opportunity for rebuttal, and if the audience keeps

silent it is because they have nothing to say. This strategy
of course paid off, because by allowing the people to *partici-*
pate in the dialogue, the people were thereby helped to live
finally with the difficult answers that inevitably had to be
given.

Chiasmus in the Larger Book of Jeremiah

In this section we will see how chiastic structures control material larger than the Jeremianic speech. The examples
will be varied. Some are collections of more than one poem.
Others are prose compilations. We will look at Jeremiah's Letters to the Exiles (ch. 29) and finally at two clusters of biographical prose in chs. 24ff.

We begin with the chapter that opens the book, the chapter that records Jeremiah's call.

1: Jeremiah's Call

This chapter is usually taken as a compilation of separate fragments, yet a unity of the whole is recognized. The
final verses (17-19) pick up the second person "you" from vv.
4-10, making it appear that they are an extension of the call.[87]
These are all personal words of Yahweh to Jeremiah. In the center are two visions. The first is the vision of the almond rod
(11-12). Everyone recognizes the play on שָׁקֵד and שֹׁקֵד, but to
my knowledge no one is quite sure what the vision really means
or how it relates to the rest of the chapter. The explanation
of Bright is common: "This [vision] suggests that Jeremiah had
already been active for some time, and had begun to be troubled
about the fulfillment of the word (of judgment) that he was pro-
claiming."[88] The second vision begins at v. 13 and is custom-
arily extended to v. 16. This vision and its interpretation
speak of the judgment to come upon Judah by the Foe from the
North.

So arranged a basic continuity is recognized within the
chapter. I would agree that the vision of the boiling pot (13-
14) leads into the explanation of judgment which follows, and
also that the end of the chapter has continuity with the beginning. But the structure is much more than this.

Let us begin by proposing a slightly different outline
which will do more justice to the content and can be more easily defended. There are four basic parts to the chapter: 1)
Jeremiah's call (4-10); 2) the vision of the almond rod (11-12);

3) the vision of the boiling pot (13-14); and 4) a further promise to Jeremiah (15-19). No one disputes the call of 4-10.
Neither is there any difficulty isolating the vision of the almond rod (11-12). But from this point on a reconstruction is
necessary. The second vision we limit to 13-14. Although not
containing a word-play quite like the almond rod vision, it is
nevertheless tied together by key words: the boiling pot tipped
"away from the north" (מפני צפונה)[89] refers metaphorically to
the enemy who will come "from the north" (מצפון). It is true
that this vision leads into what follows, but we must first show
how 15-19 holds together before discussing the connection.
Scholars are not correct in breaking after v. 16. *All of 15-19*
contains the promise to Jeremiah. These verses set up an important contrast between Jeremiah and the men of Judah which cannot
be put aside. A close look at the text will make this clear.

In the promise Yahweh tells Jeremiah that the enemy will
come

(ו)על כל־חומתיה סביב
(ו)על כל־ערי יהודה

> against all its *walls* round about
> against all the *cities* of Judah (v. 15)

Yet Yahweh will make Jeremiah a "fortified *city*" (לעיר מבצר)
"and bronze *walls* (ולחמות נחשת) to protect him from his enemies
(v. 18). The key words here point up the contrast very well and
one will note also that they are nicely inverted when repeated.
The coming of the Foe from the North will set off a chain reac-
tion. The people of Jerusalem will try to defend the city
against the enemy but in the end will fail. They in turn will
fight against Jeremiah who is announcing their defeat. But to
Jeremiah Yahweh promises what he does not promise to the others:
salvation. The section closes with Yahweh repeating the words
given earlier to Jeremiah at the time of his call (v. 19; cf.
v. 8).

Now that we have shown the unity of 15-19 we can return
to the vision of the boiling pot to see how it relates to the
promise. As we mentioned before, scholars have always recognized a link between the vision and vv. 15-16. Actually vv.
15-16 do little more than expand upon 14 giving us the judgment
in more detail. But there is also a word-play which connects
the two. In the vision the verb פתח (to open) is used so awk-
wardly that the English versions are unable to translate it
literally. The Hebrew reads, "Out of the north evil will *open*

upon all the inhabitants of the land" (v. 14). But we see why
this verb is used when we read on into the promise: thrones are
going to be placed by the enemy at the *opening* (פתח) of the
gates of Jerusalem (v. 15). Thus we agree that the second vision is firmly linked to the promise, but the promise we take to
be all of 15-19.

We now return to the first vision and the call. Our
thesis here is that this vision looks *back* to the call of 4-10
and is to be taken as part of that call. To my knowledge no
commentator has recognized this. The word-play within the vision has all but obscured the link that exists between the vision and the call. The link is a key word: דבר. In the vision
Yahweh is said to be watching over his דבר to perform it (v. 12).
What is this word? It is more than a general word of judgment
(so Bright). The answer lies in the verses above where the entire focus is upon the verb דבר (to speak) and the noun דבר
(word). Jeremiah complains like Moses before him that he is
unable to speak.[90] He says, הנה לא-ידעתי דבר, "Behold, I do not
know how to *speak*" (v. 6). But Yahweh answers, ואת כל-אשר אצוך
תדבר, "Whatever I command you, you shall *speak*" (v. 7b), and
says further in v. 9: הנה נתתי דברי בפיך, "Behold, I have put
my *words* in your mouth." Jeremiah will be able to speak because Yahweh will provide the דבר. The *word* then that Yahweh
is watching over becomes the *words* placed in Jeremiah's mouth.
The vision and the call are one event. This appears to be cor-
roborated even by the introductory formulas. Verses 4 and 11
begin ויהי דבר-יהוה אלי לאמר whereas v. 13 begins ויהי דבר-יהוה
אלי שנית לאמר, "And the word of Yahweh came to me *a second time*
saying..." There are thus only *two* events in chapter 1: a call
and a subsequent promise. Both were accompanied by visions,
but because visions contain messages that are terse and opaque
they need a more complete articulation. And in each case this
articulation is given, only we have all been misled because in
the call the normal order of the material is inverted. If it
were arranged the same way the promise is arranged, the almond
rod vision would come just prior to v. 4. Instead it comes
after v. 10.

Chapter 1 is then built into a chiasmus:

> A   Articulation of the Call (4-10)
>> B   Vision of the Call (11-12)
>> B' Vision of the Promise (13-14)
> A' Articulation of the Promise (15-19)

The structure in this case is done for a definite reason. We showed earlier how the opening verses of the call were used to make an inclusio with 20:18. The chiastic structure now makes that possible. If the almond rod vision were placed first the inclusio could not be made. So by inverting the order of the call material, Baruch or Jeremiah created two rhetorical structures, a chiasmus in chapter 1 and an inclusio for 1-20.

One final point. We realize now for the first time that Jeremiah's call came with a vision, which is how the calls of both Isaiah and Exekiel were received (Isa 6; Ezek 1-3).

8:22-9:10 [Eng. 9:11]

Two of the poems in this complex have already been examined, 9:2-5 and 9:9b-10. There are two more. One is a nicely balanced poem which we have not discussed (8:22-9:1).[91] The other is a fragment in 9:6-7 to which has been attached the stereotyped v. 8. Taken together these four poems with their supplements are built into a chiasmus based upon key words. The center poems are about lying *tongues* (לשון). As we noted earlier the tongue in 9:2 was compared to a bent bow; in 9:7 it is a "deadly arrow." The outer poems in the complex are about *weeping*. In 8:23 Jeremiah says,

> Oh that my head were waters
> and my eyes a fountain of tears
> That I might *weep* day and night (ואבכה)
> for the slain of the daughter of my people

The companion poem (9:9b-10) says nothing about weeping, but an introductory line has been prefixed to the poem (9a)[92] which reads:

> I will take up *weeping* and wailing (אשא בכי ונהי)
> for the mountains[93]
> and a lamentation for the pastures
> of the wilderness

It is now possible to explain why 9a was prefixed to 9b-10. This line contains the key word enabling 9-10 to be balanced with the first poem in 8:22-9:1. The cluster as a whole can be outlined as follows:

A   Jeremiah *weeping* for the slain people (8:22-9:1)

  B   Jeremiah warning about evil *tongues* (9:2-5)

  B'   Jeremiah warning about evil *tongues* (9:6-8)

A'   Jeremiah *weeping* for the entire creation (9:9-10)

Since the cluster is within 1-20 we are no doubt looking
at a structure created by Jeremiah as a mnemonic device when he
kept the early poems together in his head.

11:18-20; 12:1-3

These poems together with intervening commentary (11:21-
23) and what follows in 12:4-6 have been the subject of much
discussion. Following Cornill, some commentators propose that
12:1-6 be placed before 11:18-23.[94] That however is unnecessary.
Upon close examination we see that two poems have been deliberately placed end to end to make another inversion. Both are
2:2:2 and written very much alike, the main difference being
that one begins where the other ends and vice versa. Earlier
we noted that two poems, 6:1-7 and 6:8-12, contained key words
in identical collocations and were even juxtaposed in the collection process, and we called these "companion poems." The
two poems here appear also to be companion poems, the only difference being the inversion which is created.

A	ויהוה הודיעני ואדעה אז הראיתני מעלליהם	18
	ואני ככבש אלוף יובל לטבוח ולא־ידעתי כי־עלי	19
B	חשבו מחשבות נשחיתה עץ בלחמו	
	ונכרתנו מארץ חיים ושמו לא־יזכר עוד	
C	ויהוה צבאות שפט צדק בחן כליות ולב	20
	אראה נקמתך מהם כי אליך גליתי את־ריבי	
C'	צדיק אתה יהוה כי אריב אליך אך משפטים אדבר אותך	1
	מדוע דרך רשעים צלחה שלו כל־בגדי בגד	
B'	נטעתם גם־שרשו ילכו גם־עשו פרי	2
	קרוב אתה בפיהם ורחוק מכליותיהם	
A'	ואתה יהוה ידעתני תראני ובחנת לבי אתך	3
	התקם כצאן לטבחה והקדשם ליום הרגה	

```
18          Yahweh made it known to me, and I knew
                then you made me see their evil deeds
19      A   For I was like a gentle ram led to the slaughter
                For I did not know it was against me

            They devised schemes (saying)
        B    'Let us destroy the tree with its yield
            Let us cut him off from the land of the living
                that his name be remembered no more'

20              But O Yahweh of Hosts, who judges righteously
        C         who tries the heart and the mind
                Let me see your vengeance upon them
                    for to you I have committed my suit
```

1   *Righteous are you O Yahweh, yet I bring suit* [95]
                                          to you

    C'   yet I speak *judgment* against you
         Why does the way of the wicked prosper?
         why do all who are treacherous thrive?

2   You plant them, and they take root
    B'   they grow and bring forth *fruit*
         You are near in their mouth
         but far from their heart

3   But you O *Yahweh know me* and *see me*
    A'   and try my mind toward yourself
         Pull them out *like sheep* for the *slaughter*
         and sanctify them for the day of the killing

As one can see the two poems literally swarm with balanced vocabulary. To what we have underlined could be added בחן כליות ולב in v. 20 which has counterparts in ורחוק מכליותיהם of v. 2 and ובחנת לבי אתך of v. 3. Verse 20 is repeated almost verbatim in 20:12. Whether it is original there or not we cannot say, but it certainly must be kept in this context. So also must התקם כצאן לטבחה of v. 3 which is lacking in Greek.

Together the poems argue a single point, viz., that Yahweh in his righteousness should judge Jeremiah's enemies in a way that will suit their wrongdoing. In other words their punishment should fit the crime. This view of justice was common in antiquity as we know from Judges 1:6-7 and especially II Maccabees (4:26,38; 5:9-10; 8:33; 9:5-6; 13:3-8).

22:6-23

In the previous chapter we established the outer limits of the collection of speeches to kings.[96] In its final form this collection contained an inclusio which contrasted the future messianic king to Zedekiah. Now we will look at the center of the collection where a chiastic structure in the poetry isolates the core. This core is made up of three major poems, and two fragments directed to Kings Shallum (Jehoahaz) and Jehoiakim. Two of the major poems, 22:6-7 and 22:20-23, were analyzed fully in the previous chapter,[97] so we will present the core in skeleton form only:

        You are as Gilead to me
         as the summit of *Lebanon* (הלבנון)
  A   ....
        ....
    And they shall cut down your choicest *cedars* (ארזיך)
        and cast them into the fire
             (22:6-7)

```
          Weep not for him who is dead...[i.e., Josiah]
   B      but weep bitterly for him who goes away
          ..........................[Jehoahaz]
                        (22:10)


          Woe to him who builds his house...
          ..............................
          He cuts for it windows, paneling it in cedar (בארז)
   C      Do you think you are a king because you compete
                              in cedar? (בארז)
          ..............................
          and for practicing oppression and violence
                        (22:13-17)


  B'      They shall not lament for him
          ......................[Jehoiakim]
                        (22:18-19)


          Go up to Lebanon and cry out (הלבנון)
          and lift up your voice in Bashan
  A'      ...........................
          O inhabitants of Lebanon (בלבנון)
          nested in the cedars (בארזים)
          ..........................
                        (22:20-23)
```

The core is a well-balanced ABCB'A' structure. Three
main poems are placed at the beginning, middle and end, with
fragments on either side of the center poem filling out the
whole. Our prior analysis of poems A and A' showed their pre-
occupation with the "cedars of Lebanon," i.e., the wooded structures of Jerusalem. Both had inclusios which used "cedars" and
"Lebanon" as key terms. Now we see that the center poem (C) is
another which rebukes one of Judah's kings (Jehoiakim?) for his
lavish use of cedar. But here the repetition of בארז comes at
the center making then the poem a pivot for the whole.

The two fragments directed to Jehoahaz and Jehoiakim
are words of lament--or non-lament--as the case may be. Here
the introductory formulas, כה־אמר יהוה אל־, are nicely inverted.
In the word to Jehoiakim (18-19) the formula is placed at the
beginning whereas in the word to Jehoahaz (10-12) it is placed
at the end together with additional comment. This might be a
trite observation were it not now known that Deuteronomic
scribes took pleasure in doing this very thing.

We conclude then that 22:6-23 constitutes the core of
the King Collection and that at one time this was an independent composition. We have other evidence too which shows that
the King Collection ended originally with 22:20-23. This

latter poem is linked by a catchword to the poem beginning the
Prophet Collection (23:9-40). We noted earlier that *opening
key words* were used to link poems in chapter 51 into a chain,[98]
and we see now the exact same thing being done here. The final
"king poem" begins:

> Go up to Lebanon and cry out
>   and lift up your voice in Bashan
> Cry from Abarim
>   for all your lovers *are broken*   כי נשברו כל-מאהביך
>   (22:20)

And the first "prophet poem" begins:

> My heart *is broken* within me   נשבר לבי בקרבי
>   all my bones shake
>   (23:9)

We thus conclude that all of 22:24-23:8 is an expansion of the
core just as 21:1-22:5 is expansion. We see also how Hebrew
literature tends *to grow out in both directions* from the center
instead of accumulating in sequential fashion only.

Having now identified the core our attempt to date it
is greatly assisted by the fact that datable kings are referred
to both inside the core and outside. The word to Jeconiah (22:
24-30) lies outside which means that the core was probably put
together sometime before his brief reign of three months. This
gives us a *terminus ad quem* of 597 B.C. The *terminus a quo* is
not far away. In 22:18-19 Jehoiakim's ignoble death is predicted, which is probably Jeremiah's response to Jehoiakim's
poor foreign and domestic policies after 604-603 B.C. This
gives us very narrow limits--a mere 6-7 years--and it puts the
composition of the core at a time immediately following the
time when the *Urrolle*--which we take to be 1-20--was written
down. That was 605 B.C. (the fourth year of Jehoiakim according to Jer 36). Since the core (along with a portion of the
Prophet Collection to which it is linked) immediately follows
1-20 in the present order of the book, we are justified in
calling this an early appendix to the *Urrolle* for Jer 36:32
specifically states: "and many similar words were added to
them." This was done when Jeremiah and Baruch were in hiding
(Jer 36:19). Then after Jehoiakim died and the young Jehoiachin (=Jeconiah) was taken off to exile, the lament over
Jehoiachin was added. It lay outside the core but still followed the earlier laments/non-laments in chronological order.
It was only in the final stage of the collection's growth that

chronology was broken, and that was done in order to make the inclusio contrasting Zedekiah to the messianic king, which framed the whole.

For what purpose was this chiastic structure made? If it had been created earlier we might consider it to be another mnemonic aid for Jeremiah. But since it comes from a time when Baruch was helping Jeremiah bring things together--and also since it follows the creation of 1-20--we think that its function was probably the same as the function of 1-20, i.e., to make the material suitable for use in worship. If Jeremiah was too modest to suggest it himself, Baruch convinced him that one day his speeches would be heard again by the descendants of those who were presently his enemies. And Baruch, being a scribe schooled in the Deuteronomic tradition, saw to it that the material was compiled in such a way that its future use would be facilitated.

29: Jeremiah's Letters to the Exiles

This chapter is not without its problems, the most serious being 1) the omission of vv. 16-20 in the Greek (except Lucian); and 2) how one is to properly interpret vv. 24-28. Verses 16-20 are words of judgment against the "bad figs" left in Jerusalem (cf. ch. 24), and are usually taken to be a late insertion,[99] although Peake admittedly finds it difficult to explain what interest the post-exilic community would have in such an addition.[100]

The other problem concerns the end of the letter. Verse 29 begins a narrative which relates a subsequent discussion that took place between Jeremiah and Zephaniah the priest. This could make v. 28 the conclusion of the letter except for the fact that this verse quotes Jeremiah's words from the same letter (v. 5). Bright therefore takes v. 23 as the conclusion of the letter,[101] and we believe this to be correct. That means that vv. 24-28--which are directed specifically to a certain Shemaiah in Babylon--must constitute another letter or more probably a *fragment* from some other letter which was appended to the original letter at a later time. We will return to discuss the fragment but let us first look at the main letter.

The main letter is contained in vv. 4-23, 1-3 being introductory and beginning in typical Deuteronomic fashion: ואלה דברי, "These are the words..." (cf. Deut 1:1; 28:69).

It breaks down into four sections which make another chiasmus.
And a count of the lines in *MT* shows that each section is of
approximately the same length. Verse 15 is out of place however in the *MT*, so we take it along with Lucian to belong prior
to 21-23 which it is meant to introduce. The letter breaks
down as follows:

    A   Welfare of *Babylon* (4-9) - 9 lines of *MT*

     B   Welfare of *Jerusalem* (10-14) - 9 lines of *MT*

     B' Judgment in *Jerusalem* (16-20) - 9+ lines of *MT*

    A' Judgment in *Babylon* (15, 21-23) - 8 lines of *MT*

    The first half of the letter is about שלום (welfare),
first the שלום of Babylon (v. 7), and second the eventual שלום
of Jerusalem (v. 11). The remainder of the letter is judgment.
But in apportioning the judgment Jeremiah reverses the order
which he used in the שלום part of the letter. The remnant in
Jerusalem is judged first (16-20), and second those prophets
in Babylon who give false hopes for a speedy return from exile
(15, 21-23). We thus argue for the inclusion of 16-20 which
the Greek omits. It most certainly belongs and is to be deleted
only at the expense of what is deliberately intended to be a
rhetorical structure.

    We return now to the fragment. Bright takes vv. 24-28
along with the narrative in 29ff as "repercussions of the letter,"[102] still assuming that we have only one letter from Jeremiah. But this cannot be. Verses 24-28 constitute a fragment
from another letter sent by Jeremiah to Babylon, and the introductory "To Shemaiah of Nehelam you shall say:" (v. 24) is a
directive from Jeremiah to the recipient of the letter in Babylon. It is not a directive from Yahweh to Jeremiah (so
Bright).[103] We say too that this is a *fragment* rather than a
whole letter because, as scholars have long noted, the ending
is abrupt.[104] Jeremiah recounts what Shemaiah has said in his
letters and then says no more. We anticipate something addi-
tional--a word of judgment perhaps--but that does not come until later when Jeremiah writes his third letter. Now it may be
that Jeremiah was acting in his usual cautious manner waiting
to hear Shemaiah's letter to Zephaniah before cursing him.[105]
But if the letter is seeking some kind of explanation from
Shemaiah, which is what appears to be the case, should we not
hear more than a mere summary of what Shemaiah has said? It
would seem so, and thus we are compelled, I believe, to see

this as only a fragment of what was originally a much longer
letter. Also, we must remember that letters in antiquity were
often semi-public containing messages for more than one person.
Jeremiah's third letter containing the curse on Shemaiah (v. 31)
was sent "to all the exiles in Babylon." Since letters had a
wider audience we can assume that only certain portions were
selected for inclusion into the biblical text. Other parts of
the letter containing material not deemed important the compiler
edited out.

We can now proceed to a reconstruction of the events as
they took place. Jeremiah began by writing a letter to the
exiles in Babylon, which we have perhaps in full in vv. 4-23.
In this letter he told the exiles to build houses and have families because the exile would be long. Shemaiah, most likely
a prophet (v. 31: יען אשר נבא לכם שמעיה) exiled in Babylon,
then wrote a number of letters[106] back to people in Jerusalem
objecting to what Jeremiah had said. In his letter to Zephaniah the priest (and perhaps in some of the other letters as
well) he demanded that Jeremiah be censured. Jeremiah had not
yet heard the letter sent to Zephaniah, but on the basis of
either the other letters or perhaps from reports which came to
him about the letter to Zephaniah, he sent a second letter to
Babylon. This conveyed the substance of Shemaiah's letter/
letters and apparently sought to find out from Shemaiah what
was going on. The fragment in vv. 24-28 is from that letter.
Now Zephaniah is finally confronted by Jeremiah and is forced
to read his letter.[107] Jeremiah hears this letter for the
first time and after hearing it dictates another letter to
Babylon cursing Shemaiah (vv. 31-32). This letter is the *third*
sent by Jeremiah to Babylon and it is not extant.

We are now ready to look at the main letter and the
fragment together. The "abrupt ending" of the fragment as we
noted earlier is a quotation from the main letter. More than
that it is a quotation from the *very beginning* of that letter.
The original letter begins:

29:5	Build houses and live in them; plant gardens and eat their produce...	בנו בתים ושבו ונטעו גנות ואכלו את-פרין

And the fragment ends:

29:28	Build houses and live in them; plant gardens and eat their produce.	בנו בתים ושבו ונטעו גנות ואכלו את-פריהן

The end of one is made to match the beginning of the other, and
the result is an inclusio. Together the two make a rhetorical
whole which is meant to convey a single point: "Settle down and
accept the exile as a thing which you must bear for a time."
And it is not unlikely that this expanded form of Jeremiah's
Letters to the Exiles was tailored as was other material for
the ongoing worship life in exile.

The Jehoiakim Cluster: 25, 26, 35 & 36

These four chapters are the only dated narrative from
Jehoiakim's reign except for 45 which is Baruch's autobiographical postscript. They appear interspersed with dated narrative
from Zedekiah's reign, together lending support to the "disarray
theory." But we should note that this interspersion takes place
only in chapters 24-36. Chapters 37-44, which conclude the
reign of Zedekiah, follow in perfect chronological order.

Our main concern is with the chapters out of chronological order, viz., 24-36. The present arrangement is of course
the final one, and while this arrangement cannot be understood
as the one that was originally intended, it can be satisfactor-
ily explained once we know something of the material's pre-history. Other structures more carefully designed existed prior
to this one, and it is these that we now want to show. The key
which unlocks the pre-history is found by *extracting the Jehoiakim chapters from the rest and looking at them separately.*
When we do this we see that these chapters form a cluster
arranged into a chiasmus. Here our primary criterion is the
date which is found in each of the superscriptions. Five dates
are given in all, four appear at the beginnings of chapters 25,
26, 35 and 36, and a fifth comes in 36:9. The date in 36:9
marks what we believe to be an expansion of 36:1-8, but more
about that in a moment. Let us look first at the cluster. The
four chapters with their dates are as follows:

          A   Ch. 25 - 4th year of Jehoiakim
            B   Ch. 26 - the beginning of Jehoiakim's reign
            B'   Ch. 35 - in the days of Jehoiakim
          A'   Ch. 36 - 4th year of Jehoiakim

Chapters 26, 35 and 36 all appear to be in chronological order.
Chapter 26 dates from the "beginning" (בראשית) of Jehoiakim's
reign and is generally given a date of ca. 609-608 B.C.[108]
Chapter 35 can also fit into the period prior to 605 B.C.,

although this is still debated.[109] Only chapter 25 is manifest-
ly out of chronological order, but again, we believe this to be
deliberate. As was the case with 21:1-23:8, so here too chronology is broken in order to make the beginning balance the end.

Were date the *sole* criterion for the identification of
this rhetorical structure we would have to call our structure
an inclusio. A and A' balance nicely but the descriptions of
date in B and B' are different. Nevertheless we note that 26
and 35 are *both* accounts of Jeremiah in the *temple*, suggesting
that the center of the structure was probably meant to be in
balance as well. Thus we take B and B' as genuine counterparts
and the whole as a chiasmus.

A word now about the superscription in 36:9. Since our
chiasmus builds primarily on dated superscriptions it becomes
necessary to explain the one remaining superscription not used
in the structure. In our judgment 36 was originally only 36:1-
8. Verses 9-32 are later expansion as one can easily tell when
reading from verses 8 to 9. Verse 8 tells in summary fashion
that Baruch did what Jeremiah commanded him to do, i.e., go
to the temple and read the scroll the two of them had prepared.
It says nothing more. But in 9ff we get a *detailed account* of
what actually took place when Baruch went. Thus it appears
that Baruch decided sometime later to expand upon what he had
said very summarily in v. 8. And when he added this he introduced it with a superscription telling us that the reading took
place in the 5th year of Jehoiakim, the ninth month (36:9).
But the Jehoiakim Cluster originally concluded with 36:1-8,
not with all 32 verses now found in our present chapter.

We can now proceed to explain Baruch's rationale in
creating the chiasmus the way he did, which in turn will enable
us to perceive the original function of 36:1-8. We realize
that Baruch broke chronology to make the chiasmus, but why 25
first and 36:1-8 last? He could have reversed the two with no
net loss. Let us look at 36:1-8 first since its position is
easiest to explain. If one looks closely at this passage he
will see that Baruch figures prominently just as he does in 45.
He is in fact the key figure. *He* takes Jeremiah's dictation
and *he* it is who reads the scroll before the temple audience.
Thus we believe that at this earlier time Baruch wanted 36:1-8
to be *his signature* just as he later wanted 45 to be the signature of the book when completed. In his own way Jeremiah identified himself in 1-20; now Baruch writes a partially concealed

colophon for that which is *his* creation.

Why Baruch placed 25 at the beginning is not so obvious. Since in his collection this chapter introduced the Oracles to Foreign Nations, it may be that he desired to place the Oracles to Foreign Nations *first* instead of last. It is true they are last in the *MT* but that is only because of Seriah's relocation. We see in Amos that they are first, although admittedly they were placed there for rhetorical reasons of a different sort.[110]

We conclude then that the Jehoiakim Cluster was originally an independent collection of prose narrative written and arranged by Baruch. Since also it contained part if not all of the Oracles to Foreign Nations, it is probably the "this book" (בספר הזה) referred to in 25:13.[111] Eventually it would be added to earlier collections for the purpose of expanding what was rapidly becoming *a book* of Jeremiah. If the *Urrolle* (1-20) be the first edition, and the second edition be the *Urrolle* plus an early version of the King and Prophet Collection, then the third edition would contain the two collections of the second edition plus the Jehoiakim Cluster. The date here must be just prior to 597 B.C. when Jeremiah and Baruch were still in hiding.

The Zedekiah Cluster: 24, 27, 28 & 29

We proceed in our analysis of the pre-history of chapters 24-36 by looking at what is left after the Jehoiakim Cluster has been taken out. What we find is another cluster--four chapters of dated Zedekiah prose prior to the Book of Comfort (30-33)--and it too is structured into a chiasmus! The chapters in this cluster are 24, 27, 28 and 29. The criteria here for the chiasmus are just exactly what they were for the Jehoiakim Cluster. The primary criterion is *date*; the secondary criterion the *subject matter* of the center units. Let us look now at the Zedekiah Cluster:

    A   Ch. 24 - after the exile of Jeconiah
      B   Ch. 27 - beginning of Zedekiah's reign [4th year][112]
      B' Ch. 28 - beginning of Zedekiah's reign (4th year)
    A' Ch. 29 - after the exile of Jeconiah

As one can see the similarity to the other cluster is almost unbelievable. A and A' are dated at the same time, and so also are B and B' despite the textual problems in 27:1. But similar subject matter in B and B' makes the chiasmus certain.

In both 27 and 28 Jeremiah gives his object lesson using the
yoke-bar. Perhaps even more interesting is a look at how the
clusters differ. We noted that in the Jehoiakim Cluster A was
out of chronological order. This cluster, however, breaks
chronology in precisely the *opposite* way: the chapter out of
order is A'. Thus we see again that Baruch enjoyed inversions
every bit as much as Jeremiah.

It is not clear why 29 should come at the end, but 24 is
a suitable beginning to this cluster because of its similarity
to chapter 1 opening the book. These two chapters, 1 and 24,
are the only chapters which record Jeremiah's visions, and in
24:3 Jeremiah is addressed with the same words appearing in 1:11
and 13: מה־אתה ראה ירמיהו, "What do you see Jeremiah?" With
such balance and consistency we believe that Baruch must have
chosen material very carefully for his collections. No doubt
there was much else to tell but because it didn't fit into the
scheme it was left out.

We might assume that the Zedekiah Cluster was added to
the Jehoiakim Cluster to make an enlarged fourth edition. But
here we are not at all certain how the book looked ca. 593 B.C.
because very soon after the Zedekiah Cluster was completed it
was interspersed with the Jehoiakim Cluster. It is to this
problem that we now turn since we must explain how clusters so
deliberately conceived were then broken up leaving us with the
disorder now prevailing. Why was not the Zedekiah Cluster
placed immediately behind the Jehoiakim Cluster? The answer
is perhaps one which we will never know for certain, but an
explanation can be given, and it is one that squares with all
we have thus far learned about Baruch's compositional methods.
We suggested earlier that Baruch had certain ideas about what
made appropriate beginnings and what made appropriate conclusions. In the Jehoiakim Cluster the autobiographical passage
had to be last, and in the Zedekiah Cluster the chapter with
Jeremiah's vision had to be first. Now one will quickly see
that any attempt to put these two together necessitates a com-
promise. If Baruch placed the Zedekiah Cluster immediately
after the Jehoiakim Cluster, 36 would no longer be the conclusion. Nor would 24 be at the beginning. He could conceivably
have placed the entire Zedekiah Cluster ahead of the Jehoiakim
Cluster and kept both his chosen beginning and conclusion, but
this would have manifest a complete disregard for chronology
and apparently Baruch ruled that out too. The only other

option was to intersperse the two and this is the option he chose. Chapter 24 became the new beginning and 36 remained as the conclusion. Chronology in the final stage was partially broken but that could not be helped. Also we recall that in 21:1-23:8 chronology likewise remained intact until the final stage when it was then broken.

We can now pick up a few loose ends and conclude our discussion of 24-36. The Book of Comfort is of course an independent collection as we have already seen. It was expanded with the addition of two chapters of Zedekiah prose (32-33) in the course of time, but we do not know exactly when this was or why the whole collection is where it is in the present text. The only chapter not yet accounted for is 34. Chronologically it fits just prior to 37, but as I have shown on another occasion, it was displaced in order to set up a contrast between Zedekiah and the Rechabites (35).[113]

The final stage of the book saw the addition of chapters 37-44, all of which are in chronological order and describe the events leading up to Jerusalem's fall. This added material now makes a fifth edition perhaps and the book is all but in its final form. For the first time 36 is no longer the conclusion, being replaced by 45. This is Baruch's final book and it is the book from which the *LXX* was translated. There is thus no longer any good reason to believe that composition and major editing of the book went on well into the exile. Seriah's text was fluid slightly longer than the text of Baruch, but the fact that Seriah keeps Baruch's text intact except for the relocation of the Oracles to Foreign Nations argues strongly for the fixing of Baruch's text very soon after the fall of Jerusalem.

One final comment. With the explanation of how chapters 24-36 came into their present state, and also with our earlier and now later discussions of the prose material on both sides, it should perhaps be pointed out that we have accounted for *all* the biographical prose in chapters 21-45, and we have done so *without any rearranging of the present text*!

This concludes the chapter and also the substance of our research. We have seen that Jeremiah and Baruch both make use of the chiasmus to structure their respective compositions. To this extent they both reflect a common rhetorical tradition. This cannot be overemphasized because Jeremiah is still too often set over against the Deuteronomic institution of his day.

That he stood opposed to much for which that institution stood
is clear enough. But like so many others who are forced to
leave home, there was something from home that he took along
with him. This was his rhetoric, for the rhetoric of Jeremiah
is clearly the rhetoric of Deuteronomy, which was also the prevailing rhetoric of the Deuteronomic institution in his day.

IV CONCLUSION

The Rhetoric of Jeremiah

The preceding pages have been filled with numerous observations about the Jeremianic speech and they cannot all be
reiterated here. Only the most important points will be drawn
together for the purpose of making a statement on the rhetoric
of Jeremiah.

We have gone to the poetry to find the Jeremianic
speeches, and consider it established that Jeremiah used rhetorical structures to control both parts and the whole of speeches.
We chose only two structures, the inclusio and the chiasmus, but
even so a significant amount of material was covered. A rough
count of poetic lines in the *MT* shows that out of approximately
1000 lines, we dealt in one way or another with over 300, which
is slightly under one-third. And much of what we left aside,
while not making use of either the inclusio or chiasmus, is
nevertheless very well-balanced, e.g., 2:14-19; 6:16-21; 17:5-8;
31:10-14; 49:28b-33a; 51:47-48, 52-53; etc. If one were to use
our data as a control in working elsewhere in the poetry, he
would no doubt come up with additional insight into the Jeremianic speeches. This in turn could be compared with the present research to see if the conclusions we are about to draw
are valid for the speeches as a whole.

We have seen that the Jeremianic speeches are controlled
not by fixed genre structures, i.e., the letter, lawsuit, hymn,
lament, judgment speech, or whatever, but by structures which
were dictated by canons of Hebrew rhetoric in the 8th-6th cc.
B.C. Jeremiah drew upon the rhetorical tradition which first
manifested itself in Deuteronomy. Heretofore it has been difficult if not impossible to compare the Jeremianic *speeches*
with the speeches in Deuteronomy because the Jeremianic speeches
are in poetry. Previous studies compared only the prose of
Jeremiah with the prose of Deuteronomy. But now we see that
even the poetic speeches of Jeremiah have an affinity with
Deuteronomy, and that affinity is one of structure.

113

If then Jeremiah took over rhetorical structures already
in use, how did he use them? We can begin by stating the obvious. He used the inclusio and the chiasmus as homiletical devices to aid him in preaching. Jeremiah's rhetoric is thus *a
preacher's rhetoric*. These devices were known to his audience
and no doubt appreciated by them. They were used with frequency
in the temple, and for all we know the temple may have been
where Jeremiah learned them in the first place. In non-argumentative poems Jeremiah achieves the same ends as the Deuteronomic
preacher. Structures alert the audience to where the preacher
is going, sometimes functioning to restore focus, other times to
give the necessary emphasis--whether in the middle or at the end.
In the case of the chiasmus, variation is sometimes necessary
when the speech builds heavily upon repetition. And for the
listeners, the inclusio and chiasmus are mnemonic devices aiding
them in retention. The audiences of Jeremiah were conditioned
to this rhetoric and they responded to it. Despite then all his
protestations to the contrary, Jeremiah *was* heard by his audience and his speeches *were* remembered.

Secondly, Jeremiah's rhetoric is *a rhetoric of totality*.
The structures of Jeremiah were used to present a total thought,
only it came forth in fragmented form. This was done deliberately and is what made possible the subtleties and added meanings Jeremiah conveyed beyond words. But even normal parallelism functions this way. A thought is broken up and given in
segments instead of all at one time. Schoettgen in his *Exergasia Sacra* saw this more clearly than Lowth. Jeremiah was also able to create anticipation by breaking up his thoughts.
The audience frequently knew it must wait for something and
when that something came the desire for totality was satisfied.
Muilenburg is then correct when he says that this sense of
totality "is as apparent in Israel's rhetoric as in her psycho-
logy."[1]

The importance of this cannot be overstated especially
in the interest of proper exegetical and theological understanding. What we are saying in essence is that one cannot properly
understand the parts of the Jeremianic speech unless he first
understands the whole. Structure is a key to meaning and interpretation. The Jeremianic speeches contain theological statements which are hidden from view when the structure is not perceived. This should then be a warning to those who apply a
purely philological or text-critical methodology to the text.

The structural method is a necessary control for these other methods and future scholars will be better exegetes and theologians if they pay this heed.

Jeremiah's rhetoric is *a rhetoric of argumentation*. We have long known that Jeremiah was a prophet of dialogue and we have also known that he was a man of contention (15:10). But we have not realized the extent to which he was argumentative because we have heretofore not been able to get from his speeches a picture of the prophet *vis à vis* his audience. Now that has all changed and we are able to see Jeremiah in quite a new light.

This perhaps more than anything else is what makes Jeremiah's rhetoric different from the rhetoric of Deuteronomy. In Deuteronomy, judgment (and reward too) is stated in conditional terms: "If you do good you will be rewarded, and if you do bad you will be punished." Thus unless the hearer was unusually sensitive to being issued a warning, he would not likely feel alienated. But Jeremiah had moved beyond Deuteronomy. It was no longer an "If/then" situation. Israel *had* broken the covenant, therefore she *would* be punished. Such a message is hard to deliver and it is no wonder that Jeremiah had an argument on his hands much of the time. His audience is surely alienated in a way that it would not be alienated by the message of Deuteronomy.

Our recognition of the argumentative character of Jeremiah's rhetoric will also force upon us a new estimation of Jeremiah the man. Previously we have been influenced by popular conceptions of the prophets in general, and Jeremiah in particular, and these have not given us a fair picture. The prophets are seen by many as merely dogmatic preachers. They receive a word directly from God and then speak it with boldness. Jotham and Elijah lend support to such a view (Jud 9; I Kings 18). One does not enter into conversation with such a man. You either take what he says or leave it, and if he speaks judgment, the latter is usually the case.

Other stereotyped views have obtained with Jeremiah only. He is the "weeping prophet" pictured as one who can do nothing more in a desperate situation than sit and lament. He is even unfairly sought out as a model by the cynic and the complainer. Still others are attracted to Jeremiah because in him they see someone who is greatly misunderstood. Only God can know his plight.

It must certainly be conceded that there is a measure of dogmatism in Jeremiah and also that Jeremiah shows more than the normal amount of pathos. The poem in 51:20-23 shows that he could be bombastic. And he also wept (8:23; 9:9 [Eng. 9:1, 10]). But Jeremiah is primarily a prophet of engagement. He meets his audience on common ground, engages them, and then takes them with him as one does when he takes another for a ride. Only Jeremiah is taking them to an undesired place and they find they must either beg to get off or stay with him. Either way they are caught. A rhetoric of argumentation has this one quality: it does not permit an audience to remain merely as onlookers.

Finally, Jeremiah's rhetoric is *a rhetoric of descent*. We have seen that the Jeremianic argument goes quite consistently in the following directions:

$$\longrightarrow$$

ironic - straightforward
figurative - literal
general - specific
abstract - concrete

It begins at a distance and gradually comes closer until it is right upon you. Throughout the speech Jeremiah *lowers* the level of abstraction and this serves a practical end. An audience is much more easily engaged by irony, generalities, well-known laws, word-plays, unusual metaphors, proverbs and observations from the natural order. Any truth whatever in abstract form gives Jeremiah common ground with his audience. But Jeremiah is delivering a message of judgment and so he must postpone the unveiling of his preferred subject until the very end—and indeed in some instances until after the end has passed. Otherwise his chance will be lost. People rarely sit around and listen for long when the finger is pointed at them.

Now that we have stated the salient features of Jeremiah's rhetoric it might be well to see if our picture squares with the picture of Jeremiah given in the prose, and also with pictures we have of other prophets engaged in controversy. Perhaps the classic confrontation found in the prose comes in chapter 28 where Jeremiah meets Hananiah. Jeremiah is not in agreement with Hananiah about the duration of the exile, nevertheless he begins the conversation by ostensibly agreeing with him: "Amen! May Yahweh do so; may Yahweh make the words which

you have prophesied come true, and bring back to this place from
Babylon the vessels of the house of Yahweh, and all the exiles"
(28:6). Micaiah had spoken the same way to Ahab (I Kings 22:15).
Jeremiah then follows with his own statement, but it is very
general. He doesn't counter Hananiah saying that the exile will
be long--which he could have done (cf. 27:7). Instead he sets
up the criterion by which a true prophet can be distinguished
from a false one. This he gets from Deut 18:22. His lack of
directness is no deterrent, however, and the controversy enters
a physical stage. Hananiah breaks the yoke-bar off Jeremiah's
neck. And what does Jeremiah do? The text tells us very terse-
ly: "But Jeremiah the prophet went his way" (28:11b). Only
later does Jeremiah return to curse Hananiah (vv. 12ff). It
took him a while, but over time Jeremiah could become very
specific. We concluded the same when Jeremiah had to deal with
Shemaiah (29), and there are other instances where the pattern
is very much the same, e.g., in 32 where Jeremiah proceeds very
cautiously with Yahweh in accepting a message of future hope.

Jeremiah's rhetoric compares in a striking way to the
rhetoric of Nathan and Amos. When Nathan convicts David of
the crime against Uriah (II Sam 12), he begins with a hypothetical case which he knows will "hook" David. Once David gives
the desired judgment Nathan can quickly make the analogy and
point the finger saying "You are the man!" His move here is
from the general to the specific, from the abstract to the concrete. Amos, on the other hand, "hooks" his audience with
sweeping world-wide judgments (Amos 1-2). We can almost hear
the audience applauding with delight as he flays one nation
after another. But in the end Amos reveals his preferred subject, i.e., Israel. All the rest was foil. And by the time
Amos comes to his preferred subject the audience is so conditioned by assenting to seven guilty verdicts that the eighth
is inescapable. Jeremiah addresses "the people" this way. He
uses prophets, priests and kings as foil, and in the end re-
veales his preferred subject, which is the people themselves.

We thus conclude that the rhetoric of Jeremiah as revealed in our analysis of the speech material is one that can
stand. The inclusio and the chiasmus--with their ability to
return the audience to the beginning in particular--were admir-
ably suited for Jeremiah's needs. Despite Jeremiah's protesta-
tion that he was unable to speak (1:6), we find on the contrary
that he could indeed speak very well.

The Rhetoric of the Book of Jeremiah

We seem to have evidence that the book of Jeremiah developed in two stages: 1) an oral stage, and 2) a written stage. The oral stage we know least about, although structures did emerge in the course of our investigation which point to such a stage prior to 605 B.C. Since we take 1-20 to be the scroll of 605 our predisposition is to consider any structure within that collection a structure created by Jeremiah during the 23 years he collected his own works. This would include the chain of poems in chapter 2 as well as the large inclusio and chiastic structures within 1-20. We are not sure about the chain in chapters 22-23. This early form of the King and Prophet Collection may have circulated orally; then on the other hand it may be the work of a writing scribe. The chain of four poems in chapter 51 is most likely a grouping prepared for a brief period of oral transmission. The entire question needs more research. But from now on we insist that so-called "tradition-complexes" be sought in the poetry, not in the biographical prose. This means 1-20, 22-23, 30-31 and 46-51. And even then corroborating evidence will certainly be necessary in order to keep such studies from becoming overly subjective. As for the current theories about the four great tradition-complexes we can dispense with them entirely. Such simply do not exist. None of the blocks proposed by either Engnell or Rietzschel can any longer be defended, nor is 1:1-25:13 by itself anything at all. The *LXX* and *MT* break at 25:13 only because of the relocation of the Oracles to Foreign Nations in the *MT*. Related to this, of course, is our judgment that the prose in 24-45 is not legend. It is historical biography written down by Baruch very soon after the events themselves took place. Whatever contribution the community made to this material--if it made any at all--was minimal. In any case it is not significant enough for the material to be called legend.

The latter stage is the written stage and about that we know significantly more than previously. The prose commences about the same time as Baruch appears on the scene, i.e., early in Jehoiakim's reign, and from 605 until 586 numerous collections are put together, eventually being joined together into a single book. The inclusio and chiastic structures of these various collections become very useful to us in marking the stages of the book's growth because they delimit units.

The history of composition may indeed be more complex than we realize, but at least we can see what took place in broad outline.

Being a Deuteronomic scribe, Baruch was a direct heir to the great rhetorical tradition in Judah of the past century or more. He was certainly familiar with how Deuteronomy was written and compiled, which means that, besides knowing how to use rhetorical structures, he knew the importance of arranging things chronologically and also had some definite ideas on how books should begin and end. We know too that he was capable of writing good biography. Because of him the *book* of Jeremiah is what it is, for it is Baruch more than Jeremiah who creates this work.

We have argued that Baruch tailored the written collections for use in temple worship. This was his main reason for using the inclusio and the chiasmus. We can assume this, because, after writing down the very first scroll from Jeremiah's dictation, he goes to the *temple* to read it. There he finds a gathered congregation, who as far as we know, heard him out in his entirety. This was a congregation accustomed to temple rhetoric, which was still basically the rhetoric of Deuteronomy. Now when they heard a collection of prophecies from Jeremiah it had a familiar ring. At the end of Baruch's reading the audience was brought back to the beginning and Jeremiah's despair was thus tempered with a strong statement of faith. The people could respond to this, not merely because they had heard judgment often enough before--which they had--but because Baruch had come to them using the rhetoric that they had heard many times before.

Now if Baruch tailored his first scroll for use in the temple we can assume that he did the same with subsequent collections. More and more Jeremiah's words were heard by audiences removed from the audience Jeremiah originally addressed. In this way the re-presentation of the Jeremianic material began, and in the process a book took shape that became more and more like Deuteronomy, which up to that time had been *the book par excellence* in Israel. Deuteronomy re-presented Moses to an audience removed in time if not in spirit from the Mosaic Age (cf. Deut 5:2-3). Now in the book of Jeremiah it is Jeremiah who becomes the "new Moses."[2]

One question remains. If Baruch was preparing material for subsequent use in worship, did either he or Jeremiah have

a future temple in mind? The first scroll and perhaps other
early scrolls were prepared for delivery in the existing temple,
but Jeremiah had predicted that temple's destruction. Was there
some hope on the part of either that it would not be destroyed?
On the other hand, if the temple's eventual destruction was con-
ceded--which is most likely--then we might well assume that Jeremiah and Baruch looked forward to the day when a new temple
would be built. No doubt both realized that worship in some
form would continue on into the exile, temple or no temple, but
the question may still be asked whether they looked beyond the
exile to a restoration back in Jerusalem (cf. 29:10). Any argument either way is of course an argument from silence, since
Jeremiah on no occasion spoke about a future temple (or lack
thereof). He said that the ark would be gone, that old confessions and proverbs would be replaced by something new, and even
that there would be a new covenant. But about a new temple
Jeremiah said nothing. Nevertheless if structure be a silent
witness to things not otherwise uttered, we may perhaps be
allowed the suggestion that Baruch and Jeremiah did indeed en-
vision a new temple. If so, the gap normally assumed between
Jeremiah and Ezekiel is at least partially narrowed.[3] It is
only that Jeremiah (and Baruch) say silently what Ezekiel pro-
claims loud and clear.

APPENDIX

CHRISTIAN SCHOETTGEN'S *EXERGASIA SACRA*

It has been customary to credit Robert Lowth with the
discovery of Hebrew parallelism even though we realize that he
did not actually discover it.[1] Lowth's primary source was an
essay on Hebrew rhythm by Azariah de Rossi, a rabbi from Ferrara,
who included this in his larger work *Me'or Enayim* published in
1574.[2]

More recent research has shown that biblical parallelism
was widely known by the end of the 17th c. Roman Jakobson has
called attention to studies done in Scandanavia 50 years before
Lowth which compared Hebrew parallelism with parallelism in Fin-
nish poetry.[3] Among Lowth's other predecessors there were two
who defined the phenomenon in rhetorical categories. One was
the Italian Alessio Simmaco Mazzocchi, the other a German named
Christian Schoettgen. Mazzocchi saw parallelism as "epesegesi,"
whereas for Schoettgen it was "exergasia." The contributions
of both scholars have been relatively unknown, although some
years ago Mazzocchi was given his redress.[4] It is now proper,
then, to give to Schoettgen what is due him.

Very little is known about Schoettgen's *Exergasia Sacra*,
and even less is known about Schoettgen himself. To make matters worse what has been passed on about Schoettgen in the English tradition is not entirely correct. The one scholar in the
English tradition who seems to have seen Schoettgen's dissertation in *Horae Hebraicae et Talmudicae* was John Jebb, who, like
Schoettgen himself, is another scholar not well known.[5] Jebb
makes numerous references to the work in his *Sacred Literature*,
but he evidently does not know the author. He discusses the
Exergasia Sacra with other works by Abarbanel and Azariah in a
paragraph entitled "Two *or three* rabbinical dissertations"
[italics mine].[6] This is cautious, but nevertheless incorrect.
Schoettgen was not a rabbi but a Christian scholar living in
the 18th c. in Germany.

Another erroneous belief has crept into English scholarship although this is not the responsibility of Jebb. Both

Charles Briggs and Theophile Meek have made statements to the effect that Lowth used the earlier work of Schoettgen's.[7] Yet nowhere in either Lowth's *Lectures on the Sacred Poetry of the Hebrews* or *Isaiah* does he even mention Schoettgen. Jebb notes this too.[8] This appears then to be decisive because Jebb knows of no writer (presumably in the English tradition) who has cited Schoettgen when discussing Hebrew poetry,[9] in addition to the fact that both Briggs and Meek appear to be ultimately dependent upon Jebb for their information.[10] Briggs seems to be the one who first made the connection, and unless evidence is forthcoming which shows that he had independent information, we are more correct to assume that Lowth worked independent of Schoettgen and did not use the *Exergasia Sacra* as one of his sources.

It is time now to set the record straight, which we can do with the help of an article on Schoettgen in *Biographie Universelle*.[11] Christian Schoettgen was a philologist born in 1687 at Wurzen in Saxony, not far from Leipzig. His father was a shoe-maker, but having had himself a literary education, was in a position to give his son the same. After early training at the gymnasiums, the young Schoettgen matriculated at the University of Leipzig for a course in theology, at which time he also began a study of the oriental languages. Nine years were spent at Leipzig giving lessons and doing literary work of one kind or another. At the request of the local library Schoettgen undertook the revision of a 1667 manuscript by Thomas Reinesius entitled *Eponymologicum*. This was a glossary explaining ancient inscriptions. Schoettgen's teaching career began in 1716 when he was named rector at the gymnasium of Frankfort on the Oder. In 1719 he became professor of literature. Then in 1728 he became rector at one of the gymnasiums at Dresden, where he remained until his death on October 15, 1751. Schoettgen was married and had eight children. He was a much respected teacher and was remembered also for his interest in fellow-citizens and strangers.

Besides being an expert in philology and historical scholarship, Schoettgen mastered to a rare degree the oriental and rabbinic literature. He was often consulted by Jewish scholars who venerated him until they found out about his desire to prove from the Old Testament that Jesus was the Messiah. The second volume of *Horae Hebraicae et Talmudicae* (1742)[12] is taken up almost entirely by a discussion of the Messiah. This work was then followed in 1748 by *Jesus le vrai Messie*.

Schoettgen published many other works. Some were up-
dated editions of works done by earlier scholars, while others
were his own. Included among the former were the works of Lam-
bert Bos on the Greek ellipsis and Walter on the Hebrew ellipsis.
Schoettgen also published a new edition of Pasor's *Lexique* on
the New Testament. In 1746 he published a better lexicon himself, and a third edition of this with later additions by Krebs
and Spohn was considered by Thomas Horne in the 19th c. to be
the best Greek-Latin lexicon of the New Testament currently
available.[13]

The first volume of *Horae Hebraica et Talmudicae* was
published in 1733 predating the Lowth Lectures by eight years.
It is mostly commentary on the books of the New Testament, with
eight dissertations on various subjects at the back. The sixth
of these is *Exergasia Sacra*. In this dissertation Schoettgen
first gives a general explanation of exergasia equating it with
the Latin figure "expolitio." The exergasia had already been
thoroughly discussed by Julius Scaliger so the reader is referred to him for further information. Then follows 10 canons
of "exergasia sacra," which we now present for the first time
in English translation. Each canon is illustrated by three
biblical texts, and in two instances--in Canons III and VII--
Schoettgen makes some additional comments. The 10 canons are
then given further demonstration following their enumeration.
Here we will present only the canons and the illustrative texts.
After we have looked at them we will conclude with some compar-
isons to Lowth's doctrine of parallelism as well as to the subsequent restatements that have come more recently.

Canon I. *Exergasia is complete when each member of the two
cola so corresponds to the other that one is neither
greater nor less than the other.*

Psalm 33:7:

Gathering together / as in a bottle / the waters of the sea
   and putting / in a storehouse / the abyss

Numbers 24:17:

It comes / a star / out of Jacob
   and it is raised / a scepter / out of Israel

Luke 1:47:

It magnifies / my soul / the Lord
   and it exults / my spirit / in God my savior

Canon II.   *Sometimes, however, in the second part of the total
             thought, the subject is not repeated, but by ellipsis
             is omitted, and by common usage is understood.*

Isaiah 1:18:

If your sins / be as scarlet / they shall be white as snow
  and if - - / red as a berry / they shall be as wool

Proverbs 7:19:

Whereas the husband / is not in his house
  - - / is gone on a distant journey

Psalm 129:3:

Upon my back plowed / the plowers
  cut their furrows long / - -

Canon III.   *Sometimes also, only part of the subject is missing.*

Psalm 37:30:

The mouth of the just / meditates / upon wisdom
  his tongue / speaks / justice

Here only part of the subject is repeated, viz., the suffix
"his," not indeed the whole subject.

Psalm 102:29:

Sons of your servants / will dwell
  and their seed / before your face will be

Isaiah 53:3:

And he / was wounded / for our transgressions
  - - / was bruised / for our sins

Canon IV.   *Examples appear, where in the repeated line of the
             exergasia, the predicate is omitted.*

Numbers 24:5:

How beautiful they are / your tents / O Jacob
  - - / your habitations / O Israel

Psalm 33:12:

Happy / that nation / whose Lord is God
  - - / that people / whom he willed in his inheritance

Psalm 123:4:[14]

It is sated / our soul / with the mockery of the arrogant
  - - / - - / with the contempt of the proud

Canon V.   *Sometimes only part of the predicate is missing.*

Psalm 57:10:[15]

I will acknowledge you / among the peoples / O Lord
  I will sing songs / among the nations / - -

Psalm 103:1:

Bless / O my soul / the Lord
   and - / all my innards / the name of his holiness

Psalm 129:7:

So that he does not fill up / his hands / the reaper
   or - - / his fists[16] / the binder of sheaves

Canon VI. *Some elements may be added in one member when not present in the other.*

Number 23:18:

Arise / Balak / and hear
   - - / son of Zippor / give ear to me

Psalm 102:29:

The children of your servants / - - / shall dwell
   and their seed / before your face / shall be established

Daniel 12:3:

And those who make people wise[17] / - - / shall shine /
                     as the brightness of the firmament
   and those who make just / many / - - / as the stars /
                                 forever

Canon VII. *Sometimes two propositions treating different things occur, but which, arranged by means of a distribution, can and should be interpreted as one general proposition.*

Psalm 94:9: [18]

The one who plants / the ear / does he not hear?
   the one who forms / the eye / does he not see?

Psalm 128:3:

Your wife / as a fruitful vine / in the company of your house
   your sons / as olive plantings / around your table

Sirach 3:16:

As a blasphemer is he / who forsakes / his father
   and cursed by the Lord / who incites to wrath / his mother

No one supposes here, that we believe the 'eye' to be the 'ear,' or the 'father' to be the 'mother,' etc., for these two propositions refine one generalization. Thus, in the first saying, the general proposition is this: 'God knows everything'; in the second: 'Fruitful will you be in marriage'; in the third: 'Unhappy is he who strikes his parents.'

Canon VIII. *Exergasia also occurs when the second proposition expresses the opposite of the first.*

126

Proverbs 15:8:

The sacrifice / of the wicked / is an abomination to the Lord
  and the prayers / of the upright / are his good pleasure

Proverbs 14:1:

The wisdom of women / builds a house
  and foolishness within her hands / destroys it

Proverbs 14:11:

The house / of the wicked / will be devastated
  and the tent / of the righteous / will flourish

Canon IX. *We also have examples of this kind of exergasia
          where whole propositions correspond, although the
          subject and predicate are for the most part not
          the same.*

Psalm 51:7:

Behold, in iniquity I was brought forth
  and in sin my mother conceived me

Psalm 119:168:

I have kept your injunctions and your testimonies
  because all my ways are before you

Jeremiah 8:22:

Is there no balm in Gilead, nor a doctor there?
  for why has the daughter of my people not come to health?

Canon X. *There occur even three-member exergasias.*

Psalm 1:1:

Blessed is the man / who has not gone / in the counsel /
                                   of the wicked
  and - - / - has not stood / in the way / of sinners
  and - - / - has not sat / in the seat / of scoffers

Psalm 130:5:

I have waited for the Lord
  my soul has waited
  and in his word have I hoped

Psalm 52:9:

Behold the man, who would not make God his help
  and - - - has confided in the multitude of his riches
  and - - - was hardy in his emptiness

        Schoettgen's canons cover all Lowth's categories:
I-VII & X are what Lowth calls "synonymous parallelism";
VIII is "antithetical parallelism"; and IX is "synthetic
parallelism." And like Lowth's third category, Canon IX is
the weakest: Psa 51:7 may perhaps fit but neither Psa 119:168

nor Jer 8:22 is exergasia. Schoettgen lists more types of
synonymous parallelism and in so doing anticipates the later
refinements of Lowth by G. B. Gray. In Gray's terminology,
Canons II-V would be "incomplete parallelism without compensation," and Canon VI "incomplete parallelism with compensation."[19]

But the real importance of Schoettgen's dissertation is
that it emphasizes the rhetorical nature of parallelism. We are
shown how parallelism strives after *totality* (Canon VII), which
is what Muilenburg continually stressed.[20] And we see too the
elliptical quality of Hebrew poetry (Canon II). This latter
observation has been made repeatedly by Dahood in his *Psalms I-
III* where he shows how all parts of speech and even suffixes
can do "double-duty" for more than one colon of poetry.[21]

Schoettgen thus deserves his rightful place alongside
Lowth. Not only does his work predate Lowth, but more important,
it shows how parallelism *functions* for the Hebrew poet.

1. In non-biblical studies, see *inter alia, New Rhetorics,*
   edited by Martin Steinman, Jr. (New York: Charles Scribner's
   Sons, 1967), especially the article by Wayne C. Booth, "The
   Revival of Rhetoric," 1-15; Thomas O. Sloan, "Restoration of
   Rhetoric to Literary Study," *ST*, 16 (1967), 91-97. For the
   Cornell tradition see Everett L. Hunt's "Introduction" to
   The Rhetorical Idiom, edited by Donald C. Bryant (New York:
   Cornell University Press, 1958), "Herbert Wichelns and the
   Cornell Tradition of Rhetoric as a Humane Study," 1-4.
   Other works defining modern rhetoric and illustrating the
   method of rhetorical criticism include William J. Brandt,
   The Rhetoric of Argumentation (New York: Bobbs-Merrill Co.,
   1970); Edward P. J. Corbett, *Classical Rhetoric for the
   Modern Student*, 2nd edition (New York: Oxford University
   Press, 1971); *Rhetorical Analyses of Literary Works*, edited
   by, (New York: Oxford University Press, 1969); Chaim Perel-
   man and L. Olbrechts-Tyteca, *The New Rhetoric*, tr. John
   Wilkinson and Purcell Weaver (Notre Dame, Indiana: University of Notre Dame Press, 1969).

2. Published in *JBL*, 88 (1969), 1-18.

3. Muilenburg was influenced early in his career by Richard G.
   Moulton's *The Literary Study of the Bible* (New York: D.C.
   Heath & Co., 1895), and his earliest work, *Specimens of Biblical Literature* (New York: Thomas Y. Crowell Co., 1923) is
   quite similar to it. Early journal articles reflect the
   same "Bible as literature" interest: "Literary Form in the
   Fourth Gospel," *JBL*, 51 (1932), 40-53; "The Literary Ap-
   proach--the Old Testament as Hebrew Literature," *JNABI*, 1
   (1933), 14-22. Later works show deeper insight into matters
   of structure and style: "The Literary Character of Isaiah
   34," *JBL*, 59 (1940), 339-365; "Psalm 47," *JBL*, 63 (1944),
   235-256; "A Study in Hebrew Rhetoric: Repetition and Style,"
   VT Supp., I (Copenhagen, 1953), 97-111; *IB: Isaiah*, 5,
   edited by G. A. Buttrick (Nashville: Abingdon-Cokesbury,
   1956), 381-773; "The Form and Structure of the Covenantal
   Formulations," *VT*, 9 (1959), 347-365; "The Linguistic and
   Rhetorical Usages of the Particle כי in the Old Testament,"
   HUCA, 32 (1961), 135-160; "A Liturgy on the Triumphs of
   Yahweh" in *Studia Biblica et Semitica*, [Essays in Honor of
   Theodoro C. Vriezen], (Wageningen: H. V. Veenman en Zonen
   N. V., 1966), 233-251.

4. Professor Brandt of the University of California, Berkeley
   is about to publish a book entitled *The Rhetoric of Poetry*.

5. Scholars of the Renaissance were fond of collecting figures
   of speech; cf. Richard E. Young and Alton L. Becker, "Toward
   a Modern Theory of Rhetoric: A Tagmemic Contribution" in *New
   Rhetorics*, 84. Young and Becker mention Henry Peacham's
   Garden of Eloquence (1577) which listed 184 schemes and
   tropes. A popular book of the same kind, only listing
   figures found in Scripture, was John Smith's *Mystery of
   Rhetoric Unveiled* (1657), Facsimile reprint (Menston,
   England: Scholar Press, 1969).

6. Figures of speech in the Bible were catalogued by E. W. Bullinger, *Figures of Speech Used in the Bible*, 2nd edition, (Grand Rapids: Baker Book House, 1969 [1st edition, 1898]), and Ed König, *Stilistik, Rhetorik, Poetik* (Leipzig: Dieterich'sche Verlagsbuchhandlung Theodor Weicher, 1900).

7. Two recent studies of structure in poetry are pioneering: Barbara Herrnstein Smith, *Poetic Closure* (Chicago: University of Chicago Press, 1970), and Leonard Nathan, "Conjectures on the Structural Principle of Vedic Poetry," forthcoming in the *Journal of Indian Philosophy*.

8. "Form Criticism and Beyond," 8.

9. *Ibid.*, 9-10; cf. *IB: Isaiah*, 385, 392. It is called "ring composition" by classicists; cf. J. A. Notopoulos, "Continuity and Interconnexion in Homeric Oral Composition," *TAPA*, 82 (1951), 81-101; Moulton called the same an "envelope figure;" *The Literary Study of the Bible*, 56-58.

10. "Form Criticism and Beyond," 11ff.

11. *Ibid.*, 11-12; cf. T. J. Meek, "The Structure of Hebrew Poetry," *JR*, 9 (1929), 549; T. H. Robinson, "Basic Principles of Hebrew Poetic Form" in *Festschrift Alfred Bertholet*, edited by Walter Baumgartner et. al. (Tübingen: J.C.B. Mohr [Paul Siebeck], 1950), 450; Charles F. Kraft, *The Strophic Structure of Hebrew Poetry* (Chicago: University of Chicago Press, 1938), 1-32.

12. "Form Criticism and Beyond," 14-16.

13. *Estudios De Poética Hebrea* (Barcelona: Juan Flors, 1963).

14. "Style, Irony and Authenticity in Jeremiah," *JBL*, 81 (1962), 44-54; "The Recovery of Poetic Passages of Jeremiah," *JBL*, 85 (1966), see especially "Theoretical Framework," 406-410; "Form and Word-play in David's Lament over Saul and Jonathan," *VT*, 20 (1970), 153-189.

15. "Form Criticism and Beyond," 8-9.

16. *Ibid.*, 10.

17. "Rhetorical Criticism and Formgeschichte: Some Methodological Considerations," *JBL*, 89 (1970), 423-424.

18. Muilenburg is aware of this; cf. "Form Criticism and Beyond," 9.

19. In BH^3, Ezekiel is 83 pages of text, Jeremiah 107 pages. Isaiah is 93 pages, but since it is taken to be two separate collections (1-39; 40-66), the size of each is substantially smaller than Jeremiah.

20. De Wette argued in his *Dissertatio critica* (1805) that Deuteronomy was the lawbook found in Josiah's temple (II Kings 22); cf. Eissfeldt, *The Old Testament: An Introduction*, tr. Peter Ackroyd, (New York and Evanston: Harper & Row, 1965), 171f. De Wette further believed that Deuteronomy must have been written shortly before it was found, which is what gave the D source a firm date in the 7th c. The date has since been pushed back. *Urdeuteronomium* is now thought to derive

from the time of Hezekiah (early 7th c.). The Deuteronomic
History, on the other hand, is dated in the time of Josiah
(late 7th c.); cf. D. N. Freedman, "Pentateuch" in *IDB*,
K-Q, 715-716; F. M. Cross, "The Structure of the Deuter-
onomic History" in *Perspectives in Jewish Learning*, 3
(Chicago: College of Jewish Studies, 1968), 9-24.

21. S. R. Driver, *ICC: Deuteronomy*, 3rd edition (Edinburgh:
T & T Clark, 1965; [1st edition 1895]), xciiff; John Bright,
"The Date of the Prose Sermons of Jeremiah," *JBL*, 70 (1951),
15-29; cf. Bright, *AB: Jeremiah* (Garden City: Doubleday &
Co., 1965), lxx-lxxiii.

22. Translated from the Latin by G. Gregory (Boston: Joseph T.
Buckingham, 1815).

23. Lecture XIX.

24. Lecture XVIII.

25. *Isaiah, Preliminary Dissertation and Notes*, 10th edition
(London: T. T. & J. Tegg, 1833).

26. *Lectures on the Sacred Poetry of the Hebrews*, 291.

27. *Jeremiah and Lamentations*, 3rd edition (London: Thomas Tegg
& Son, 1836).

28. My impression is that it takes slightly more to be poetic
than would presently be conceded, but nevertheless it is a
respectable piece of work for its day.

29. See *Fifty Years (and Twelve) of Classical Scholarship* (Oxford: Basil Blackwell, 1968), Chapter I i, "Homer and the
Analysts;" also Cedric Whitman, *Homer and the Heroic Tradition* (Cambridge: Harvard University Press, 1967), 4.

30. This is due mainly to the relocation of the Oracles to
Foreign Nations; in the *LXX* they follow 25:13 while the *MT*
places them in chapters 46-51.

31. A recently published thesis by J. Gerald Janzen entitled
Studies in the Text of Jeremiah (Cambridge: Harvard University Press, 1973) is the most recent example and contains
a useful introduction to earlier studies.

32. *Ibid.*, 2; Frank Cross, however, had recently argued that
the *MT* has a Babylonian provenance; see his article "The
History of the Biblical Text in the Light of Discoveries in
the Judaean Desert," *HThR*, 57 (1964), 297.

33. Wilhelm De Wette, *A Critical and Historical Introduction to
the Canonical Scriptures of the Old Testament*, II, 3rd
edition, translated and enlarged by Theodore Parker (Boston:
Little, Brown & Co., 1858), 416.

34. *Ibid.*, 366; cf. S. De Vries, "History of Biblical Criticism," *IDB*, A-D, 415.

35. De Wette, *A Critical and Historical Introduction...*, 403.

36. *Ibid.*, 396ff.

37. *Der Prophet Jeremia* (Leipzig: T. O. Weigel, 1862).

38. *Ibid.*, **xxxix**.

39. *HKAT: Das Buch Jeremia* (Göttingen: Vandenhoeck & Ruprecht, 1894), xv.

40. *HKAT: Das Buch Jesaia* (Göttingen: Vandenhoeck & Ruprecht, 1892); *Das Buch Jeremia* (Tübingen and Leipzig: Verlag von J. C. B. Mohr [Paul Siebeck], 1901).

41. *Die kleinen Propheten übersetzt und erklärt* (Berlin: Verlag von Georg Reimer, 1898); his views are carried over into the English *ICC* volumes on the Minor Prophets.

42. Julius Ley, *Grundzüge des Rhythmus des Vers- und Strophen-baues in der hebräischen Poesie* (Halle: Verlag der Buchhandlung des Waisenhauses, 1875); *Leitfaden der Metrik der hebräischen Poesie* (Halle: Verlag der Buchhandlung des Waisenhauses, 1887). Ed. Sievers, *Metrische Studien I* (Leipzig: B. G. Teubner, 1901).

43. He sided with Ley over Sievers choosing to count only accented syllables; see Duhm's article on "Poetical Literature" in *Encyclopaedia Biblica*, III, col. 3802. This article of Duhm's is not well-known because of a printing error attributing the article to a non-existent H. D.; see Key on p. xiv and cf. Israel Slotki, "Antiphony in Ancient Hebrew Poetry," *JQR*, 26 (1936), 199 note 3.

44. Duhm came to the conclusion that Jeremiah's words were written only in pentameter verse (3:2). After scanning Jer 2:2b as 3:2--a verse about which no one would quarrel-- he remarked: "In diesem Versmass sind sämtliche prophet-ischen Dichtungen Jeremias geschrieben;" *Jeremia*, 16. He then determined that Jeremiah's *ipsissima verba* amounted to 280 Massoretic verses, Baruch's memoirs 220 verses, while the chief contribution came from redactors, to whom the remaining 850 verses were assigned (xvi).

45. Sigmund Mowinckel, *Zur Komposition des Buches Jeremia*, (Oslo: J. Dybwad, 1914), 20ff.

46. Mowinckel, *Prophecy and Tradition* (Oslo: Jacob Dybwad, 1946), 61.

47. "Baruch's Roll," *ZAW*, 42 (1924), 209-221.

48. As a movement that is; for current use of the methodology see works cited in note 55.

49. William L. Holladay, "The Recovery of Poetic Passages of Jeremiah," 401-402.

50. Baba Bathra, 14b-15a.

51. *Prophecy and Tradition*, 61-62.

52. Janzen (*Studies in the Text of Jeremiah*, 135) concludes that the Greek text is superior, i.e., less developed. Muilen-burg thinks that the Greek order (Oracles to Foreign Nations follow 25:1-13) is more original because Jeremiah's personal word to Baruch comes at the end of chapter 51; cf. "Baruch

the Scribe" in *Proclamation and Presence* [Essays in Honour
of G. Henton Davies] (Richmond: John Knox Press, 1970), 235.

53. See T. H. Robinson's excellent article "Higher Criticism
and the Prophetic Literature," *ET* 50 (1938-39), 198-202.

54. In Jeremiah we no longer refer to Mowinckel's B and C material as "sources." Mowinckel himself modified this earlier
view in *Prophecy and Tradition*, 62. Recent Jeremianic
scholars are now questioning further the distinction between B and C; see William L. Holladay, "Prototypes and
Copies: A New Approach to the Poetry-Prose Problem in the
Book of Jeremiah," *JBL* 79 (1960), 354. E. W. Nicholson in
Preaching to the Exiles (New York: Schocken Books, 1970)
adopts a traditio-historical point of view (see ahead pp.
14-16) and takes all the prose simply as "tradition."

55. G. W. Anderson makes the point very well: "It is perhaps
not superfluous to state the obvious fact that the scientific study of the Old Testament must begin with the material which we now have in the form in which we now have it;"
"Some Aspects of the Uppsala School of Old Testament Study,"
HThR 43 (1950), 248. Klaus Koch agrees; cf. *The Growth of
the Biblical Tradition*, tr. S. M. Cupitt (New York: Charles
Scribner's Sons, 1969), 77-78.

56. It also goes by the names of *Gattungsforschung* and
Gattungsgeschichte; in New Testament studies, following
Dibelius, it is *Formgeschichte*.

57. *Genesis*, 7th edition (Göttingen: Vandenhoeck & Ruprecht,
1966); *Einleitung in die Psalmen*. Completed by J. Begrich,
2nd edition (Göttingen: Vandenhoeck & Ruprecht, 1966).

58. Grobel, "Form Criticism" in *IDB*, E-J, 320, implies this in
his statement of definition.

59. "The Close of Micah: A Prophetical Liturgy" in *What Remains
of the Old Testament and Other Essays*, tr. A. K. Dallas
(New York: Macmillan Co., 1928), 116.

60. Hugo Gressmann, "Die Literarische Analyse Deuterojesajas,"
ZAW 34 (1914), 254-297; Johannes Lindblom, "Die prophet-
ische Orakelformel," *Die literarische Gattung der prophet-
ischen Literatur* (Uppsala: A-B Lundequistska Bokhandeln,
1924)--for a summary see Claus Westermann, *Basic Forms of
Prophetic Speech*, tr. Hugh Clayton White (Philadelphia:
Westminster Press, 1967), 34-36; Walter Baumgartner, *Die
Klagegedichte des Jeremia* (Giessen: Verlag von Alfred
Töpelmann, 1917).

61. *Deutsche Literaturzeitung*, 29 (1906), cols. 1797-1800; 1861-
1866; tr. later as "Fundamental Problems of Hebrew Literary
History" in *What Remains of the Old Testament*, 57-68.

62. "Fundamental Problems of Hebrew Literary History," 61-62.

63. Yet he was not deficient in his psychological understanding;
cf. "The Secret Experiences of the Prophets," *The Expositor*,
9th series, 1 (1924), 356-366; 427-435; 2 (1924), 23-32.

64. See James Muilenburg, "The Gains of Form Criticism in Old
Testament Studies," *ET* 71 (1959-60), 229-233.

65. See *The Legends of Genesis* which is a translation of the Introduction to his *Genesis* commentary (New York: Schocken Books, 1966), 38. Gunkel's evolutionary views on the prophets manifest the same belief; cf. p. 8.

66. "Fundamental Problems of Hebrew Literary History," 60.

67. Eduard Norden, in his *Antike Kuntsprosa*, I (Stuttgart: B. G. Teubner, 1958) argued that Buffon's famous saying, "le style est l'homme même" could not be applied to men of antiquity: "Der Stil war im Altertum nicht der Mensch selbst, sondern ein Gewand, das er nach Belieben wechseln konnte," 11-12. Cf. Gunkel, "Fundamental Problems of Hebrew Literary History," 58-59.

68. *Ibid.*, 60.

69. Koch, *The Growth of the Biblical Tradition*, 3ff; Gene M. Tucker, *Form Criticism of the Old Testament* (Philadelphia: Fortress Press, 1971), 1ff.

70. This latest work was completed by Joachim Begrich; (see note 57). Gunkel's earlier works included *Ausgewählte Psalmen übersetzt und erklärt*, 3rd edition (Göttingen: Vandenhoeck & Ruprecht, 1911) and an article in *Old Testament Essays* entitled "The Poetry of the Psalms: Its Literary History and Its Application to the Dating of the Psalms," 118-142.

71. The influence of the Grimm brothers is best seen in his *Das Märchen im Alten Testament* (Tübingen: J. C. B. Mohr [Paul Siebeck], 1921) where he traces the genre of the folktale throughout the Old Testament. Olrik published articles showing how oral saga follows regular laws of expression: "Episke Love i Folke-digtningen," *Danske Studier*, 5 (1908), 69-89, and the later German article, "Epische Gesetze der Volksdichtung," *ZDA*, 51 (1909), 1-12. This latter article was used liberally by Gunkel in the 3rd edition of his *Genesis*; cf. xxxvi-liv.

72. *Legends of Genesis*, 43.

73. Koch, *The Growth of the Biblical Tradition*, 210; the same was done by Mowinckel; cf. *Prophecy and Tradition*, 45.

74. "Fundamental Problems of Hebrew Literary History," 62.

75. Gunkel says, "Just as we see the development of our children's minds in the gradually increasing amount that they can take in at a time, so we can trace one feature of the growth of civilization in the gradual increase of the literary units in Israel;" "Fundamental Problems of Hebrew Literary History," 63.

76. In explaining the reason for the long dialogues in Job, Herder says, "We are accustomed to prefer brevity in the dialogue, and a more obvious sequence of ideas, than we find here. The Orientals in their social intercourse heard each other quietly through, and were even fond of prolonged discourses, especially in verse;" *The Spirit of Hebrew Poetry*, I, tr. James Marsh (Burlington: Edward Smith, 1833), 81.

77. "Schriftstellerei und Formensprache der Propheten" in *Die Propheten* (Göttingen: Vandenhoeck & Ruprecht, 1917), 116.

78. "Propheten II B. Propheten Israels seit Amos," RGG^2, IV, col. 1548.

79. "Schriftstellerei und Formensprache der Propheten," 116-117.

80. *Ibid.*, 112: "Inzwischen aber hatte sich die Zeit verändert; das allmählich zu höherer Kultur heranreifende Israel begann immer mehr zu schreiben. Und auch die Prophetie war, ... eine andere geworden: ihr Gesichtskreis umfassender, ihre Einsichten tiefer, ihre Ziele weiter. So haben sich die Propheten der Schriftstellerei zugewandt."

81. Note how Mowinckel gives customary lip-service to the form-critical maxim of brief units when discussing this passage, but goes on to say that the passage makes more sense when treated as a unity; *Prophecy and Tradition*, 56-57.

82. "Schriftstellerei und Formensprache der Propheten," 117-118.

83. Gunkel thought that Psalm 1 was an imitation of this poem; *The Psalms: A Form-Critical Introduction* [Facet Books, Biblical Series, # 19] (Philadelphia: Fortress Press, 1967), 27.

84. *Legends of Genesis*, 80.

85. "Fundamental Problems of Hebrew Literary History," 64.

86. Theophile J. Meek, "The Poetry of Jeremiah," *JQR*, New Series, 14 (1923-24), 283.

87. Herder spoke of "pearls from the depths of the ocean loosely arranged;" cf. *The Spirit of Hebrew Poetry*, I, 81.

88. So Tucker, *Form Criticism of the Old Testament*, 64.

89. "The impression he gains is one of extreme disarray;" *Jeremiah*, lvi.

90. See the comments of Israel Slotki as he contrasts treatments by Gunkel and Charles Briggs on Psalm 136; cf. "The Stichometry and Text of the Great Hallel," *JThS*, 29 (1928), 255-256.

91. *Basic Forms of Prophetic Speech*.

92. *Ibid.*, 26, where Westermann quotes Gunkel with approval; cf. Gunkel, "Fundamental Problems of Hebrew Literary History," 60.

93. Westermann did an earlier study of the salvation speech entitled "The Way of the Promise through the Old Testament" in *The Old Testament and Christian Faith*, edited by Bernhard W. Anderson (New York: Harper & Row, 1963), 200-224.

94. *Basic Forms of Prophetic Speech*, 115-128.

95. Earlier source critics de-emphasized this aspect of prophecy. Gunkel, on the other hand takes Deut 18:22 seriously; cf. "The Secret Experiences of the Prophets," I, 433.

96. *Basic Forms of Prophetic Speech*, 175.

97. In Amos 4:1-2; Micah 3:1-2,4; 9-12 it is a call to hear, while in Micah 2:1-4 the word "Woe" has been extrapolated to meet the need; other speeches are without an "Introduction;" cf. *ibid.*, 174-175.

98. *Ibid.*, 137.

99. In 22:24-27, what did Coniah do wrong? See also 22:30, 37:17.

100. 20:1-6; 28:12-16.

101. This problem is noticed by Tucker and causes him to reject such detailed structures; cf. *Form Criticism of the Old Testament*, 64, note 94.

102. Gunkel believed that most of the genres used by the prophets did not originate with the prophets but were borrowed and appropriated to a new use. This they did because of a burning desire to win over the hearts of people who had a natural receptivity to such forms: "Für diese Geschichte aber ist die grundlegende Erkenntnis diese, dass die meisten der genannten Gattungen nicht ursprünglich p[rophet]isch sind, sondern dass die Prophetie fremde Gattungen in weitestem Umfange aufgenommen hat...Und auch der Grund, warum sie das geworden sind, ist deutlich: es ist der brennende Wunsch der P[rophet]en, Macht über das Gemüt ihres Volkes zu gewinnen, der sie dazu getrieben hat;" "Propheten II B. Propheten Israels seit Amos," col. 1550.

103. *Basic Forms of Prophetic Speech*, 199-204.

104. For a study of this term, see James Limburg, "The Root ריב and the Prophetic Lawsuit Speeches," *JBL*, 88 (1969), 291-304.

105. *Einleitung in die Psalmen*, 329.

106. *Ibid.*, 364-365.

107. "The Covenant Lawsuit in the Prophets," *JBL*, 78 (1959), 285-295. Preceding Huffmon B. Gemser did an earlier study entitled "The 'RĪB' or Controversy-Pattern in Hebrew Mentality" in *Wisdom in Israel and in the Ancient Near East* [VT Supp., 3] (Leiden: E. J. Brill, 1955), 120-137.

108. *Law and Covenant in Israel and the Ancient Near East* (Pittsburgh: Presbyterian Board of Colportage, 1955).

109. See William L. Holladay, "Jeremiah and Moses: Further Observations," *JBL*, 85 (1966), 17-27. For a separate analysis of Deut 32 as a lawsuit, see G. Ernest Wright, "The Lawsuit of God: A Form-Critical Study of Deuteronomy 32" in *Israel's Prophetic Heritage*, edited by Bernhard W. Anderson and Walter Harrelson (New York: Harper & Brothers, 1962), 26-67.

110. "Le 'RĪB-Pattern' Réquisitoire Prophétique sur la Rupture de l'Alliance," *Biblica*, 43 (1962), 172-196.

111. "The Prophetic Reproach," *JBL*, 90 (1971), 267-278.

112. In Amos 4:6-12 the phrase "yet you did not return to me" repeated five times impresses him as a structural feature;

cf. *ibid.*, 267-268.

113. Perhaps this is why Huffmon leaves out these verses.

114. In Jeremiah, Huffmon limits the pericope to 2:4-13; Harvey
takes all of 2:2-37, and Gemser extends the lawsuit all
the way to 4:4! With Deut 32, Huffmon takes the whole
poem, for which he is to be commended, while Harvey omits
vv. 26-43 leaving a good bit of the poem unexplained.

115. *Einleitung in die Psalmen*, 364; cf. Huffmon, "The Covenant
Lawsuit in the Prophets," 288.

116. *Ibid.*

117. In Huffmon's analysis, besides the admission that compo-
nents are in a different order, it is not clear what difference exists between the speech of the plantiff (II) and
the accusation to the defendant (II C 1). Huffmon considers v. 5 as "accusation" (p. 288), and I would ask if this
doesn't continue on through to v. 8. The only verse where
Yahweh speaks in the first person about his mighty acts is
v. 7. Also where is the indictment? And why does v. 13
reiterate the accusation of v. 9? It is clear that Yahweh
is accusing Israel of wrong--yes even breach of covenant--
but a comparison of the Jeremianic text with the Gunkel-
Huffmon outline is by no means clear. With Harvey the
situation is much worse. Beginning in the middle of his
"Indictment" (III) and continuing through the "Declaration
of Guilt" (V) there is no direct correspondence to the
Jeremianic text. The only part of Harvey's outline which
rings true--and here it does so in both Jer 2:5ff and
Deut 32:4ff--is the first part of the Indictment, where it
is clear in both texts that Yahweh's gracious deeds are
followed by Israel's ingratitude. But this correspondence
will not support Harvey's entire scheme. To begin with,
the inclusion of vv. 14-19 is doubtful since this is generally taken to be a separate poem (so Gunkel; cf. p. 8
above). If it is to be included, then Yahweh's goodness
and Israel's ingratitude is hardly the main thought. The
point here is rather the futility of continued political
alliances with Egypt and Assyria (vv. 18-19) especially in
light of past failures (vv. 15-17). Within vv. 20-28, we
have such a contrast in 21 alone, but nowhere else in the
unit. In vv. 29-30 I do not see the contrast at all. As
for IV--The Uselessness of Ritual Expiation--there is nothing in vv. 26-28 which stands out from the rest of the
chapter. The mention of idolatry appears in vv. 5, 8, 11,
13, 19, 20 and 23 in one form or another--indeed it is the
theme of the entire chapter. The same is true with V--
The Declaration of Guilt: it is mentioned in vv. 7, 9, 13,
19, 22, 23 etc. There is thus no reason to isolate vv.
31-37 as a specific reference to judgment and destruction.

118. Muilenburg, "Form Criticism and Beyond," 5, says that
2:1-4:4 contains *several* examples of the lawsuit, although
he agrees that the biblical text does not give a complete
reproduction of this genre as it was carried on in the
courtyard. He calls them "imitations of a Gattung." But
is even this necessary? Only after we provide a better
analysis of structure can this question be answered.

119. "Jeremiah's Lawsuit with God," *Int.*, 17 (1963), 280-287.

120. "The Prophetic Summons to Repentance," *ZAW*, 83 (1971), 30-48.

121. "The Form and Significance of the Call Narratives," *ZAW*, 77 (1965), 297-323.

122. Raitt says, "In the transition from an oral to a written representation--to say nothing of the continual tendency to re-work early speech elements to fit the needs of a later situation--any hypothetical speech-form is subject to the possibility of modifications and adaptations;" "The Prophetic Summons to Repentance," 37. It is one thing to say this when we have a known prototype and some known deviations, but in the absence of both, such reasoning goes in a circle.

123. In the call of Jeremiah, the "sign" is actually not present; vv. 9-10 can hardly be forced into this category. In the call of Isaiah, besides the modification which Habel admits for the beginning, the Introductory Word (II) does not fit the text. The words of the seraphim are to each other, not to Isaiah. Secondly, the "Woe is me" phrase (v. 5) comes much closer to an objection than "How long, O Yahweh" (v. 11). In any case, Isaiah does not offer an objection like Moses and Jeremiah; he accepts the call readily: "Here am I, send me" (v. 8). Also, the final Sign (VI) is missing in Isaiah's call as it is in the call of Jeremiah. We note too a problem of non-descript categories like those of Westermann, e.g., the Introductory Word can cover almost anything. If we are asked to take the call as a separate genre, we must insist that outlines be rejected which do not fit the text. Muilenburg issues a warning in this regard to those who would overly conventionalize the prophetic calls; cf. "The 'Office' of the Prophet in Ancient Israel" in *The Bible in Modern Scholarship*, edited by J. Philip Hyatt (Nashville & New York: Abingdon Press, 1965), 89.

124. "Formen und Stoffe," *Deuterojesaja (Jesaja 40-55) Stilkritisch Untersucht* [BZAW, 37] (Giessen: Verlag von Alfred Topelmann, 1923), 102-142.

125. Gustav Hölscher, *Die Propheten* (Leipzig: J. C. Hinrichs'sche Buchhandlung, 1914). Hölscher takes Jeremiah too as an ecstatic, frequently appearing in the temple court where he is under the discipline of the priests (Jer 20:2; 29:26). Like other prophets of his day he could appear mad and disturbed (29:26ff), and in ecstasy could hear sounds and see images (3:21; 4:13,15; etc.). Jeremiah also does not always have ready access to the word of Yahweh; sometimes he must wait many days for the spirit to grip him; cf. 294.

126. See Martin Noth, "History and the Word of God in the Old Testament," *BJRL*, 32 (1950), 197ff; also Herbert Huffmon, "Prophecy in the Mari Letters," *BA* 31 (1968), 101-124.

127. I Kings 20:3,5; II Kings 9:18.

128. Jeremiah later distinguished himself from the false prophets by claiming to have stood in Yahweh's council where he

was then given Yahweh's message. Others were quick enough
to run and deliver, but they had not been sent (Jer 23:
18, 21-22).

129. Westermann, *Basic Forms of Prophetic Speech*, 98ff; James
F. Ross, "The Prophet as Yahweh's Messenger" in *Israel's
Prophetic Heritage*, 98-107.

130. Westermann, *Basic Forms of Prophetic Speech*, 111.

131. "The Poetry of Jeremiah," 281-282.

132. T. H. Robinson, *Prophecy and the Prophets in Ancient
Israel*, 2nd edition (London: Gerald Duckworth & Co.,
1953), 52-53.

133. So Klaus Koch, *The Growth of the Biblical Tradition*,
201ff, and Martin Kessler, "Form-Critical Suggestions on
Jer 36," *CBQ*, 28 (1966), 390.

134. "The Secret Experiences of the Prophets," I, 434: "It is
clear that many of these narratives [i.e., the narratives
of Elijah and Elisha] are popular tales, for it is significant that the biography of Jeremiah, included in his
book, *which is extraordinarily faithful* [italics mine],
contains no such magical deeds concerning him."

135. "Baruch the Scribe," 233. Muilenburg here cites Kessler
for support, but as we have just shown (note 133), Kessler
stated that the material was legend.

136. Just to read Koch's description of the material is to wonder why he uses the term. He refers to this prose as "the
first prophetic biography composed in Israel" and agrees
it is completely reliable; cf. *The Growth of the Biblical
Tradition*, 204. He also agrees that the "legends" were
not collected by a circle of the prophet's disciples--
which was the case with the Elijah-Elisha legends--and
passed on then by oral transmission (p. 203). How then
can he call such "legend" and say on p. 201 that it is
similar to the Elijah-Elisha narratives?

137. Mowinckel pointed out quite rightly that the prophetic
literature has no real counterpart in the literature of
the *ANE*; see his article, "Literature," *IDB*, K-Q, 142.

138. Westermann, *Basic Forms of Prophetic Speech*, 115ff.

139. Of course the form-critics could always say that by Jeremiah's time the forms were breaking up. Gunkel believed
that forms have their own history: they are born, they
flourish for a time, then they decay and die, after which
come the imitations; cf. Fundamental Problems of Hebrew
Literary History," 65-66. Von Rad in fact says this quite
specifically about Jeremiah: "In Jeremiah all the forms of
expression to be found in classical prophecy are obviously
breaking up;" cf. Gerhard von Rad, *Old Testament Theology*
II, tr. D. M. G. Stalker (Edinburgh & London: Oliver and
Boyd, 1967), 193. Yet it should be noted that Gunkel's
desire to write a history of Israelite literature died
with him and is now forgotten; see Koch, *The Growth of the
Biblical Tradition*, 103. Furthermore, the so-called
"forms of classical prophecy" have yet to be shown.

140. There are three good surveys of this school: G. W. Anderson, "Some Aspects of the Uppsala School of Old Testament Study;" C. R. North, "The Place of Oral Tradition in the Growth of the Old Testament," *ET*, 61 (1949-50), 292-296; and Walter E. Rast, *Tradition History and the Old Testament* (Philadelphia: Fortress Press, 1972).

141. *Studien zum Hoseabuche* (Uppsala: Lundequistska Bokhandeln, 1935).

142. Geo Widengren, *Literary and Psychological Aspects of the Hebrew Prophets* (Uppsala: Lundequistska Bokhandeln, 1948), 68ff; 122. See also Solomon Gandz, "Oral Tradition in the Bible" in *Jewish Studies in Memory of George A. Kohut* (New York: Alexander Kohut Memorial Foundation, 1935), 251ff, and James Muilenburg, "Baruch the Scribe," 215ff.

143. J. Weingreen, "Oral Torah and Written Records" in *Holy Book and Holy Tradition*, edited by F. F. Bruce and E. G. Rupp (Grand Rapids: Eerdmans Press, 1968), 67. The suggestion by Moses Buttenwieser in *The Prophets of Israel* (New York: Macmillan Co., 1914), 133, that Jeremiah was unable to write, is not at all implied by Jer 36.

144. See Edwin Good's "The Composition of Hosea," *SEÅ*, 31 (1966), 21-63.

145. Harris Birkeland, *Zum Hebräischen Traditionswesen* (Oslo: Jacob Dybwad, 1938), 43ff; Mowinckel, *Prophecy and Tradition*, 61. For a summary of Engnell's late study on Jeremiah and the method he employed, see T. R. Hobbs, "Some Remarks on the Composition and Structure of the Book of Jeremiah," *CBQ*, 34 (1972), 263ff.

146. *Ibid.*, 43.

147. See p. 5.

148. The views of Engnell and Claus Rietzschel (see note following) are conveniently summarized by Hobbs, "Some Remarks on the Composition and Structure of the Book of Jeremiah," 267ff.

149. See *Das Problem der Urrolle* (Gütersloh: Gütersloher Verlagshaus Gerd Mohn, 1966), 17.

150. Kessler, "Form-Critical Suggestions on Jer 36," 389; Hobbs, "Some Remarks on the Composition and Structure of the Book of Jeremiah," 267-268.

151. The comment of Edwin Good ("The Composition of Hosea," 21) is to the point: "We have too often been satisfied merely to apply our own canons of logic to the Old Testament, and we are still groping after an understanding of the Old Testament's own logic."

152. *Das Problem der Urrolle*, 24.

153. As proposed by Martin Kessler in his unpublished dissertation, "A Prophetic Biography: A Form-Critical Study of Jer 26-29, 32-45" (Ph.D. thesis, Brandeis, 1965).

154. Leon Liebreich, "The Compilation of the Book of Isaiah,"
JQR, 46 (1956), 259-277; 47 (1956), 114-138.

155. Professor Lohfink kindly sent me a copy of his *Lectures
in Deuteronomy*, tr. S. McEvenue S. J., (Rome: Pontifical
Biblical Institute, 1968), in which he notes inclusios in
Deut 14:1-21 and 14:22-15:23; cf. 24, 26. But there are
others. Chapter 12 is framed by the words חשמרון לעשות
(12:1) and חשמרו לעשות (13:1). The *RSV* and *NEB* correctly
take the latter as the concluding verse of chapter 12
(against both *MT* and the *LXX*!). Also the liturgical-type
injunction found duplicated in 6:6-9 and 11:18-20 (with
the center sections inverted!) may likewise be an inclusio for 6-11. Two other inclusios are overlooked by
Lohfink due to his view that Deuteronomy in its final
form was modeled on an archive (*Lectures*, 7-9). According to this view four documents are placed side by side,
each being introduced by a superscription. The four
superscriptions would be 1:1; 4:44; 28:69 and 33:1. But
4:44 and 28:69 are *not* superscriptions. They are *subscriptions*--or in the case of 4:44 part of a subscrip-
tion--which link up to 1:1-5 to make inclusios. It is
true that the *LXX* takes *MT* 28:69 as 29:1, but Driver is
quite correct in taking the verse as a subscription. He
says it looks back to 5-26,28 and not ahead to 29ff; cf.
S. R. Driver, *Deuteronomy*, 319. To show further that this
verse makes an inclusio with 1:1-5 we need only notice the
following key words: אלה הדברים (1:1) and אלה דברי (28:
69); also בארץ מואב in both 1:5 and 28:69. This suggests
then that Deuteronomy was not modeled on an archive but
had instead a rhetorical form even at this late stage.
We also believe that 4:44-49 is yet another inclusio with
1:1-5. Here we lack the support of Driver and others
(although Driver does admit that 4:44-49 is "superfluous"
after 1:1-5; *Deuteronomy*, 79) but a close look at both
pericopes will show that they are indeed intended as a
frame for 1-4. 1:1-5 ends with את־התורה הזאת (this law)
while 4:44-49 begins with וזאת התורה (And this is the
law). The terms are nicely inverted too. Also there is
mention of the "Arabah" at the beginning of 1:1-5 and at
the end of 4:44-49. And both pericopes have "beyond the
Jordan" at beginning and end. It is clear I think that
4:44-49 looks *back* to the events of chapters 2-3 just as
28:69 looks back to the covenant contained in 1-28. Both
pericopes (1:1-5 and 4:44-49) reiterate the sojourn from
Horeb to Moab, the high point being the victories over
Sihon and Og. These victories are described more fully
in chapters 2-3. Thus we conclude that both 4:44-49 and
28:69 were meant to form inclusios with 1:1-5 giving Deut
1-28 an overall rhetorical form.

156. Mitchell Dahood, *AB: Psalms I-III* (Garden City: Doubleday
& Co., I, 1966; II, 1968; III, 1970). See I, 5 and in-
dices for specific passages.

157. "The Structure of Job 3," *Biblica* 49 (1968), 503-508.
The inclusio of Hosea 8:9-13 is shown in the Prolegomenon
to G. B. Gray's *The Forms of Hebrew Poetry* (New York:
KTAV Publishing House, 1972), xxxvi-xxxvii.

158. Albert Condamin, *Le Livre de Jérèmie*, 3rd edition (Paris:
Librairie Lecoffre, 1936).

142

159. *The Forms of Hebrew Poetry*, xxxvi.

160. Also called "introverted parallelism" by John Jebb in his
     Sacred Literature (London: T. Cadell & W. Davies, 1820),
     53ff, and John Forbes in *The Symmetrical Structure of
     Scripture* (Edinburgh: T & T Clark, 1854), 35ff. Roman
     Catholic scholars call the larger panels "concentric
     structures; so Dennis J. McCarthy, "Moses' Dealings with
     Pharaoh: Ex 7,8--10,27," *CBQ* 27 (1965), 338. Lohfink re-
     fers to the same as "chiastische" or "konzentrische" in
     Das Hauptgebot (Rome: Pontifical Biblical Institute,
     1963), 67, 181, *et passim*. In his *Lectures in Deuter-
     onomy* the translated term is "concentric inclusion;" cf.
     11, *et passim*. Aaron Mirsky considers the chiasmus as an
     expanded form of "anadiplosis," which he says is used
     often in the Mishnah, and even defined elsewhere in the
     Talmud (Vide Nazir, ii); see "The Origin of the *Anadiplo-
     sis* in Hebrew Literature" [Hebrew with English summary],
     Tarbiz 28 (1958-59), 171-180; cf. iv.

161. See Sheridan Baker, *The Complete Stylist* (New York:
     Thomas Y. Crowell Co., 1966), 4, 326; Edward P. J. Cor-
     bett, *Classical Rhetoric for the Modern Student*, 478.
     Brandt uses the Latin term, "commutatio;" cf. *The Rheto-
     ric of Argumentation*, 162-163.

162. Lund argued that the *LXX* translators showed awareness of
     a chiastic structure in Amos 2:14-16 by choosing words
     which were euphonic; cf. "The Presence of Chiasmus in the
     New Testament," *JR* 10 (1930), 92. It has also been argued
     that chiastic structures appear in some Qumran documents;
     cf. Barbara Thiering, "The Poetic Forms of the Hodayot,"
     JSS 8 (1963), 189-209; Jacob Licht, "An Analysis of the
     Treatise of the Two Spirits in DSD" in *Scripta Hiero-
     solymitana* IV, edited by C. Rabin and Y. Yadin (Jerusalem:
     Magnes Press, 1965), 88-100; Ed. Parish Sanders, "Chiasmus
     and the Translation of I Q Hodayot VII, 26-27," *RQ* 23
     (1968), 427-431.

163. By Jebb and Forbes; see above, note 160.

164. *Chiasmus in the New Testament* (Chapel Hill: University of
     North Carolina Press, 1942).

165. *Outline Studies in the Book of Revelation* [Covenant Graded
     Lessons], (Chicago: Covenant Book Concern, 1935), 4;
     Chiasmus in the New Testament, viii.

166. *Chiasmus in the New Testament*, 93.

167. See *inter alia*, Dennis J. McCarthy, "Moses' Dealings with
     Pharaoh: Ex 7,8--10,27;" Stephen Bertman, "Symmetrical
     Design in the Book of Ruth," *JBL* 84 (1965), 165-168;
     Bezalel Porten, "The Structure and Theme of the Solomon
     Narrative (I Kings 3-11)," *HUCA* 37 (1967), 93-128; Norman
     K. Gottwald, "Samuel, Book of," *EJ* 14, 796-797.

168. In Isaiah, see Luis Alonso-Schökel, *Estudios de Poética
     Hebrea*, 319-336; Fredrik Holmgren, "Chiastic Structure
     in Isaiah LI 1-11," *VT* 19 (1969), 196-201; elsewhere in
     the Prophets: William L. Holladay, "Chiasmus, the Key to
     Hosea XII 3-6," *VT* 16 (1966), 53-64; R. Pesch, "Zur kon-
     zentrischen Struktur von Jona 1," *Biblica* 47 (1966),

577-581; John T. Willis, "The Structure of Micah 3-5 and the Function of Micah 5:9-14 in the Book," *ZAW* 81 (1969), 191-214.

169. See *Das Hauptgebot*. In *Lectures in Deuteronomy*, 15, Lohfink shows a chiasmus of *speaker* in Deut 1:20-31. This is an important discovery as we will see after having looked at many of the same type of structures in Jeremiah.

170. The remarks of Hans Dieter Betz in *JBL* 89 (1970), 126 are over-reactionary to an author's views of inspiration, and thus basically uncritical. Less scholarly still are the remarks of John Elliott, *CBQ* 34 (1972), 371.

171. Gordis says of chiasmus: "it is the key to many difficult passages in Biblical literature, the value of which have not yet been fully explored;" cf. "On Methodology in Biblical Exegesis," *JQR* 61 (1970), 115.

172. "Style, Irony and Authenticity in Jeremiah," 45, 51-52.

173. "The Recovery of Poetic Passages of Jeremiah," 434.

174. *Chiasmus in the New Testament*, 25.

175. The most complete restatement is by G. B. Gray in *The Forms of Hebrew Poetry*.

176. 2 Vols., I (Leipzig & Dresden: Christoph. Hekelli B. Sons, Booksellers, 1733); II (Leipzig & Dresden: Fridericum Hekel Booksellers, 1742). In the first volume is a treatise entitled "Exergasia Sacra" (Dissertatio VI), 1249-1263, in which he discusses his insights into Hebrew poetry.

177. John Smith, *Mystery of Rhetoric Unveiled* (1657), 221-222; Sheridan Baker, *The Complete Stylist* (1966), 327.

178. See especially, Perelman and Olbrechts-Tyteca, *The New Rhetoric*, and Brandt, *The Rhetoric of Argumentation*.

179. William L. Holladay, "The Recovery of Poetic Passages of Jeremiah," 403-404; cf. W. F. Albright, "The Old Testament and Canaanite Language and Literature," *CBQ* 7 (1945), 19-22; *Yahweh and the Gods of Canaan* (Garden City: Doubleday & Co., 1968), 1-52.

180. Muilenburg retains "strophe" because of its wide usage, but also agrees that it has these unfortunate connotations; "Form Criticism and Beyond," 12.

181. One exception is Condamin's work on Lamentations 1-2 where his concentric structure had the advantage of being found within an acrostic. The acrostic provides a valuable control for stanza division, and thus Condamin's insight is substantiated; cf. "Symmetrical Repetitions in *Lamentations* Chapters I and II," *JThS* 7 (1905), 137-140.

182. Lowth's position was that Hebrew poetry was indeed metrical, but since the true pronunciation was lost when Hebrew ceased to be a living language, we are now unable to recover the original meter; *Lectures on the Sacred Poetry of the Hebrews*, 44.

183. David Noel Freedman, "Archaic Forms in Early Hebrew Poetry," *ZAW* 72 (1960), 101-107; more recently see the Prolegomenon to Gray's *The Forms of Hebrew Poetry*, vii-xlvi; "The Structure of Psalm 137" in *Near Eastern Studies in Honor of William Foxwell Albright*, edited by Hans Goedicke (Baltimore: John Hopkins Press, 1971), 187-205; "Acrostics and Metrics in Hebrew Poetry," *HThR* 65 (1972), 367-392. See also Mitchell Dahood, "A New Metrical Pattern in Biblical Poetry," *CBQ* 29 (1967), 574-579.

1. Liebreich, "The Compilation of the Book of Isaiah," 276-277.

2. See note 155 on p. 141.

3. W. F. Albright, *Yahweh and the Gods of Canaan*, 1ff.

4. *Studies in Deuteronomy* (London: SCM Press, 1963).

5. "Deuteronomy," *IDB*, A-D, 836.

6. *Studies in Deuteronomy*, 14.

7. See Moshe Weinfeld, "Deuteronomy--the Present State of Inquiry," *JBL* 86 (1967), 249-262.

8. *Lectures in Deuteronomy*, 6.

9. *Ibid.*, 7.

10. See note 155 on p. 141.

11. *Lectures in Deuteronomy*, 5.

12. Von Rad took the "original Deuteronomy" to end at chapter 26 after the formula of commitment to the covenant (vv. 16-19); cf. "Deuteronomy," *IDB*, 831. Driver includes chapter 28; cf. *Deuteronomy*, ii. Our inclusio tying 1-28 together supports Driver. Chs. 29-34 form a supplement.

13. So Freedman, "Pentateuch," *IDB*, K-Q, 715.

14. *BDB* under חָנָה, 244.

15. *BDB*, 633. The name "Neriah" does not occur in the OT outside Jeremiah, and since Baruch is also "son of Neriah, son of Mahseiah" (32:12) we can assume he and Seriah were brothers.

16. He is recorded, however, as going in the 4th year of Zedekiah (51:59), which means that the rest of the biographical prose (37-44) must have followed him at a later time. Since there was frequent travel between Jerusalem and Babylon (cf. chapter 29), this would not be an impossibility.

17. Cross has come to this conclusion as a result of his study of text recensions; cf. note 32 on p. 131. For a recent challenge to Cross, however, see George Howard, "Frank Cross and Recensional Criticism," *VT* 21 (1971), 440-450.

18. There it comes in 28:59-64.

19. So Janzen on the *MT*; see *Studies in the Text of Jeremiah*, 135.

20. While commentators generally take 1-25:13 as the first major collection, Rudolph (*Jeremia*, xix) recognizes that

21-24 comes from a later period than 1-20. Rietzschel takes 1-20 as an *Überlieferungsblock* within 1-25:15 (*Das Problem der Urrolle*, 17, 128). He also thinks that Jeremiah's personal word to Baruch (ch 45) stood originally after 20:18.

21. *Old Testament Theology* II, 204.

22. This was required by the Massoretes; see Liebreich, "The Compilation of the Book of Isaiah," 277.

23. Muilenburg, "Baruch the Scribe," 231; Bright, *Jeremiah*, lvii-lviii, 162-163; S. R. Driver, *The Book of the Prophet Jeremiah* (London: Hodder and Stoughton, 1908), xlvii.

24. Rietzschel, *Das Problem der Urrolle*, 136; cf. Rudolph, *Jeremia*, xix; Philip Hyatt, "The Deuteronomic Edition of Jeremiah" in *Vanderbilt Studies in the Humanities* I (Nashville: Vanderbilt University Press, 1951), 93.

25. Not only does 8:12 conclude with אמר יהוה, but 8:10-12 less the first line is duplicated in 6:13-15. This suggests that 8:10-12 was originally independent.

26. No need to revocalize with Bright (*Jeremiah*, 61); Jeremiah is engaging in word-play with two verbs that sound alike, אסף, meaning "to gather," and סוף, meaning "to make an end of" (H stem).

27. *Le Livre de Jérémie*, 82-83. Bright takes "gather" as a catchword linking 9:21 with 10:17.

28. *Basic Forms of Prophetic Speech*, 95-96.

29. "A Problem in Jeremiah," *ET* 26 (1914-15), 429; Bright agrees; cf. *Jeremiah*, 144.

30. Bright, *Jeremiah*, 213ff.

31. Condamin, *Le Livre de Jérémie*, 177, following Cornill and Giesebrecht. More recently see Holladay, "The Covenant with the Patriarchs Overturned: Jeremiah's Intention in 'Terror on Every Side' (Jer 20:1-6)," *JBL* 91 (1972), 314.

32. Holladay argues (*ibid.*) that Jeremiah is playing the same kind of word game with the name Pashhur.

33. "Jer xxxi 22b Reconsidered: 'The Woman Encompasses the Man'," *VT* 16 (1966), 236-239.

34. See the Holladay article (*ibid.*) for a survey of other explanations. Holladay himself takes the line to be a word to the personified daughter of Israel which bids her to return from exile.

35. "Style, Irony and Authenticity in Jeremiah," 53-54.

36. I have outlined the structure of the core in an earlier study entitled "Patterns of Poetic Balance in the Book of Jeremiah" (Unpublished B. D. Thesis, North Park Theological Seminary, 1967), 66-67.

37. See Theodore M. Ludwig, "The Shape of Hope: Jeremiah's Book
of Consolation," *CTM* 39 (1968), 526-541. Ludwig follows
the lead of Volz although not accepting an early date for
all the hope poems in 30-31.

38. Bright wants to date the collection in the middle of the
exilic period or thereabouts, which I think is too late.

39. Add באים with Qere; omission due to haplography.

40. The *MT* prefixes לאמר which Bright fills out with the complete formula "The word of Yahweh came to me saying...";
cf. *Jeremiah*, 19. One Ms., the *LXX* and Syriac omit;
Rudolph suggests we delete.

41. Hyatt, in his *Jeremiah* commentary (*IB* 5, 829), ends the
unit at 3:20. Muilenburg ("Hebrew Rhetoric: Repetition
and Style," 105) and Bright (*Jeremiah*, 25) follow Volz and
take all of 3:1-4:4 as a single unit. Giesebrecht (*Jeremia*, 13), however, takes 1-5 as a self-contained unit.

42. Granted the "if" is understood, but there is nothing wrong
with reading simply "Behold." "Behold" can carry the conditional element even in English.

43. Bright, *Jeremiah*, 19; cf. Volz, *Der Prophet Jeremia* [KAT],
(Leipzig: A. Deichertsche Verlagsbuchhandlung, 1928), 35.

44. For an important discussion of this text, see Reuven Yaron,
"The Restoration of Marriage," *JJS* 17 (1966), 1-11.

45. Brandt (*The Rhetoric of Argumentation*, 130) calls the same
a *contrarium*.

46. Yaron ("The Restoration of Marriage," 8) argues that the
law of Deut 24:1-4 is designed to *preserve* the second
marriage. If this is the case, then Jeremiah is taking
it out of its legal context and using it to make a different point. It seems unlikely that Jeremiah would want
Israel's second, third and fourth marriages to be preserved, unless of course he is being highly ironic.

47. See James D. Martin, "The Forensic Background to Jeremiah
III 1," *VT* 19 (1969), 82-92. Yaron's translation "yet return again to me" (*ibid.*, 3) does not take the Hebrew as
having interrogative force. This interpretation goes back,
as Yaron points out, to the Talmud where this text was used
to show how Yahweh's mercy is not subject to law. But see
the modern Jewish commentary by Rabbi Harry Freedman, *Jeremiah* [Soncino Books of the Bible] (London: Soncino Press,
1961), 18, which translates the Hebrew as a question. For
a more complete discussion of the omission of the interrogative ה, see H. G. Mitchell, "The Omission of the Interrogative Particle" in *Old Testament and Semitic Studies in
Memory of William Rainey Harper* I (Chicago: University of
Chicago Press, 1908), 115-129.

48. See note above.

49. Bright, *Jeremiah*, 42.

50. Professor Freedman reminds me that the Dead Sea Scrolls
show the open and closed sections to be very old, dating
from at least pre-Christian times.

51. Although made in a slightly different context, David Daube's comments about long final lines are a warning to those who would require all the lines of a poem to be of the same length; cf. David Daube, "Three Questions of Form in Matthew V," *JThS* 45 (1944), 21-22.

52. This colon has long been a crux because of the אֹל‎־. Older commentators deleted it, as they also deleted the לֹא‎־ in 4:27 (so Volz and Rudolph). We know now from Ugaritic, however, that אַל‎ (like לֹא‎) can have asseverative meaning, i.e., it can mean "surely." That seems to be the meaning here. On the asseverative אַל‎, see C. H. Gordon, *Ugaritic Textbook* (Rome: Pontifical Biblical Institute, 1965), 357; also M. Dahood, "Hebrew-Ugaritic Lexicography I," *Biblica* 44 (1963), 293-294.

53. My translation of this colon does not reflect the fact that the Hebrew verb is N stem and should be translated passively: "thus it will be done to them." I wanted, however, to force the link between עשׂה‎ here and in v. 10, which the poet intends.

54. Bright, *Jeremiah*, 37.

55. See note 52, above.

56. Text obscure; see commentaries.

57. For a different reading, see W. L. Holladay, "'The Priests Scrape Out On Their Hands,' Jeremiah V 31," *VT* 15 (1965), 111-113.

58. The use of "cap" and "foil" to analyze poetic structure is developed by Professor Brandt in his forthcoming book, *The Rhetoric of Poetry* (Chapter V, "The Structures of Lyric Poetry").

59. A more complete analysis will be published jointly with Professor Freedman at some future date.

60. So Volz, *Der Prophet Jeremia*, 162; Bright, *Jeremiah*, 102.

61. "The Covenant with the Patriarchs Overturned...," 307ff.

62. Holladay leaves מגור‎ untranslated because of a three-fold meaning which he believes Jeremiah intends for it.

63. Jeremiah uses the verb אהב‎ and its cognate nouns with ironic meaning in 2:33; 5:31; 22:20,22; and 30:14.

64. Condamin, *Le Livre de Jérémie*, 164.

65. So Bright.

66. Bright ingeniously recognizes that "Terror On Every Side" is here a nickname which Jeremiah has been given; cf. *Jeremiah*, 132-133.

67. See Chapter III, p. 68.

68. On the subject of textual omissions, Albright has said the following: There is "increasing evidence from the Qumran

Scrolls that our Hebrew originals, once edited in antiquity, suffered far more from omissions by copyists than from additions"; cf. W. F. Albright, "Some Remarks on the Song of Moses in Deuteronomy XXXII," *VT* 9 (1959), 341.

69. One cannot help but wonder if the lost colon beginning v. 17 was not omitted intentionally since it no doubt named the one who could have killed Jeremiah while he was still in the womb. This may have been too offensive, especially if Yahweh was in any way implied.

70. See 15:16 and also my translation of 8:18 discussed in Chapter III, p. 85.

71. For later metaphorical uses of "Lebanon" in the Targums, see Geza Vermes, "The Symbolical Interpretation of 'Lebanon' in the Targums: The Origin and Development of an Exegetical Tradition," *JThS* 9 (1958), 1-12.

72. עיר can mean "temple quarter"; see L. R. Fisher "The Temple Quarter," *JSS* 8 (1963), 34-41.

73. So Volz, Condamin, Hyatt, Bright, etc.

74. Condamin sees the "Lebanon" balance; *Le Livre de Jérémie*, 172.

75. See also 2:33; 20:4,6 (although in discussing 20:4,6 we used Holladay's translation of "dear ones") and 30:14.

76. So Condamin and Bright.

77. See note 102 on p. 136.

78. So Bright.

79. When the poem is taken as a 3:3:3 structure, some other nice balancing terms emerge, e.g., נמשך (v. 30) and נפשי (v. 31). Also, although we did not identify this as an inclusio poem, it may very well be one with מקול beginning the first stanza (v. 29) and כי קול beginning the third stanza (v. 31).

80. Bright, *Jeremiah*, 31.

81. *The Root ŠÛBH in the Old Testament* (Leiden: E. J. Brill, 1958).

82. *Ibid.*, 1.

83. Bright (*Jeremiah*, 60) omits; Volz (*Der Prophet Jeremia*, 107) retains.

84. Bird names are not known for certain; see the commentaries.

85. Massoretic closed sections mark off 19-21 as a unit. Bright calls these verses a soliloquy in which Jeremiah speaks for the nation; cf. *Jeremiah*, 73.

86. In the apparatus to BH^3 he suggests that it is probably added from 4:20.

87. So *BDB* 452; *KBH* 193.

88. See pp. 49-50.

89. A good example is the word-play on ראה and ירא in balancing stanzas of Jer 17:5-8; cf. Holladay, "Style, Irony and Authenticity in Jeremiah," 52.

90. So Bright, *Jeremiah*, 286, although he breaks at v. 17 as do other commentators. I would however see 16-18 as another 4:2 structure just like 12-15. This structure predominates in these poems: 30:5-7 is 4:2, while its companion piece in 30:10-11 is 2:4. I also take 30:19-20 as 4:2. Outside the Book of Comfort, we noted earlier that 10:19-21 was 2:4 (see p. 55).

91. This is Bright's translation; for a discussion of the textual difficulties, see Bright, *Jeremiah*, 271.

92. See p. 47.

93. Commentators are not agreed on the limits of this poem. If we take it as a 4:4:4 structure, then some rather impressive balancing features emerge. Each final line begins with כי and each stanza has a simile at the beginning.

94. Read בה for the second בא with 100 Mss., Greek and Syriac.

1. For a chiastic structure in II Kings 1-2 see my article
    "Elijah's Chariot Ride," *JJS*, 24 (1973), 39-50.

2. *Chiasmus in the New Testament*, 59.

3. *Ibid.*, **44**.

4. *Lectures in Deuteronomy*, 15.

5. *Ibid.*, 5.

6. "The Recovery of Poetic Passages of Jeremiah," 409.

7. No need to omit ובחחפנחס with the Greek; also against
    Rudolph I take אמרו with the previous colon.

8. See earlier analysis of this verse on p. 52.

9. The following five bi-cola are all of one type and demon-
    strate the sequence well:

Yet you have *a harlot's brow*	ומצח אשה זונה היה לך
you refuse to be ashamed (3:3)	מאנת הכלם
They have made *their faces harder than rock*	חזקו פניהם מסלע
they refuse to repent (5:3)	מאנו לשוב
Behold, *their ears are uncircumcised*	הנה ערלה אזנם
they cannot listen (6:10)	ולא יוכלו להקשיב
They hold fast to deceit	החזיקו בתרמת
they refuse to repent (8:5)	מאנו לשוב
They have loved to wander thus	כן אהבו לנוע
they have not restrained their feet (14:10)	רגליהם לא חשכו

10. This verse is in Aramaic and intends a word-play with עבדו
    and יאבדו.

11. Dahood uses the term "double-duty" in his *Psalms*; see I,
    17 and the index in III; also cf. "A New Metrical Pattern
    in Biblical Poetry."

12. See prior discussion of 8:5a on pp. 53-54.

13. In David's lament over Saul and Jonathan (II Sam 1:20),
    two cola beginning with פן־ *end* a 4-cola unit.

14. *The Symmetrical Structure of Scripture*, 37.

15. "Style, Irony and Authenticity in Jeremiah," 51-52.

16. The gates *lift up* their heads in Psalm 24:7,9.

17. See p. 47.

18. We looked at 14:7-9 earlier; see p. 44.

19. I would divide up 14:2-6 as follows:

2 אבלה יהודה ושעריה אמללו
   קדרו לארץ וצוחת ירושלם עלתה

3 ואדריהם שלחו צעוריהם למים באו על־גבים
   לא־מצאו מים שבו כליהם ריקם

4 בשו והכלמו וחפו ראשם
   בעבור האדמה חתה כי לא־היה גשם בארץ

5 בשו אכרים חפו ראשם
   כי גם־אילת בשדה ילדה ועזוב כי לא־היה דשא

6 ופראים עמדו על־שפים שאפו רוח כתנים
   כלו עיניהם כי־אין עשב

20. On 19ab see p. 67; on 22 see p. 52.

21. Against the *RSV*, we read the *MT* which preserves the archaic 2fs form שמעתי "you have heard"; Jeremiah is in conversation with himself (cf. 3:19; 5:4-5).

22. See p. 13.

23. Some but not all of the key words are noted by Condamin.

24. Delete המוליך אתנו במדבר as an explanatory gloss. Its function is to clarify the ב of the following בארץ. Without it not only is the transition from Egypt to the Wilderness abrupt, but there could also be ambiguity about which land is being talked of, the *land of Egypt* or the *land of the Wilderness*. The gloss clears this up: the land of desert and pits, drought and death-shadows is the Wilderness. The gloss appears to be a conflation of לכתך אחרי במדבר.. in 2:2 (part of which is lacking in the *LXX* but which is nevertheless genuine) and בעת מוליכך בדרך in 2:17 (which is absent in the *LXX* and is definitely itself a gloss). The H Stem of הלך is here the mark of an editor. For a more complete explanation of this expansion see the discussion to follow.

25. Delete בארץ לא־עבר בה איש ולא־ישב אדם שם as more expansion perhaps intended to fill out a standard liturgical confession; see the discussion to follow and cf. note 85 for a similar expansion following ארץ ציה וערבה in 51:43.

26. A few Mss. and the Vulgate omit בני.

27. Condamin, "Symmetrical Repetitions in *Lamentations* Chapters I and II"; cf. note 181 on p. 143.

28. See p. 68.

29. See p. 42.

30. Verses 10-13 must be a separate poem since v. 14 begins a new poem extending to v. 19 (so Gunkel and others; cf. p. 8).

31. Bright, *Jeremiah*, 18: "Finally, in vv. 29-37 there is a

further unit of two parts (vss. 29-32, 33-36 [sic]), which
were probably of separate origin..."

32. Condamin, *Le Livre de Jérémie*, 20.

33. In his article, "A New Metrical Pattern in Biblical Poetry,"
Dahood notes how a term doing "double-duty" can make a
short center for the bi-colon. Dahood is counting syllables, but in most cases the center is about *one-half* of
what remains on either side.

34. *LXX* omits אביונים; Bright and *JB* follow.

35. Bright, *Jeremiah*, 16.

36. *Ibid.*, 41.

37. Rudolph in *BH*[3] suggested we delete ואסלח לה from 5:1
(*propheta loquitur* in 1-6), but in the new *BHS* this suggestion is given up in favor of another which would allow
Yahweh to be the speaker in v. 1. He now proposes that at
the end of v. 1 we add נאם-יהוה. Neither change is necessary. The chiastic structure to be shown makes it clear
that Yahweh is the speaker in vv. 1-2.

38. Much discussion has been generated about the identity of
the "Foe from the North" (1:13ff), whether it refers to
roving bands of marauders (Jer 18:22; II Kings 24:2), the
Scythians mentioned by Herodotus in his *Histories* (Book I,
105), or the Babylonian army. For a balanced discussion
of the problem, see H. H. Rowley, "The Early Prophecies of
Jeremiah in Their Setting," *BJRL*, 45 (1962-63), 206ff.

39. In Gen 18-19 the Yahwist has reworked an earlier version
of the story. Note the different designations for the
arsonists. They are called אנשים (men) in 18:2,16,22; 19:
5,8,12,16; and מלאכים (messengers/angels) in 19:1,15. In
19:18 Lot addresses them as אדני (lords), and if it is to
one of them that Abraham speaks in 18:23-33, then we have
three additional occurrences of אדני in vv. 30-32. These
strands of saga show a gradual progression of theological
understanding. In the beginning it was *men* who set the
city on fire. But such were later perceived not as ordinary but as divine men, thus the designation "messengers."
In the final version, which is the work of the Yahwist,
Yahweh is the one who destroys Sodom and Gomorrah (19:24).

40. Law 1 says that "The centre is always the turning point";
cf. *Chiasmus in the New Testament*, 40ff.

41. Omit אליה יבאו רעים ועדריהם as an explanatory gloss providing the subject for תקעו.

42. Omit כי כה אמר יהוה צבאות as editorial similar to v. 9;
cf. note 45.

43. Robert Gordis, "Quotations as a Literary Usage in Biblical,
Oriental and Rabbinic Literature," *HUCA* 22 (1949), 177.

44. Recall the break-up of "cedars of Lebanon" in 22:6-7 (cf.
p. 48). An excellent article has been published on this
phenomenon by Ezra Zion Melamed entitled, "Break-up of
Stereotype Phrases as an Artistic Device in Biblical

154

Poetry" in *Scripta Hierosolymitana*, 8 (Jerusalem: Hebrew University, 1961), 115-153.

45. Omit כה אמר יהוה צבאות as editorial; cf. note 42. Also read עוֹלָל for יְעוֹלְלִי with Rudolph and most commentators.

46. Cf. note 89 on p. 150 regarding the sound balance in Jer 17:5-8.

47. The closing formula is lacking in the Greek, but we need not delete with Rudolph.

48. Greek omits ואתן להם יעברום and Rudolph suggests we delete. Bright (*Jeremiah*, 61) does not translate. Our earlier analysis (p. 66) would seem to indicate that a nicely balanced 4-cola unit has been expanded.

49. The final colon sounds prosaic (cf. 3:25) and perhaps should be deleted; see discussion following.

50. See Lund's third law of chiastic structures in *Chiasmus in the New Testament*, 41. Lund refers in this law to *ideas* instead of key words, nevertheless most all his chiastic structures are based on the distribution of key words.

51. In chapter II; see p. 30.

52. This view goes back to Duhm (*Jeremia*, 92), who is followed by Rudolph (*Jeremia*, 64-65) and Volz (*Der Prophet Jeremia*, 110-112).

53. Delete שועת בת-עמי מארץ מרחקים as a gloss; see discussion to follow.

54. Volz, Rudolph and Hyatt all excised C (19b) as a gloss. Holladay, however, has rightly argued for its genuineness; cf. "The So-called Deuteronomic Gloss in Jeremiah 8:19b," *VT* 12 (1962), 494-498.

55. So *BDB*, 114; *KBH*, 40.

56. עלה can also have the meaning "to go away" (I Kings 15:19).

57. Bright following the *RSV* translates "far and wide through the land" (*Jeremiah*, 62,64), but Volz "aus fernem Land" with the following comment: "Da die Leute im Land sind und die Worte nicht bedeuten können 'im Lande weit und breit' müssen die Worte als Glosse (oder als aus 8,14-17 versprengt) ausgeschieden werden"; cf. *Der Prophet Jeremia*, 111.

58. See Roland de Vaux, *Jerusalem and the Prophets* (Cincinnati: Hebrew Union College Press, 1965); also *Ancient Israel*, II (New York: McGraw-Hill Book Co., 1965), 327.

59. "The Recovery of Poetic Passages of Jeremiah," 404-406.

60. One is tempted to leave בת-עמי (daughter of my people) in v. 19a since the term appears again in v. 21. But 19a is definitely a gloss; also we will see another poem, 17:13-16a (ahead pp. 88-89), which has a chiasmus of speaker but *no* key word balance.

61. "Style, Irony and Authenticity in Jeremiah," 48. S. R. Driver pointed it out too as one of Jeremiah's characteristic expressions; cf. Driver, *An Introduction to the Literature of the Old Testament* (Cleveland and New York: World Publishing Co., 1967), 275.

62. Both are lacking in the Greek and Rudolph suggests we delete. Our analysis however will argue for their retention.

63. See p. 67.

64. This translation is Professor Holladay's and came to me in a letter dated Nov. 18, 1966. See discussion to follow.

65. Hebrew unintelligible; all versions and commentaries follow the Greek.

66. Bright, *Jeremiah*, 119.

67. Delete את־יהוה; see discussion to follow.

68. Qere form is וסורי; Rudolph proposes נָסוֹרֶיךָ in the new *BHS* (in *BH³*, וְסוּרֶי). *RSV* emends to 2nd p. suffix. For another reading of lines 1-2, see Dahood, "The Metaphor in Jeremiah 17,13," *Biblica* 48 (1967), 109-110.

69. Rudolph now agrees in *BHS*; in *BH³* he was not sure.

70. Both Hyatt (*Jeremiah*, 993) and Bright (*Jeremiah*, 152) are aware of this possibility but prefer to leave them in.

71. Delete וישמע with the Greek as a gloss. A problem was apparently created by the use of ראה (to see) with את־דברו (his word). Yet we take this to be the original reading. In 2:31 we also have ראו דבר־יהוה. Professor Freedman calls my attention to Ex 20:18: וכל־העם ראים את־הקולת ....ראת הלפידם ואת קול השפך, and to this we can add Amos 1:1: דברי...אשר חזה. Yahweh's word was often received by vision as we know from Jer 1 and 24, but visions were later disparaged in light of Jeremiah's comments in 23:23ff.

72. Reading here the Qere with all modern versions so as to harmonize with את־דברו in the previous colon. The Kethib, however, is probably original; see discussion to follow.

73. The first poem in the chain is 51:1-10, marked by the chapter division at one end and delimited at the other by the independence of vv. 11-14 (see pp. 50-51). This poem begins הנני מעיר על בבל.....רוח משחית, "Behold, I will stir up against Babylon...the spirit of a *destroyer*." The first verse of 51:11-14 also contains שחת: כי־על־בבל מזמתו להשחיתה, "because concerning Babylon his purpose is to *destroy* it." This appears to be editorial comment which would indicate that 11-14 has been expanded to fit into the chain. We skip over 51:15-19 since it is a duplication of 10:12-16 and is probably a later interpolation into the text. 51:20-23 is the poem just analyzed. The next poem, beginning in 51:25 (so Massoretic divisions), begins הנני אליך הר המשחית, "Behold, I am against you O *destroying* mountain..." Again שחת. In all there are four poems which either begin with שחת or have the verb supplied at the beginning.

74. Professor Freedman has called my attention to a number of deliberate variations made in sequences of repeated terms, all of them in poetry. In Amos 1-2 שלחתי אש occurs six times (1:4,7,10,12; 2:2,5) and הצתי אש once (1:14). Gen 49:25-26 has ויברכך and then five repetitions of ברכת followed by תאות. In Deut 33:13-16 ממגד occurs five times and מראש once.

75. In Jer 50:35-38 the variation is primarily for sound effect: five repetitions of חֶרֶב and at the end חֹרֶב.

76. Janzen, *Studies in the Text of Jeremiah*, 118.

77. For the translation of בתולה with a meaning broader than "virgin," see G. J. Wenham, "Be^{TÛLÂH} 'A Girl of Marriageable Age'," *VT* 22 (1972), 326-348.

78. In 6:6-9 the unit beginning "And you shall teach them diligently to your children" and ending "when you lie down and when you rise" comes before the unit "And you shall bind them as a sign upon your hand, and they shall be as frontlets between your eyes." In 11:18-20 these units are *reversed*.

79. When Peter quotes the prophecy from Joel 3:1-2 [Eng. 2:28-29] at Pentecost (Acts 2:17-18) he inverts the two center lines. Since the Hebrew and Greek texts of Joel are the same we must attribute the inversion to Peter.

80. Jer 5:17 has a similar distribution of terms:

> They shall eat up your *harvest* and your *food*
> They shall eat up your *sons* and your *daughters*
> They shall eat up your *flocks* and your *herds*
> They shall eat up your *vines* and your *fig trees*

The terms at the extremes are all produce, whereas the center terms are people and animals, which are normally grouped together in the OT.

81. Bright (*Jeremiah*, 359) takes as three separate poems: 1) 34-37; 2) 38-40; and 3) 41-45, but he acknowledges that the divisions are difficult to make.

82. Reading the Qere here and throughout the verse with all modern versions.

83. Delete לכן כה אמר יהוה as expansion.

84. ששך is an Athbash for בבל.

85. Delete ארץ לא-ישב בהו כל-איש ולא-יעבר בהן בן-אדם as expansion (see also the expansion of 2:6 in note 25).

86. Sheldon H. Blank, "Men Against God: The Promethean Element in Biblical Prayer," *JBL* 72 (1953), 1-13.

87. Bright, *Jeremiah*, 6-7.

88. *Ibid.*, 7.

89. The Hebrew as it now stands is not precise. The locative *he* on צָפוֹנָה would render the term "towards the north," yet

מפני means "from." But common sense tells us that the pot must be tipped *away* from the north if the metaphor is to refer to the Foe from the North.

90. Ex. 4:10ff.

91. This poem was analyzed in my earlier study, "Patterns of Poetic Balance in the Book of Jeremiah," 51-53.

92. See p. 42.

93. No reason to read an imperative here with the Greek and Syriac (so *RSV*); Hebrew text is correct.

94. See H. H. Rowley, "The Text and Interpretation of Jer 11: 18-12:6," *AJSLL* 42 (1926), 219ff; cf. Bright, *Jeremiah*, 89.

95. For the translation of this line, see Holladay, "Jeremiah's Lawsuit with God," 280-287.

96. See pp. 31-32.

97. See pp. 48-50.

98. See pp. 91-92 and note 73 above.

99. So Bright, *Jeremiah*, 211; cf. A. S. Peake, *Jeremiah and Lamentations*, II (New York: Henry Frowde, 1911), 60-61.

100. *Ibid.*

101. *Jeremiah*, 211.

102. *Ibid.*, 206-207; 211-212.

103. *Ibid.*, 212.

104. Peake, *Jeremiah and Lamentations*, II, 64-65; Bright (*ibid.*) speaks of an oracle to Shemaiah which is interrupted and never resumed.

105. The caution which Jeremiah displayed in dealing with Hananiah (ch. 28) is instructive. After their first encounter, which ended without the dispute being resolved, we are told that Jeremiah "went his way" (v. 11). Only later did he return to curse Hananiah (vv. 12ff).

106. Bright argues that the plural "letters" can refer to just one letter (*Jeremiah*, 206); so also Volz (*Der Prophet Jeremiah*, 276). This is forced and we see no reason to so read the text.

107. The interpretation here hangs on the antecedent of "this letter" (את-הספר-הזה) in v. 29. The Greek omits הזה too which does not help. But Bright is undoubtedly correct in taking this letter to be the letter sent by Shemaiah to Zephaniah about Jeremiah; cf. *Jeremiah*, 212.

108. Bright, *Jeremiah*, 169.

109. Bright dates ch. 35 ca. 599/598 B.C. which I believe is too late. A date prior to 605 B.C. is historically defensible since Nebuchadnezzar made his first campaign

into Palestine in 604 B.C. On this occasion he destroyed
Ashkelon; see Bright, *A History of Israel*, 2nd edition
(Philadelphia: Westminster Press, 1972), 325-326. This
date easily satisfies the military threat implied in 35:11,
which is the basis on which Bright proposes his date (*Jeremiah*, 189-190). More important, a date prior to 605
would avoid our having to ask the obvious question of how
Jeremiah could be in the temple (in 599/598 according to
Bright) after he was debarred in 605 (so 36:5). It is not
only unlikely that Jeremiah went into the temple from 604
to 598, but it is unlikely that he (and Baruch) *went anywhere at all* during this period. We know the fate of another prophet less able to avoid the grasp of King Jehoiakim (cf. 26:20-23), which indicates that this was the
only course to follow so long as Jehoiakim was still alive.

110. The deliberate judgment of nations leading up to Israel in
Amos 1-2 has long been recognized; see Lund, *Chiasmus in
the New Testament*, 87-88; A. Bentzen, "The Ritual Background of Amos i 2-ii 16," *OS* 8 (1950), 85-99.

111. Numerous scholars take 25:13 to be the conclusion to the
first collection of Jeremiah's prophecies; cf. Eissfeldt,
The Old Testament: An Introduction, 350-351; Bright, *Jeremiah*, lvii, 162-163.

112. The 4th year is derived from the superscription in 28:1
which reads, ויהי בשנה ההיא, "In that same year..." The
entire verse is problematic. The *LXX* omits, while the *MT*
reads "Jehoiakim," which cannot be correct. On the basis
of a few Mss, the Syriac and Arabic, all modern English
versions (*RSV*, *NEB*, *JB*) correct to "Zedekiah."

113. This was in a paper entitled "Scribal Contributions to Old
Testament Theology: Composition by Contrast" given at the
International Congress of Learned Societies in the Field
of Religion, Los Angeles, September, 1972.

1. "A Study in Hebrew Rhetoric: Repetition and Style," 99; cf. Appendix.

2. For the development of this thesis, see Holladay, "The Background of Jeremiah's Self-Understanding: Moses, Samuel and Psalm 22," *JBL*, 83 (1964), 153-164. This thesis was also presented by James Muilenburg in the unpublished Nils Lund Memorial Lectures (North Park Theological Seminary, 1963) entitled, "The Mediators of the Covenant."

3. For the usual distinctions typically drawn by source-critics between prophet and priest, see T. J. Meek, "Was Jeremiah a Priest?", *The Expositor*, 8th series, 25 (1923), 215-222.

1. For the most recent article on Lowth see Aelred Baker,
   "Parallelism: England's Contribution to Biblical Studies,"
   CBQ 35 (1973), 429-440.

2. מאור עינים [The Light of the Eyes], (Volna: R. M. Romma
   Press, 1866); see chapter 60 "Essays in Criticism"
   (אמרי בינה), 477-485.

3. "Grammatical Parallelism and Its Russian Facet," *Language*
   42 (1966), 403.

4. See Ugo Bonamartini, "L'epesegesi nella S. Scrittura,"
   Biblica 6 (1925), 424-444; cf. Baker, "Parallelism: England's Contribution to Biblical Studies," 433.

5. See Frederick Bussby, "Bishop Jebb, A Neglected Biblical
   Scholar," *ET* 60 (1948-49), 193.

6. *Sacred Literature*, 14-15.

7. Briggs, *ICC: Psalms*, I (Edinburgh: T & T Clark, 1952),
   xxxv; Meek, "The Structure of Hebrew Poetry," *JR* 9 (1929),
   528.

8. *Sacred Literature*, 14.

9. *Ibid.*

10. Brigg's remarks about Schoettgen are immediately followed
    by a reference to Jebb's *Sacred Literature*. Meek in his
    discussion then repeats what Briggs says almost verbatim.

11. Ed. J. Fr. Michaud, 38 (Ganz, Austria: Akademische Druck--
    u. Verlagsanstalt, 1969), 409.

12. In the biographical article in *Biographie Universelle* (see
    note above), Schoettgen's second volume is given a publi-
    cation date of 1740. The second volume in my possession
    is dated 1742.

13. Thomas H. Horne, *An Introduction to the Critical Study
    and Knowledge of the Holy Scriptures*, II, 4th edition
    (Philadelphia: E. Littell, 1831), 705-706.

14. Correction; Schoettgen text has 123:6.

15. Correction; Schoettgen text has 57:11.

16. Compare "bosom" in both the Hebrew and the Vulgate. Is
    he striving after a more exact parallelism with "hands"?

17. Schoettgen supplies *reddunt* to render the Hebrew H Stem
    (compare modern English versions).

18. Correction; Schoettgen text has 94:8.

162

19. *The Forms of Hebrew Poetry*, 74. Lowth had also recognized this, however; cf. *Lectures on the Sacred Poetry of the Hebrews*, 262-263.

20. "A Study in Hebrew Rhetoric: Repetition and Style," 99.

21. See especially *Psalms III*, 429-444.

BIBLIOGRAPHY

Abrams, M. H. *The Mirror and the Lamp: Romantic Theory and the Critical Tradition* (New York: Oxford University Press, 1953).

Ackroyd, Peter. "Historians and Prophets," *SEÅ* 33 (1968), 18-54.

Albright, William F. "The Old Testament and Canaanite Language and Literature," *CBQ* 7 (1945), 5-31.

_____. "Some Remarks on the Song of Moses in Deuteronomy XXXII," *VT* 9 (1959), 339-346.

_____. *Yahweh and the Gods of Canaan* (Garden City: Doubleday & Co., 1968).

Alonso-Schökel, Luis. "Die stilistische Analyse bei den Propheten," *VT Supp.* 7 (Oxford, 1959), 154-164.

_____. *Estudios de Poética Hebrea* (Barcelona: Juan Flors, 1963).

Anderson, Bernhard W., and Walter Harrelson (eds.). *Israel's Prophetic Heritage* [Essays in Honor of James Muilenburg] (New York: Harper & Bros., 1962).

Anderson, G. W. "Some Aspects of the Uppsala School of Old Testament Study," *HThR* 43 (1950), 239-256.

Aristotle. *The "Art" of Rhetoric*, translated with an introduction and notes by John Henry Freese [Loeb Classical Library] (Cambridge, Massachusetts: Harvard University Press, 1947).

Baker, Aelred. "Parallelism: England's Contribution to Biblical Studies," *CBQ* 35 (1973), 429-440.

Baker, Sheridan. *The Complete Stylist* (New York: Thomas Y. Crowell Co., 1966).

Baldwin, Charles Sears. *Ancient Rhetoric and Poetic* (Gloucester, Massachusetts: Peter Smith, 1959).

Baumgartner, Walter. *Die Klagegedichte des Jeremia* [*BZAW* 32] (Giessen: Verlag von Alfred Topelmann, 1917).

Bentzen, Aage. "The Ritual Background of Amos i 2 - ii 16," *OS* 8 (1950), 85-99.

Berridge, John M. *Prophet, People, and the Word of Yahweh: An Examination of Form and Content in the Proclamation of the Prophet Jeremiah* [Basel Studies of Theology 4] (Zurich: EVZ-Verlag, 1970).

Bertman, Stephen. "Symmetrical Design in the Book of Ruth," *JBL* 84 (1965), 165-168.

164

_____. "Structural Symmetry at the End of the Odyssey," *GRBS* 9 (1968), 115-123.

Bewer, Julius A. "Critical Notes on Old Testament Passages," in *Old Testament and Semitic Studies in Memory of William Rainey Harper*, Vol. II (Chicago: University of Chicago Press, 1908), 207-226.

Birkeland, Harris. *Zum Hebräischen Traditionswesen* (Oslo: Jacob Dybwad, 1938).

_____. *Jeremia, Profet og dikter* (Oslo: Gyldendal Norsk Forlag, 1950).

Black, Edwin. *Rhetorical Criticism: A Study in Method* (New York: Macmillan Co., 1965).

Blank, Sheldon H. "Men against God - The Promethean Element in Biblical Prayer," *JBL* 72 (1953), 1-13.

Blayney, Benjamin. *Jeremiah and Lamentations*, 3rd ed. (London: Thomas Tegg & Son, 1836).

Blenkinsopp, Joseph. "The Prophetic Reproach," *JBL* 90 (1971), 267-278.

Bloomfield, Maurice. *Rig-Veda Repetitions* [Harvard Oriental Series, 20] (Cambridge, Massachusetts: Harvard University Press, 1916).

Boling, Robert G. "'Synonymous' Parallelism in the Psalms," *JSS* 5 (1960), 221-255.

Bonamartini, Ugo. "L'epesegesi nella S. Scrittura," *Biblica* 6 (1925), 424-444.

Booth, Wayne C. "The Revival of Rhetoric," in *New Rhetorics*, edited by Martin Steinmann Jr. (New York: Scribner's, 1967), 2-15.

Bowra, C.M. *Ancient Greek Literature* (New York: Oxford University Press, 1960).

Boys, Thomas. *Key to the Book of the Psalms*, revised and enlared edition with an introduction by E. W. Bullinger (London: St. Paul's Churchyard, 1890).

Brandt, William J. *The Rhetoric of Argumentation* (New York: Bobbs-Merrill Co., 1970).

Briggs, Charles A. "Hebrew Poetry," *Hebraica* 2 (1885-86), 164-170.

_____, and Emilie Grace Briggs. *The Book of Psalms* [ICC] I (Edinburgh: T. & T. Clark, 1952).

Bright, John. "The Date of the Prose Sermons of Jeremiah," *JBL* 70 (1951), 15-29.

_____. *Jeremiah* [AB] (Garden City: Doubleday & Co., 1965).

_____. "Jeremiah's Complaints: Liturgy, or Expressions of Personal Distress?" in *Proclamation and Presence* [Essays in Honour of G. Henton Davies] (Richmond: John Knox Press, 1970), 189-214.

_____. *A History of Israel*, 2nd ed. (Philadelphia: Westminster Press, 1972).

Bryant, Donald C. "Rhetoric: Its Function and Scope," in *The Province of Rhetoric*, edited by Joseph Schwartz and John A. Rycenga (New York: Ronald Press Co., 1965), 3-36.

_____ (ed.). *The Rhetorical Idiom* (Ithaca: Cornell University Press, 1958).

Budde, K. "Poetry (Hebrew)," *HDB* 4, 2-13.

Bullinger, E. W. *Figures of Speech Used in the Bible*, 2nd ed. (Grand Rapids: Baker Book House, 1969).

Burney, C. F. *The Poetry of Our Lord* (Oxford: Clarendon Press, 1925).

Bussby, Frederick. "Bishop Jebb, A Neglected Biblical Scholar," *ET* 60 (1948-49), 193.

Buttenwieser, Moses. *The Prophets of Israel* (New York: Macmillan Co., 1914).

Buttrey, T. V. "Accident and Design in Euripides' 'Medea'," *AJP* 79 (1958), 1-17.

Carney, T. F. "Plutarch's Style in the 'Marius'," *JHS* 80 (1960), 24-31.

Carrubba, R. W. "The Technique of the Double Structure in Horace," *Mnemosyne*, Series IV, 20 (1967), 68-75.

Casanowicz, Immanuel M. *Paronomasia in the Old Testament* (Boston: Norwood Press, 1894).

Cheyne, T. K., and J. Sutherland Black (eds.). *Encyclopaedia Biblica*, Vol. 3 (New York: Macmillan Co., 1913).

[Cicero]. *Rhetorica Ad Herennium*, translated with an introduction and notes by Harry Caplan [Loeb Classical Library] (Cambridge, Massachusetts: Harvard University Press, 1968).

Clark, Donald L. *Rhetoric and Poetry in the Renaissance* (New York: Columbia University Press, 1922).

Collins, John J. "Chiasmus, the 'ABA' Pattern and the Text of Paul," in *Studiorum Paulinorum Congress Internationalis Catholicus*, Vol. II (Rome: Pontifical Biblical Institute, 1961), 575-583.

Colunga, R. P. Alberto, and Laurentio Turrado (eds.). *Biblia Sacra Iuxta Vulgatam Clementinam*, 3rd ed. (Madrid: Biblioteca de Autores Cristianos, 1959).

166

Condamin, Albert. "Symmetrical Repetitions in *Lamentations* I and II," *JThS* 7 (1905), 137-140.

_____. *Poems de la Bible*, 2nd ed. (Paris: Gabriel Beauchesne et ses Fils, 1933).

_____. *Le Livre de Jérémie*, 3rd ed. (Paris: Librairie Lecoffre, 1936).

Corbett, Edward P. J. (ed.). *Rhetorical Analyses of Literary Works* (New York: Oxford University Press, 1969).

_____. *Classical Rhetoric for the Modern Student*, 2nd ed. (New York: Oxford University Press, 1971).

Cornill, D. Carl Heinrich. *Das Buch Jeremia* (Leipzig: Chr. Herm. Tauchnitz, 1905).

_____. *Introduction to the Canonical Books of the Old Testament*, translated from the 5th ed. of *Einleitung in das Alte Testament* by G. H. Box (New York: G. P. Putnam's Sons and London: Williams & Norgate, 1907).

Croft, Albert J. "The Functions of Rhetorical Criticism," *QJS* 42 (1956), 283-291.

Cross, Frank M. *Studies in Ancient Yahwistic Poetry* (Baltimore, 1950).

_____. "The History of the Biblical Text in the Light of Discoveries in the Judaean Desert," *HThR* 57 (1964), 281-299.

_____. "The Structure of the Deuteronomic History," in *Perspectives in Jewish Learning*, Vol. III (Chicago: College of Jewish Studies, 1968).

Cummins, Patrick. "Jeremias Orator," *CBQ* 11 (1949), 191-201.

Dahood, Mitchell. "Hebrew-Ugaritic Lexicography I," *Biblica* 44 (1963), 289-303.

_____. *Psalms I-III* [AB] (Garden City: Doubleday & Co., I, 1966; II, 1968; III, 1970).

_____. "The Metaphor in Jeremiah 17,13," *Biblica* 48 (1967), 109-110.

_____. "A New Metrical Pattern in Biblical Poetry," *CBQ* 29 (1967), 574-579.

Daube, David. "A Rhetorical Principle in the Gospels," *ET* 54 (1942-43), 305-306.

_____. "Three Questions of Form in Matthew V," *JThS* 45 (1944), 21-31.

_____. "Rabbinic Methods of Interpretation and Hellenistic Rhetoric," *HUCA* 22 (1949), 239-264.

De Vries, Simon. "Biblical Criticism, History of," *IDB* A-D, 413-418.

Driver, G. R. "Linguistic and Textual Problems: Jeremiah," *JQR* 28 (1937-38), 97-129.

_____. "Problems and Solutions," *VT* 4 (1954), 225-245.

Driver, S. R. "The Double Text of Jeremiah," *The Expositor*, 3rd Series, 9 (1889), 321-337.

_____. *An Introduction to the Literature of the Old Testament* (Cleveland: World Publishing Co., 1967).

_____. *Deuteronomy* [ICC], 3rd ed. (Edinburgh: T. & T. Clark, 1965).

_____. *The Book of the Prophet Jeremiah*, 2nd ed. (London: Hodder & Stoughton, 1908).

Duckworth, George E. *Foreshadowing and Suspense in the Epics of Homer, Apollonius and Vergil* (Princeton: Princeton University Press, 1933).

_____. *Structural Patterns and Proportions in Vergil's Aeneid* (Ann Arbor: University of Michigan Press, 1962).

Duhm, D. Bernhard. *Das Buch Jesaia* [HKAT], 2nd revised ed. (Göttingen: Vandenhoeck und Ruprecht, 1902).

_____. *Das Buch Jeremia* [Kurzer Hand-Commentar zum Alten Testament] (Tübingen and Leipzig: J. C. B. Mohr, 1901).

_____. "Poetical Literature," in *Encyclopaedia Biblica*, Vol. III, edited by T. K. Cheyne (New York: Macmillan Co., 1913), cols. 3793-3804.

Eissfeldt, Otto. *The Old Testament: An Introduction*, translated from the German by Peter R. Ackroyd (New York: Harper & Row, 1965).

Engnell, Ivan. *Gamla Testamentet I: En Traditionshistorisk Inledning* (Stockholm: Svenska Kyrkans Diakonistyrelses Bokförlag, 1945).

Exum, Cheryl, and Charles Talbert. "The Structure of Paul's Speech to the Ephesian Elders (Acts 20, 18-35)," *CBQ* 29 (1967), 233-236.

Fenton, J. C. "Inclusio and Chiasmus in Matthew," in *Texte und Untersuchungen zur Geschichte der Altchristlichen Literatur* [Studia Evangelica, 73], edited by Kurt Aland (Berlin: Akademie-Verlag, 1959), 174-179.

Fisher, Loren R. "The Temple Quarter," *JSS* 8 (1963), 34-41.

Flight, John W. "The Present State of Studies in the History of Writing in the Near East," in *The Haverford Symposium on Archaeology and the Bible* (New Haven: American Schools of Oriental Research, 1938), 111-135.

Forbes, John. *The Symmetrical Structure of Scripture* (Edinburgh: T. & T. Clark, 1854).

Freedman, David Noel. "Archaic Forms in Early Hebrew Poetry," *ZAW* 72 (1960), 101-107.

168.

_____. "Pentateuch," *IDB*, K-Q, 711-727.

_____. "On Method in Biblical Studies: The Old Testament," *Int.* 17 (1963), 308-318.

_____. "Divine Commitment and Human Obligation," *Int.* 18 (1964), 419-431.

_____. "The Structure of Job 3," *Biblica* 49 (1968), 503-508.

_____. "The Structure of Psalm 137," in *Near Eastern Studies in Honor of William Foxwell Albright*, edited by Hans Goedicke (Baltimore: John Hopkins Press, 1971), 187-205.

_____. "Acrostics and Metrics in Hebrew Poetry," *HThR* 65 (1972), 367-392.

Freedman, Harry. *Jeremiah* [Soncino Books of the Bible] (London: Soncino Press, 1949).

Gaechter, Paul. "Semitic Literary Forms in the Apocalypse and Their Import," *TS* 8 (1947), 547-573.

Gandz, Solomon. "Oral Tradition in the Bible," in *Jewish Studies in Memory of George A. Kohut* (New York: Alexander Kohut Memorial Foundation, 1935), 248-269.

Garland, D. David. "Exegesis of Jeremiah 2:10-13," *SJT* 2 (1959-1960), 27-32.

Gemser, B. "The 'RĪB' or Controversy-Pattern in Hebrew Mentality," in *Wisdom in Israel and in the Ancient Near East* [VT Supp, 3] (Leiden: E. J. Brill, 1955) 120-137.

Gevirtz, Stanley. "The Ugaritic Parallel to Jeremiah 8:23," *JNES* 20 (1961), 41-46.

_____. *Patterns in the Early Poetry of Israel* (Chicago: University of Chicago Press, 1963).

Giesebrecht, D. Fredrich. *Das Buch Jeremia* [HKAT] (Göttingen: Vandenhoeck und Ruprecht, 1894).

Gilula, M. "An Egyptian Parallel to Jeremiah I 4-5," *VT* 17 (1967), 114.

Ginsburg, Christian D. *Introduction to the Massoretico-Critical Edition of the Hebrew Bible*, with a Prolegomenon by Harry M. Orlinsky (New York: KTAV Publishing House Inc., 1966).

Ginsberg, H. L. "The Rebellion and Death of Ba'lu," *Orientalia* 5 (1936), 161-198.

_____. "Ugaritic Studies and the Bible," *BA* 8 (1945), 41-58.

Glasson, T. Francis. "Chiasmus in St. Matthew vii. 6," *ET* 68 (1956-57), 302.

Gonda, J. *Stylistic Repetition in the Veda* (Amsterdam: N. V. Noord-Hollandsche Uitgevers Maatschappij, 1959).

Good, Edwin M. *Irony in the Old Testament* (Philadelphia: West-
      minster Press, 1965).

_____. "The Composition of Hosea," *SEÅ* 31 (1966), 21-63.

Gordis, Robert. "A Rhetorical Use of Interrogative Sentences in
      Biblical Hebrew," *AJSLL* 49 (1933), 212-217.

_____. "Quotations in Wisdom Literature," *JQR* 30 (1939-40),
      123-147.

_____. "Quotations as a Literary Usage in Biblical, Oriental
      and Rabbinic Literature," *HUCA* 22 (1949), 157-219.

_____. "On Methodology in Biblical Exegesis," *JQR* 61 (1970),
      93-118.

Gordon, A. R. "Pioneers in the Study of Old Testament Poetry,
      I, Lowth," *ET* 22 (1910-11), 444-448.

_____. "Pioneers in the Study of Old Testament Poetry, II,
      Herder," *ET* 24 (1912-13), 227-232.

Gordon, Cyrus H. *Ugaritic Textbook* [Analecta Orientalia, 38]
      (Rome: Pontificum Institutum Biblicum, 1965).

Gottwald, Norman K. *Studies in the Book of Lamentations*
      [Studies in Biblical Theology, 14] (Chicago: Alec R.
      Allenson Inc., 1954).

_____. "Lamentations," *Int.* 9 (1955), 320-338.

_____. "Samuel," *EJ* 14 (1971), 788-797.

Goulder, M. D. "The Chiastic Structure of the Lucan Journey,"
      in *Studia Evangelica* [Papers of the Second Internation-
      al Congress on New Testament Studies, Oxford, 1961],
      Vol. II, edited by F. L. Cross (Berlin: Akademie Verlag,
      1964), 195-202.

Graf, Karl Heinrich. *Der Prophet Jeremia* (Leipzig: T. O.
      Weigel, 1862).

Gray, George Buchanan. *The Forms of Hebrew Poetry*, Prole-
      gomenon by David Noel Freedman (New York: KTAV, 1972).

Greenwood, David. "Rhetorical Criticism and Formgeschichte:
      Some Methodological Considerations," *JBL* 89 (1970),
      418-426.

Gressmann, Hugo. "Die literarische Analyse Deuterojesajas,"
      ZAW 34 (1914), 254-297.

Grobel, K. "Form Criticism," *IDB*, E-J, 320-321.

Gross, Karl. "Hoseas Einfluss auf Jeremias Anschauungen,"
      Neue Kirchliche Zeitschrift 42 (1931), 241-256; 327-
      343.

Guillaume, D. F. "Paronomasia in the Old Testament," *JSS* 9
      (1964), 282-290.

Gunkel, Hermann. *Genesis übersetzt und erklärt* (Göttingen: Vandenhoeck & Ruprecht, 1966).

_____. *The Legends of Genesis*, translation of the Introduction to *Genesis* with an introduction by William F. Albright (New York: Schocken Books, 1966).

_____. *Ausgewählte Psalmen übersetzt und erklart*, 3rd ed. (Göttingen: Vandenhoeck & Ruprecht, 1911).

_____. "Die Grundprobleme der israelitischen Literaturgeschichte," *Deutsche Literaturzeitung* 29 (1906), cols. 1797-1800; 1861-1866.

_____. *Die Propheten* (Göttingen: Vandenhoeck & Ruprecht, 1917).

_____. *Das Märchen im Alten Testament* (Tübingen: J. C. B. Mohr [Paul Siebeck], 1921).

_____. "The Secret Experiences of the Prophets," *The Expositor*, 9th Series, 1 (1924), 356-366; 427-435; 2 (1924), 23-32.

_____. "The Poetry of the Psalms: Its Literary History and Its Application to the Dating of the Psalms," in *Old Testament Essays*, edited by D. C. Simpson (London: Charles Griffin & Co., 1927), 118-142.

_____. *The Psalms: A Form-Critical Introduction* [Facet Books, Biblical Series, 19], translated by Thomas M. Horner; Introduction by James Muilenburg (Philadelphia: Fortress Press, 1967).

_____. *What Remains of the Old Testament and Other Essays*, translated by A. K. Dallas (London: George Allen & Unwin Ltd., 1928).

_____. "Propheten: IIB. Propheten Israels seit Amos," in *RGG*2, Vol. IV (Tübingen: Verlag von J. C. B. Mohr [Paul Siebeck], 1930), cols. 1538-1554.

_____. *Einleitung in die Psalmen*, completed by Joachim Begrich, 2nd ed. (Göttingen: Vandenhoeck & Ruprecht, 1966).

Habel, Norman. "The Form and Significance of the Call Narratives," *ZAW* 77 (1965), 297-323.

_____. *Literary Criticism of the Old Testament* (Philadelphia: Fortress Press, 1971).

Hahn, Herbert F. *The Old Testament in Modern Research* (Philadelphia: Fortress Press, 1966).

Hals, Ronald M. "Legend: A Case Study in OT Form-Critical Terminology," *CBQ* 34 (1972), 166-176.

Harvey, Julien. "Le 'RÎB-Pattern,' Réquisitoire Prophétique sur la Rupture de L'Alliance," *Biblica* 43 (1962), 172-196.

Held, Moshe. "The Action-Result (Factitive-Passive) Sequence of Identical Verbs in Biblical Hebrew and Ugaritic," *JBL* 84 (1965), 272-282.

_____. "Rhetorical Questions in Ugaritic and Biblical Hebrew," *Eretz-Israel* 9 (1969), 71-79.

Herder, J. G. *The Spirit of Hebrew Poetry*, 2 vols., translated by James Marsh (Burlington: Edward Smith, 1833).

Herodotus. *Histories, Books I-II*, Vol. I, translated with an introduction and notes by A. D. Godley [Loeb Classical Library] (Cambridge, Massachusetts: Harvard University Press, 1946).

Heschel, Abraham J. *The Prophets* (New York & Evanston: Harper & Row, 1962).

Hobbs, T. R. "Some Remarks on the Structure and Composition of the Book of Jeremiah," *CBQ* 34 (1972), 257-275.

Hölscher, Gustav. *Die Propheten* (Leipzig: J. C. Hinrichs'sche Buchhandlung, 1914).

Holladay, William L. *The Root ŠŪBH in the Old Testament* (Leiden: E. J. Brill, 1958).

_____. "Prototypes and Copies: A New Approach to the Poetry-Prose Problem in the Book of Jeremiah," *JBL* 79 (1960), 351-367.

_____. "Style, Irony and Authenticity in Jeremiah," *JBL* 81 (1962), 44-54.

_____. "The So-Called 'Deuteronomic Gloss' in Jer VIII 19b," *VT* 12 (1962), 494-498.

_____. "Jeremiah's Lawsuit with God: A Study in Suffering and Meaning," *Int.* 17 (1963), 280-287.

_____. "The Background of Jeremiah's Self-Understanding: Moses, Samuel and Psalm 22," *JBL* 83 (1964), 153-164.

_____. "'The Priests Scrape Out on Their Hands,' Jeremiah V 31," *VT* 15 (1965), 111-113.

_____. "Chiasmus, the Key to Hosea XII 3-6," *VT* 16 (1966), 53-64.

_____. "Jeremiah XXXI 22B Reconsidered: The Woman Encompasses the Man," *VT* 16 (1966), 236-239.

_____. "Jeremiah and Moses: Further Observations," *JBL* 85 (1966), 17-27.

_____. "The Recovery of Poetic Passages of Jeremiah," *JBL* 85 (1966), 401-435.

_____. "Form and Word-play in David's Lament over Saul and Jonathan," *VT* 20 (1970), 153-189.

_____. "The Covenant with the Patriarchs Overturned:

172

Jeremiah's Intention in 'Terror on Every Side' (Jer 20: 1-6)," *JBL* 91 (1972), 305-320.

Holman, Jan. "The Structure of Psalm CXXXIX," *VT* 21 (1971), 298-310.

Holmgren, Fredrick. "Chiastic Structure in Isaiah LI 1-11," *VT* 19 (1969), 196-201.

Horne, Thomas Hartwell. *An Introduction to the Critical Study and Knowledge of the Holy Scriptures*, II, 4th ed. (Philadelphia: E. Littell, 1831).

Howard, George. "Frank Cross and Recensional Criticism," *VT* 21 (1971), 440-450.

Howell, Wilber Samuel. "Renaissance Rhetoric and Modern Rhetoric: A Study in Change," in *The Rhetorical Idiom*, edited by Donald C. Bryant (New York: Cornell University Press, 1958), 53-70.

Howes, Raymond F. (ed.). *Historical Studies of Rhetoric and Rhetoricians* (Ithaca: Cornell University Press, 1961).

Hudson, Hoyt H. "'Compendium Rhetorices' by Erasmus: A Translation," in *Studies in Speech and Drama* [Essays in Honor of Alexander M. Drummond], edited by Herbert A. Wichelns (Ithaca: Cornell University Press, 1944), 326-340.

_____. "The Field of Rhetoric," in *Historical Studies of Rhetoric and Rhetoricians*, edited by Raymond F. Howes (Ithaca: Cornell University Press, 1961), 3-15.

Huffmon, Herbert B. "The Covenant Lawsuit in the Prophets," *JBL* 78 (1959), 285-295.

_____. "Prophecy in the Mari Letters," *BA* 31 (1968), 101-124.

Humbert, Paul. "La formule hébraïque en *hineni* suivi d'un participe" in *Opuscules D'Un Hébraïsant* (Neuchatel: Secrétariat de L'Université, 1958), 54-59.

Hunt, Evertt L. "Herbert Wichelns and the Cornell Tradition of Rhetoric as a Humane Study," in *The Rhetorical Idiom*, edited by Donald C. Bryant (Ithaca: Cornell University Press, 1958), 1-4.

Hyatt, J. Philip. "The Deuteronomic Edition of Jeremiah," in *Vanderbilt Studies in the Humanities*, Vol. I (Nashville: Vanderbilt University Press, 1951), 71-95.

_____. "Jeremiah," in the *Interpreter's Bible*, Vol. V., edited by George A. Buttrick (New York: Abingdon Press, 1956), 777-1142.

Immerwahr, Henry R. *Form and Thought in Herodotus* [Philological Monographs, 23] (Cleveland: Western Reserve University Press, 1966).

Irwin, W. A. "The Face of the Pot, Jeremiah 1:13b," *AJSLL* 47 (1930-31), 288-289.

Jakobson, Roman. "Grammatical Parallelism and Its Russian Facet," *Language* 42 (1966), 399-429.

Janzen, J. Gerald. "Double Readings in the Text of Jeremiah," *HThR* 60 (1967), 433-447.

_____. *Studies in the Text of Jeremiah* (Cambridge: Havard University Press, 1973).

Jebb, John. *Sacred Literature* (London: T. Cadell and W. Davies, 1820).

Jeremias, Joachim. "Chiasmus in den Paulusbriefen," *ZNW* 49 (1958), 145-156.

Johnson, A. R. "The Prophet in Israelite Worship," *ET* 47 (1935-36), 312-319.

Johnson, Sherman E. "The Preaching to the Dead," *JBL* 79 (1960), 48-51.

Kautzsch, E. (ed.). *Gesenius' Hebrew Grammar*, 2nd English ed., revised and translated by A. E. Cowley (Oxford: Clarendon Press, 1963).

Kennedy, George. "The Rhetoric of Advocacy in Greece and Rome," *AJP* 89 (1968), 419-436.

Kessler, Martin. "Form-Critical Suggestions on Jer 36," *CBQ* 28 (1966), 389-401.

Koch, Klaus. *The Growth of the Biblical Tradition*, translated from the 2nd German edition by S. M. Cupitt (New York: Charles Scribner's Sons, 1969).

Köhler, Ludwig. *Deuterojesaja (Jesaja 40-55) Stilkritisch Untersucht* [BZAW, 37] (Giessen: Verlag von Alfred Töpelmann, 1923).

König, Ed. *Stilistik, Rhetorik, Poetik in Bezug auf Die Biblische Litteratur* (Leipzig: Dieterich'sche Verlagsbuchhandlung, 1900).

_____. "Style of Scripture," *HDB*, Extra Vol. (1904), 156-169.

Kosmala, Hans. "Form and Structure in Ancient Hebrew Poetry," *VT* 14 (1964), 423-445; 16 (1966), 152-180.

Kraft, Charles F. *The Strophic Structure of Hebrew Poetry* (Chicago: University of Chicago Press, 1938).

_____. "Some Further Observations Concerning the Strophic Structure of Hebrew Poetry," in *A Stubborn Faith*, edited by Edward C. Hobbs (Dallas: Southern Methodist University Press, 1956), 62-89.

Kramer, Samuel Noah. "Schooldays: A Sumerian Composition Relating to the Education of a Scribe," *JAOS* 69 (1949), 199-215.

Ley, Julius. *Grundzüge des Rhythmus des Vers- und Strophenbaues in der hebräischen Poesie* (Halle: Verlag der Buchhandlung des Waisenhauses, 1875).

_____. *Leitfaden der Metrik der hebräischen Poesie* (Halle: Verlag der Buchhandlung des Waisenhauses, 1887).

Licht, Jacob. "Time and Eschatology in Apocalyptic Literature and in Qumran," *JJS* 16 (1965), 177-182.

_____. "An Analysis of the Treatise of the Two Spirits in DSD," in *Scripta Hierosolymitana*, Vol. IV, edited by C. Rabin and Y. Yadin, 2nd ed. (Jerusalem: Magnes Press, Hebrew University, 1965), 88-100.

Liebreich, Leon J. "The Compilation of the Book of Isaiah," *JQR* 46 (1956), 259-277; 47 (1956), 114-138.

Limburg, James. "The Root ריב and the Prophetic Lawsuit Speeches," *JBL* 88 (1969), 291-304.

Lindblom, Johannes. *Die literarische Gattung der prophetischen Literatur* [UUÅ, 1924:1] (Uppsala: A-B Lundequistska Bokhandeln, 1924).

_____. *Prophecy in Ancient Israel* (Philadelphia: Fortress Press, 1965).

Loewenstamm, Samuel E. "The Expanded Colon in Ugaritic and Biblical Verse," *JSS* 14 (1969), 176-196.

Lohfink, Norbert. *Das Hauptgebot* (Rome: Pontifical Biblical Institute, 1963).

_____. *Lectures in Deuteronomy*, translated by S. McEvenue (Rome: Pontifical Biblical Institute, 1968).

Lohr, Charles H. "Oral Techniques in the Gospel of Matthew," *CBQ* 23 (1961), 403-435.

Lord, Albert Bates. "Composition by Theme in Homer and South-slavic Epos," *TAPA* 82 (1951), 71-80.

_____. *The Singer of Tales* (New York: Atheneum, 1968).

Lowth, Robert. *Lectures on the Sacred Poetry of the Hebrews*, translated from the Latin by G. Gregory (Boston: Joseph T. Buckingham, 1815).

_____. *Isaiah, Preliminary Dissertation and Notes*, 10th ed. (London: T. T. & J. Tegg, 1833).

Ludwig, Theodore M. "The Shape of Hope: Jeremiah's Book of Consolation," *CTM* 39 (1968), 526-541.

Lund, Nils W. "The Presence of Chiasmus in the Old Testament," *AJSLL* 46 (1930), 104-126.

_____. "The Presence of Chiasmus in the New Testament," *JR* 10 (1930), 74-93.

_____. "The Literary Structure of Paul's Hymn to Love," *JBL* 50 (1931), 266-276.

_____. "The Influence of Chiasmus upon the Structure of the Gospels," *AThR* 13 (1931), 27-48.

_____. "The Influence of Chiasmus upon the Structure of the Gospel according to Matthew," *AThR* 13 (1931), 405-433.

_____. "Chiasmus in the Psalms," *AJSLL* 49 (1933), 281-312.

_____. *Outline Studies in the Book of Revelation* (Chicago: Covenant Book Concern, 1935).

_____. *Chiasmus in the New Testament* (Chapel Hill: University of North Carolina Press, 1942).

_____. "The Significance of Chiasmus for Interpretation," *Crozer Quarterly* 20 (1943), 105-123.

_____. *Studies in the Book of Revelation* (Chicago: Covenant Press, 1955).

Lundbom, Jack R. "Elijah's Chariot Ride," *JJS* 24 (1973), 39-50.

Mandelkern, Solomon. *Veteris Testamenti Concordantiae Hebraicae atque Chaldaicae* (Jerusalem and Tel Aviv: Schocken, 1967).

Marcus, Ralph. "Alphabetic Acrostics in the Hellenistic and Roman Periods," *JNES* 6 (1947), 109-115.

Martin, James D. "The Forensic Background to Jeremiah III 1," *VT* 19 (1969), 82-92.

Meek, Theophile J. "Was Jeremiah a Priest?" *The Expositor*, 8th Series, 25 (1923), 215-222.

_____. "The Poetry of Jeremiah," *JQR* 14 (1923-24), 281-291.

_____. "The Structure of Hebrew Poetry," *JR* 9 (1929), 523-550.

Melamed, Ezra Zion. "Break-Up of Stereotype Phrases as an Artistic Device in Biblical Poetry," in *Scripta Hierosolymitana*, Vol. VIII (Jerusalem: Hebrew University, 1961), 115-153.

Mendenhall, George E. *Law and Covenant in Israel and the Ancient Near East* (Pittsburgh: Presbyterian Board of Colportage, 1955).

Metzger, Bruce M. (ed.) *The Apocrypha of the Old Testament: Revised Standard Version* (New York: Oxford University Press, 1965).

Michaud, J. Fr. (ed.). *Biographie Universelle*, Vol. 38 (Graz, Austria: Akademische Druck - u. Verlagsanstalt, 1969).

Mielziner M. "The Talmudic Syllogism or the Inference of Kal Vechomer," *Hebrew Review* 1 (1880-81), 42-53.

Milgrom, Jacob. "The Date of Jeremiah Chapter 2," *JNES* 14 (1955), 65-69.

176

Mirsky, Aaron. "The Origin of Anadiplosis in Hebrew Literature" [Modern Hebrew with English summary], *Tarbiz* 28 (1958-59), 171-180.

Mitchell, Hinckley G. "The Omission of the Interrogative Particle," in *Old Testament and Semitic Studies in Memory of William Rainey Harper*, Vol. I (Chicago: University of Chicago Press, 1908), 115-129.

Möller, H. "Strophenbau der Psalmen," *ZAW* 50 (1932), 240-256.

Moran, William L. "New Evidence from Mari on the History of Prophecy," *Biblica* 50 (1969), 15-56.

Morgenstern, Julian. "The Loss of Words at the Ends of Lines in Manuscripts of Biblical Poetry," *HUCA* 25 (1954), 41-83.

Moulton, Richard G. *The Literary Study of the Bible* (New York: D. C. Heath & Co., 1895).

Mowinckel, Sigmund. *Zur Komposition des Buches Jeremia* (Oslo: J. Dybwad, 1914).

_____. "Die Komposition des deuterojesajanischen Buches," *ZAW* 49 (1931), 87-112.

_____. *Prophecy and Tradition* (Oslo: Jacob Dybwad, 1946).

_____. "Literature," *IDB*, K-Q, 139-143.

_____. "Tradition, Oral," *IDB*, R-Z, 683-685.

Müller, D. H. *Die Propheten in ihrer ursprünglichen Form* (Wein: Alfred Hölder, 1896).

_____. *Komposition und Strophenbau* [Biblische Studien, III] (Wien: Alfred Hölder K.U.K. Hof- und Universitäts Buchhändler, 1907).

Muilenburg, James. *Specimens of Biblical Literature* (New York: Thomas Y. Crowell Co., 1923).

_____. "Literary Form in the Fourth Gospel," *JBL* 51 (1932), 40-53.

_____. "The Literary Approach - the Old Testament as Hebrew Literature," *JNABI* 1 (1933), 14-22.

_____. "The Literary Character of Isaiah 34," *JBL* 59 (1940), 339-365.

_____. "Psalm 47," *JBL* 63 (1944), 235-256.

_____. "A Study in Hebrew Rhetoric: Repetition and Style," *VT Supp.* I (Copenhagen, 1953), 97-111.

_____. "Isaiah," in the *Interpreter's Bible*, Vol. V, edited by George A. Buttrick (New York: Abingdon Press, 1956), 381-773.

_____. "The Form and Structure of the Covenantal Formulations," *VT* 9 (1959), 347-365.

_____. "The Gains of Form Criticism in Old Testament Studies," *ET* 71 (1959-60), 229-233.

_____. "The Linguistic and Rhetorical Usages of the Particle כי in the Old Testament," *HUCA* 32 (1961), 135-160.

_____. "Jeremiah," *IDB*, E-J, 823-835.

_____. "The 'Office' of the Prophet in Ancient Israel," in *The Bible in Modern Scholarship*, edited by J. Philip Hyatt (New York: Abingdon Press, 1965), 74-97.

_____. "A Liturgy on the Triumphs of Yahweh," in *Studia Biblica Et Semitica* [Essays in Honor of Theodoro C. Vriezen] (Wageningen: H. V. Veenman en Zonen N. V., 1966), 233-251.

_____. "Form Criticism and Beyond," *JBL* 88 (1969), 1-18.

_____. "Baruch the Scribe," in *Proclamation and Presence* [Essays in Honour of G. Henton Davies] (Richmond: John Knox Press, 1970), 215-238.

_____. "The Terminology of Adversity in Jeremiah," in *Translating and Understanding the Old Testament* [Essays in Honor of Herbert Gordon May] (New York: Abingdon Press, 1970), 42-63.

Myres, John L. "The Last Book of the 'Illiad'," *JHS* 52 (1932), 264-296.

_____. "The Structure of Stichomythia in Attic Tragedy," *PBA* 34 (1948), 199-231.

_____. "The Pattern of the Odyssey," *JHS* 72 (1952), 1-19.

_____. *Herodotus: Father of History* (Oxford: Clarendon Press, 1953).

McCarthy, Dennis J. "Moses' Dealings with Pharoah: Ex 7,8 - 10,27," *CBQ* 27 (1965), 336-347.

Nethercut, William R. "Notes on the Structure of Propertius Book IV," *AJP* 89 (1968), 449-464.

Newman, Louis L, and William Popper. *Studies in Biblical Parallelism* (Berkeley: University of California Press, 1918).

Nicholson, E. W. *Preaching to the Exiles: A Study of the Prose Tradition in the Book of Jeremiah* (New York: Schocken Books, 1971).

Norden, Eduard. *Die Antike Kunstprosa*, 2 Vols. (Stuttgart: B. G. Teubner Verlagsgesellschaft, 1958).

North, C. R. "The Place of Oral Tradition in the Growth of the Old Testament," *ET* 61 (1949-50), 292-296.

Norwood, Gilbert. "Vergil, *GEORGICS* iv, 453-527," *CJ* 36 (1940-41), 354-355.

_____. *Pindar* (Berkeley: University of California Press, 1945).

Noth, Martin. "History and the Word of God in the Old Testament," *BJRL* 32 (1950), 194-206.

Notopoulos, James A. "Continuity and Interconnexion in Homeric Oral Composition," *TAPA* 82 (1951), 81-101.

Nyberg, H. S. *Studien zum Hoseabuche* [UUÅ, 1935:4] (Uppsala: A. B. Lundequistska Bokhandeln, 1935).

Olrik, Axel. "Episke Love i Folkedigtningen," *Danske Studier* 5 (1908), 69-89.

_____. "Epische Gesetze der Volksdichtung," *ZDA* 51 (1909), 1-12.

Oppenheim, A. Leo. "A Note on the Scribes in Mesopotamia," in *Studies in Honor of Benno Landsberger* [Assyriological Studies, 16] (Chicago: Oriental Institute, University of Chicago, 1965), 253-256.

Parks, E. Patrick. *The Roman Rhetorical Schools as a Preparation for the Courts under the Early Empire* (Baltimore: John Hopkins Press, 1945).

Parry, Milman. "Studies in the Epic Technique of Oral Verse-Making, I. Homer and Homeric Style," *HSCP* 41 (1930), 73-147.

_____. "Studies in the Epic Technique of Oral Verse-Making, II. The Homeric Language as the Language of an Oral Poetry," *HSCP* 43 (1932), 1-50.

Peake, A. S. *Jeremiah* [CB], 2 Vols. (New York: Henry Frowde, 1911).

Pedersen, Johs. *Israel, Its Life and Culture*, I-II (London: Oxford University Press, 1964).

Perelman, Chaim. "The New Rhetoric: A Theory of Practical Reasoning," in *The Great Ideas Today, 1970*, translated by E. Griffin-Collart and O. Bird (Chicago: Encyclopaedia Britanica Inc., 1970), 273-312.

_____, and L. Olbrechts-Tyteca. *The New Rhetoric*, translated by John Wilkinson and Purcell Weaver (Notre Dame, Indiana: University of Notre Dame Press, 1971).

[Platnauer, Maurice (ed.)]. *Fifty Years (And Twelve) of Classical Scholarship* (Oxford: Basil Blackwell, 1968).

Popper, William. "Notes on Parallelism," *HUCA* 2 (1925), 63-85.

Porten, Bezalel. "The Structure and Theme of the Solomon Narrative (I Kings 3-11)," *HUCA* 38 (1967), 93-128.

Poteat, Hubert Mc Neill. "The Functions of Repetition in Latin Poetry," *Classical Weekly* 18 (1919), 139-142; 145-150.

Quintilian. *Institutio Oratoria*, Vol. I, translated with an introduction and notes by H. E. Butler [Loeb Classical Library] (Cambridge, Massachusetts: Harvard University Press, 1969).

von Rad, Gerhard. "Deuteronomy," *IDB*, A-D, 831-838.

_____. *Studies in Deuteronomy* (London: SCM Press, 1963).

_____. *Old Testament Theology*, Vol. II, translated by D. M. G. Stalker (Edinburgh and London: Oliver & Boyd, 1967).

Radday, Yehuda T. "Chiasm in Samuel," *LB* 9-10 (1971), 21-31.

_____. "Chiasm in Tora," *LB* 19 (1972), 12-23.

Raitt, Thomas M. "The Prophetic Summons to Repentance," *ZAW* 83 (1971), 30-49.

Rast, Walter E. *Tradition History and the Old Testament* (Philadelphia: Fortress Press, 1972).

Rietzschel, Claus. *Das Problem der Urrolle* (Gütersloh: Gütersloher Verlagshaus, Gerd Mohn, 1966).

Rife, J. Merle. "The Literary Background of Revelation II-III," *JBL* 60 (1941), 179-182.

Ringgren, Helmer. "Oral and Written Transmission in the O. T.," *Studia Theologica* 3 (1949), 34-59.

Roberts, W. Rhys. *Greek Rhetoric and Literary Criticism* (New York: Longmans, Green & Co., 1928).

Robinson, T. H. "The Structure of the Book of Jeremiah," *The Expositor*, 8th Series, 20 (1920), 17-31.

_____. "Baruch's Roll," *ZAW* 42 (1924), 209-221.

_____. "Anacrusis in Hebrew Poetry," in *Werden und Wesen des Alten Testaments* [BZAW, 66], edited by Paul Volz et al. (Berlin: Verlag von Alfred Töpelmann, 1936), 37-40.

_____. "Higher Criticism and the Prophetic Literature," *ET* 50 (1938-39), 198-202.

_____. "Basic Principles of Hebrew Poetic Form," in *Festschrift Alfred Bertholet*, edited by Walter Baumgartner et al. (Tübingen: J. C. B. Mohr [Paul Siebeck], 1950), 438-450.

_____. "Hebrew Poetic Form: The English Tradition," *VT Supp.* I [Congress Volume, Copenhagen, 1953], 128-149.

_____. *Prophecy and the Prophets in Ancient Israel*, 2nd ed. (London: Gerald Duckworth & Co. Ltd., 1953).

Ross, James F. "The Prophet as Yahweh's Messenger," in *Israel's Prophetic Heritage*, edited by Bernhard W. Anderson and Walter Harrelson (New York: Harper & Bros., 1962), 98-107.

_____. "Prophecy in Hamath, Israel and Mari," *HThR* 63 (1970), 1-28.

de Rossi, Azariah ben Moses. מאור עינים [The Light of the Eyes] (Volna: R. M. Romma Press, 1866).

Rowley, H. H. "The Text and Interpretation of Jer. 11:18-12:6," *AJSLL* 42 (1926), 217-227.

_____. "The Nature of Prophecy in the Light of Recent Study," *HThR* 38 (1945), 1-38.

_____. "The Early Prophecies of Jeremiah in Their Setting," *BJRL* 45 (1962-63), 198-234.

Rudd, Niall. "Colonia and Her Bridge: A Note on the Structure of Catullus 17," *TAPA* 90 (1959), 238-242.

Rudolph, Wilhelm. *Jeremia* [Handbuch zum Alten Testament] (Tübingen: J. C. B. Mohr [Paul Siebeck], 1968).

Sanders, Ed. Parish. "Chiasmus and the Translation of *I Q Hodayot* VII, 26-27," *RQ* 23 (1968), 427-431.

Saydon, P. P. "Assonance in Hebrew as a Means of Expressing Emphasis," *Biblica* 36 (1955), 36-50; 287-304.

Schoettgen, Christian. *Horae Hebraicae et Talmudicae*, 2 Vols. (I, Leipzig and Dresden: Christoph. Hekelii B. Sons, 1733; II, Leipzig and Dresden: Fridericum Hekel, 1742).

Schwartz, Joseph, and John A. Ryenga (eds.). *The Province of Rhetoric* (New York: Ronald Press Co., 1965).

Sievers, Eduard. *Metrische Studien I* (Leipzig: B. G. Teubner, 1901).

Sloan, Thomas O. "Restoration of Rhetoric to Literary Study," *ST* 16 (1967), 91-97.

Slotki, Israel. "The Stichometry and Text of the Great Hallel," *JThS* 29 (1928), 255-268.

_____. "Forms and Features of Ancient Hebrew Poetry," *JMEOS* 14 (1929), 31-49.

_____. "Antiphony in Ancient Hebrew Poetry," *JQR* 26 (1936), 199-219.

Smith, Barbara Herrnstein. *Poetic Closure: A Study of How Poems End* (Chicago: University of Chicago Press, 1968).

Smith, H. P. "Old Testament Notes," *JBL* 24 (1905), 30.

Smith, John. *The Mystery of Rhetoric Unveiled*, Facsimile Reprint (Menston, England: Scholar Press, 1969).

Steele, R. B. "Chiasmus in the Epistles of Cicero, Seneca, Pliny and Fronto," in *Studies in Honor of Basil L. Gildersleeve* (Baltimore: John Hopkins Press, 1902), 339-352.

Steinmann, Martin Jr. (ed.). *New Rhetorics* (New York: Scribner's, 1967).

Streane, A. W. *The Double Text of Jeremiah* (Cambridge: Deighton Bell & Co., 1896).

Talbert, Charles H. "Artistry and Theology: An Analysis of the Architecture of Jn 1,19 - 5,47," *CBQ* 32 (1970), 341-366.

Thiering, Barbara. "The Poetic Forms of the Hodayot," *JSS* 8 (1963), 189-209.

_____. "The Acts of the Apostles as Early Christian Art," in *Essays in Honour of Griffithes Wheeler Thatcher*, edited by Evan C. B. MacLaurin (Sidney: Sidney University Press, 1967), 139-189.

Topel, L. John. "A Note on the Methodology of Structural Analysis in Jn 2:23-3:21," *CBQ* 33 (1971), 211-220.

Tucker, Gene M. *Form Criticism of the Old Testament* (Philadelphia: Fortress Press, 1971).

de Vaux, Roland. *Ancient Israel*, Vol. II (New York: McGraw-Hill Book Co., 1965).

_____. *Jerusalem and the Prophets* [Goldenson Lecture, 1965] (Cincinnati: Hebrew Union College Press, 1965).

Vermes, Geza. "The Symbolical Interpretation of *Lebanon* in the Targums: The Origin and Development of an Exegetical Tradition," *JThS* 9 (1958), 1-12.

_____. *Scripture and Tradition in Judaism* [Studia Post-Biblica, 4] (Leiden: E. J. Brill, 1961).

Volz, Paul. *Studien zum Text des Jeremia* [BWAT] (Leipzig: J. C. Hinrichs'sche Buchhandlung, 1920).

_____. *Der Prophet Jeremia* [KAT] (Leipzig: A. Deichertsche Verlagsbuchhandlung, 1928).

Walker, H. H., and Nils W. Lund. "The Literary Structure of the Book of Habakkuk," *JBL* 53 (1934), 355-370.

Weinfeld, Moshe. "Deuteronomy - The Present State of Inquiry," *JBL* 86 (1967), 249-262.

Weingreen, J. "Oral Torah and Written Records," in *Holy Book and Holy Tradition*, edited by F. F. Bruce and E. G. Rupp (Grand Rapids: Eerdmans Press, 1968), 54-67.

Welch, Adam C. "A Problem in Jeremiah," *ET* 26 (1914-15), 429-430.

Wellhausen, Julius. *Prolegomena to the History of Ancient Israel* (Cleveland and New York: Meridian Books, World Publishing Co., 1965).

_____. *Die Kleinen Propheten übersetzt und erklärt* (Berlin: Verlag von Georg Reimer, 1898).

Wenham, Gordon J. "B^eTŪLĀH 'A Girl of Marriageable Age'," *VT* 22 (1972), 326-348.

Westermann, Claus. "The Way of the Promise through the Old Testament," in *The Old Testament and Christian Faith*, edited by Bernhard W. Anderson (New York and Evanston: Harper & Row, 1963), 200-224.

_____. *Basic Forms of Prophetic Speech*, translated by Hugh Clayton White (Philadelphia: Westminster Press, 1967).

de Wette, Wilhelm. *A Critical and Historical Introduction to the Canonical Scriptures of the Old Testament*, Vol. II, 3rd ed., translated and enlarged by Theodore Parker (Boston: Little, Brown & Co., 1858).

Whitman, Cedric H. *Homer and the Heroic Tradition* (Cambridge, Massachusetts: Harvard University Press, 1958).

Wichelns, Herbert A. "The Literary Criticism of Oratory," in *Studies in Rhetoric and Public Speaking in Honor of James Albert Winans* (New York: The Century Co., 1925), 181-216.

_____. "Some Differences between Literary Criticism and Rhetorical Criticism," in *Historical Studies of Rhetoric and Rhetoricians*, edited by Raymond F. Howes (Ithaca: Cornell University Press, 1961), 217-224.

Widengren, Geo. *Literary and Psychological Aspects of the Hebrew Prophets* [UUÅ, 1948:10] (Uppsala: A-B Lunde-quistska Bokhandeln, 1948).

Willis, John T. "The Structure of Micah 3-5 and the Function of Micah 5:9-14 in the Book," *ZAW* 81 (1969), 191-214.

Wohlberg, Joseph. "The Structure of the Laodamia Simile in Catullus 68b," *CP* 50 (1955), 42-46.

Wright, Addison G. "Structure of the Book of Wisdom," *Biblica* 48 (1967), 165-184.

Wright, G. Ernest. "Deuteronomy," in the *Interpreter's Bible*, Vol. II, edited by George A. Buttrick (New York: Abing-don Press, 1953), 311-537.

_____. "The Lawsuit of God: A Form-Critical Study of Deuter-onomy 32," in *Israel's Prophetic Heritage*, edited by Bernhard W. Anderson and Walter Harrelson (New York: Harper & Bros., 1962), 26-67.

Yaron, Reuven. "The Restoration of Marriage," *JJS* 17 (1966), 1-11.

Yellin, David. "The Use of Ellipsis in 'Second Isaiah'," *JPOS* 1 (1920-21), 132-137.

Yoder, Perry B. "A - B Pairs and Oral Composition in Hebrew Poetry," *VT* 21 (1971), 470-489.

Young, Richard E., and Alton Becker. "Towards a Modern Theory of Rhetoric: A Tagmemic Contribution," in *New Rhetorics*, edited by Martin Steinman Jr. (New York: Scribner's, 1967), 77-107.

Zeitlin, Solomon. "Hillel and the Hermeneutic Rules," *JQR* 54 (1963-64), 161-173.

Unpublished Material

Brandt, William J. *The Rhetoric of Poetry* (to be published).

Kessler, Martin. "A Prophetic Biography: A Form-Critical Study of Jer. 26-29, 32-45," unpublished Ph.D. dissertation (Brandeis University, 1965).

Lundbom, Jack R. "Patterns of Poetic Balance in the Book of Jeremiah," unpublished B.D. thesis (North Park Theological Seminary, 1967).

_____. "Scribal Contributions to Old Testament Theology: Composition by Contrast," paper read at the International Congress of Learned Societies in the Field of Religion, Los Angeles, September, 1972.

Muilenburg, James. "The Mediators of the Covenant," unpublished Nils Lund Memorial Lectures given at North Park Theological Seminary, 1963.

Nathan, Leonard E. "Conjectures on the Structural Principle of Vedic Poetry" (forthcoming article in the *Journal of Indian Philosophy*).

Raitt, Thomas 12,138

Rast, Walter E. 140

Reinesius, Thomas 122

Rietzschel, Claus 15,118,140,146

Robinson, T.H. 5,130,133,139

Ross, James F. 139

de Rossi, Azariah 121

Rowley, H.H. 153,157

Rudolph, Wilhelm 39-40,53,56,70,
80,85,88,94,145-148,151,153-
155

Rupp, E.G. 140

Sanders, Ed. Parish 142

Scaliger, Julius 123

Schoettgen, Christian 19,64,114,
121-123,126-127,161

Sievers, Eduard 4,132

Sloan, Thomas O. 129

Slotki, Israel 132,135

Smith, Barbara H. 130

Smith, John 129,143

Spohn, G.L. 123

Stalker, D.M.G. 139

Steinman Jr., Martin 129

Thiering, Barbara 142

Tucker, Gene M. 134-136

de Vaux, Roland 154

Vermes, Geza 149

Volz, Paul 38-39,41-42,48,
52,70,82,89,92,147-149,
154,157

Vriezen, Theodoro C. 129

Walter, Christoph. T. 123

Weaver, Purcell 129

Weinfeld, Moshe 145

Weingreen, J. 140

Welch, Adam 31

Wellhausen, Julius 4

Wenham, G.J. 156

Westermann, Claus 9-11,31,
133,135,138-139

de Wette, Wilhelm 3,130-131

White, Hugh C. 133

Whitman, Cedric 131

Wichelns, Herbert 129

Widengren, Geo 140

Wilkinson, John 129

Willis, John T. 143

Wright, G. Ernest 136

Yadin, Y. 142

Yaron, Reuven 147

Young, Richard E. 129

INDEX OF BIBLICAL PASSAGES

Jeremiah